D1554861

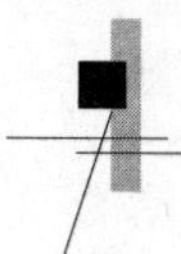

ROTH FAMILY FOUNDATION

Music in America Imprint

Michael P. Roth
and Sukey Garcetti
have endowed this
imprint to honor the
memory of their parents,
Julia and Harry Roth,
whose deep love of music
they wish to share
with others.

Paul Bowles on Music

Paul Bowles on Music

Includes the last interview with Paul Bowles

....

EDITED BY TIMOTHY MANGAN

AND IRENE HERRMANN

UNIVERSITY OF CALIFORNIA PRESS BERKELEY LOS ANGELES LONDON

University of California Press
Berkeley and Los Angeles, California

University of California Press, Ltd.
London, England

Library of Congress Cataloging-in-Publication Data

Bowles, Paul, 1910–1999
Paul Bowles on music / Paul Bowles ; edited by Timothy Mangan and Irene Herrmann.
p. cm.
Includes bibliographical references (p.) and index.
ISBN 0-520-23655-6 (alk. paper).
1. Music—History and criticism. 2. Music—Philosophy and aesthetics. 3. Bowles, Paul, 1910—Interviews. 4. Composers—United States—Interviews. I. Mangan, Timothy. II. Herrmann, Irene. III. Title.

ML60 .B7985 2003
780'.9—dc21 2002155795

Manufactured in the United States of America
12 11 10 09 08 07 06 05 04 03
10 9 8 7 6 5 4 3 2 1

The paper used in this publication is both acid-free and totally chlorine-free (TCF). It meets the minimum requirements of ANSI/NISO Z39.48–1992 (R 1997) (*Permanence of Paper*).∞

Contents

Introduction

......

TIMOTHY MANGAN

Early in the novel *The Sheltering Sky*, Paul Bowles introduces the reader to his itinerant trio of characters, Port, Tunner, and Kit. They sit drinking in a North African café.

> Across the street a radio was sending forth the hysterical screams of a coloratura soprano. Kit shivered. "Let's hurry up and get there," she said. "Maybe we can escape that."
>
> They listened fascinated as the aria, drawing to a close, made the orthodox preparations for the inevitable high final note.
>
> Presently Kit said: "Now that that's over, I've got to have another bottle of Oulmès."

It is just a passing moment, but an interesting one. The aria serves as an obvious symbol for what the three Americans are leaving behind—Western civilization—as they journey ever deeper into the Sahara. In writing the passage, the author also betrays a certain amount of musical learning. The phrase "orthodox preparations" is a give-away. Indeed, the passage might be considered as yet another nod towards autobiography (in a book teeming with it). For Bowles had literally left music behind, quitting the New York musical scene where he had been an admired and prolific composer (of ballets, incidental music for plays, concert works) to take up the life of the expatriate fiction writer. The novel was written in Fez, Tangier, and the Sahara in nine months in 1947–48. After New York, the silence of these locales, among other things, appealed to the writer. The coloratura soprano becomes an auditory irritation. And Bowles knew all about auditory irritations.

Paul Bowles was a music critic. From 1939 through the first part of 1945, in fact, he published nothing in prose but music criticism, and quite a substantial amount of it. From 1931, he had contributed translations of articles on music, then his own music criticism, to the journal *Modern Music,* a publication of the League of Composers. Aaron Copland, Bowles's teacher, friend and, probably, one-time lover, was the guiding light of both the League and the journal. Then, from 1942 through early 1946, Bowles served on the music reviewing staff of the *New York Herald Tribune,* where another friend and teacher, Virgil Thomson, reigned as chief critic. In his three and a half years there, he wrote more than four hundred music reviews and columns.[1]

Until now, however, Bowles's stint as a music critic has received scant attention. It has been considered a minor episode in the life of the composer (whose music is now garnering renewed interest) and the celebrated writer of fiction. Bowles himself never spoke of it much and remained modest about his accomplishments. His biographers, when treating it at all, have generally glossed over the subject.

Bowles discouraged discussion of the subject by often asserting the complete separateness of the two pursuits, writing and composing music. "I always put it that they're in two different rooms," he told biographer Millicent Dillon.[2] "And I go out of one, shut the door, and go into the other. And in there it's different." But he was comparing, of course, the creation of fiction with that of music. The music criticism represents something different; it is much more easily identified as the product, stylistically speaking, of the elegant, charming, and aphoristic composer. It does not baffle in that regard. What's more, it forms a kind of passageway between Bowles's "two different rooms." Were it not for the music criticism, Bowles might never have become the novelist and short-story writer.

"The work gave Bowles invaluable experience in producing a straightforward narration of events and in putting nonverbal experiences into verbal expression" is how one commentator neatly sums up the role of music criticism in his career.[3] Dillon sees his daily review writing for the *Herald Tribune* as "a process that reinforced his already awesome self-discipline." Perhaps Bowles put it most succinctly in a 1953 interview: "I only returned to writing through music criticism."[4]

It was Gertrude Stein who had caused him to give up writing. While the young writer was staying with her in Paris in 1931, she took a dim view of the experimental poetry Bowles had been writing. He still remembered Stein's reaction vividly some forty years later when he wrote his autobiography, *Without Stopping*:

> "Well, the only trouble with all this is that it isn't poetry."
> "What is it?" I demanded.
> "How should I know what it is? You wrote it. You tell me what it is. It's not poetry. Look at this." She pointed to a line on the top page. "What do you mean, *the heated beetle pants?* Beetles don't pant. Basket [Stein's dog] pants, don't you, Basket? But beetles don't. And here you've got purple clouds. It's all false."
> "It was written without conscious intervention," I told her sententiously. "It's not my fault. I didn't know what I was writing."[5]

When, a week later, Stein asked if he had done any work on the poems she had criticized and Bowles said he hadn't, for her it was proof. "'You see?' she cried. 'I told you you were no poet. A real poet, after one conversation, would have gone upstairs and at least tried to recast them, but you haven't even looked at them.'"

Bowles had to agree. Traveling with Copland around Europe and Morocco at the time, his writing of poetry and fiction dwindled to a halt as he concentrated on musical composition.

Copland was already writing articles for *Modern Music,* so it would have been a simple step for Bowles to do so as well. But, perhaps still smarting from Stein's judgement, he was at first reluctant. Recovering in a Paris hospital from typhoid in 1932, he wrote a letter to his mother:

> I became ambitious the other day, and wrote an article for *Modern Music.* They used to pay $20. What it is now, I don't know. Probably the same. The editor, as you know, has asked me two or three times to do some articles, and I have always shunned the task. It's an easy enough job if one has something to say, I discovered.[6]

Among the most important music journals of its day, *Modern Music* still makes lively reading. Published from 1924 to 1946 by the League of Composers, an organization that promoted the interests of living composers, the quarterly largely concerned itself with new music. Though academics and critics also wrote for the journal, composers were its leading contributors. Their essays were letters from the front—an insider's view of contemporary music—and thus remain valuable as primary documents.

Minna Lederman (1896–1995), a graduate of Barnard College who had studied piano at Juilliard, served as the editor of *Modern Music* from its inception to its death. She is often credited with nurturing a generation of composer-critics. ("My own debt to her is enormous," wrote Virgil Thomson.) Though its circulation was never large, *Modern Music* attempted to appeal to a somewhat broader audience than just composers. Lederman, it turned out, was a staunch exponent of clear, clean prose. She enlisted Joel Lifflander, a journalist who had helped develop the *New York Times* style book, as an assistant in her battle for plain English.[7] Copland, Thomson, and Roger Sessions were among her regular stable of writers, but the roster was a virtual who's who of art music at the time. Arnold Schoenberg contributed many articles, as did Colin McPhee, Henry Cowell, Elliott Carter, Marc Blitzstein, Lou Harrison, and others; many more wrote occasional submissions. Stravinsky, though he never wrote for the magazine, was one of its favorite topics. And, by a shrewd strategy, *Modern Music*'s influence proved greater than its circulation numbers. "We sent most of the copies to the press," Lederman would later recall. "The press was our real target and the press fell in love with the magazine."[8]

Not including his early translations of texts in French and Italian, Bowles wrote twenty-two articles for *Modern Music* between 1935 and 1946, most of them in 1940 and 1941. His ceaseless traveling served him well: he produced several penetrating examinations of indigenous folk music for the magazine. He also wrote extensively on film and theatre music (he was active as a composer in both genres) and on jazz. His first contribution, as it would happen, was a review of a new work by Virgil Thomson.

In the late 1930s and early 1940s, Bowles junketed between exotic locales (mostly in Mexico) and New York City, where he fulfilled commissions to write incidental music for plays produced by The Group and Orson Welles's Mercury Theater, and written by Tennessee Williams and William Saroyan, among others. In late 1942, Thomson invited him to join the staff of the *New York Herald Tribune* as a music critic. The paper, though second to the *Times* in circulation, was admired for the quality of its news coverage, the literacy of its writing, and the affluence of its readership. In the words of Thomson, it was "a gentleman's paper." Thomson had arrived there in 1940, immediately establishing himself as a brilliant stylist and fearless, iconoclastic critic, equally adept at bursting the bubbles of established stars (Toscanini and Heifetz received famous putdowns) and championing his own causes. Over the years, Thomson hired a number of composer-critics for the *Herald Tribune* staff, most of them, as it turned out, veterans of *Modern Music.* Eventually Harrison, Carter, Arthur Berger, Peggy Glanville-Hicks, John Cage, and Lester Trimble worked there. No other American newspaper has ever assembled a more illustrious team of composer-critics.

It came, however, with its own set of perils. While composers have shown themselves to be perhaps the most penetrating of all music critics (Berlioz, Schumann, Thomson), they cannot be said to be particularly impartial. Thomson could be cavalier in his disregard of conflict of interest, regularly extolling the virtues of performers who programmed his music, as well as his compositional colleagues. None of the composer-critics at the *Herald Tribune* was asked to give up their careers in composing, Bowles included. This led to a curious situation, to say the least, one in which Bowles, for instance, would find himself assigned to review the music of his boss. One can only wonder what readers must have thought when Olin Downes in the *Times* and Oscar Thompson in the *Sun* gave the premiere of Thomson's *Symphony on a Hymn Tune* (with Thomson conducting) negative reviews, while Bowles praised it in the *Herald Tribune.*[9] What's more, Bowles reviewed the music of friends, such as Copland and Leonard Bernstein, who had conducted the premiere of Bowles's zarzuela *The Wind Remains.* On a couple of occasions, Bowles even reviewed concerts during which songs of his own were performed. That he (and Thomson, as well) generally managed to overcome the incestuous nature of his assignments by the perceptiveness of his remarks is undeniable, however.

Bowles had met Thomson in Paris in 1931, when both were members of Stein's circle. The younger writer, then only twenty, had dazzled the older. They would remain lifelong friends. Bowles later became a member of Thomson's arty "Little Friends" entourage, "all young and a quarter mad." Thomson helped Bowles get composing jobs and served as something of a composition teacher too, though Bowles was never much of a student. When Bowles was offered the position at the *Herald Tribune,* though, he wasn't sure he could handle it. "The idea was interesting, but I was worried by the time element," he wrote in *Without Stopping.* He had never written a review on a tight deadline. "Forty-five minutes, which on average was about the length of time available for turning out a piece, did not seem very much in which to organize and write a literate critical report."[10] This was in the days of the overnight review, when critics, in order to make deadline, sometimes had to leave an event they were reviewing even before it ended.

That worry is typical of young critics, of course. Gena Dagel Caponi relates an illustrative anecdote. Shortly after Bowles had started the job, a pianist spotted him pacing in the lobby during the intermission of a concert. The pianist greeted Bowles, who looked up in panic and said, "What am I going to say? What am I going to say?"[11]

"Only after a year, when I no longer felt any tension connected with the activity, did I come to enjoy the *Herald Tribune* routine," Bowles wrote. He eventually felt comfortable enough to propagandize for both jazz and folk-music columns, which appeared sporadically on Sundays. Bowles later mentioned being "vain enough" to enjoy having a regular by-line in the paper, but he considered composing his primary activity. Still, if criticism is a form of autobiography, as H. L. Mencken asserted, we know what Bowles did most nights—he went to concerts and wrote. In 1943 and 1944, his two busiest years as a music critic, he wrote some 280 articles for the *Herald Tribune,* most of them concert reviews. In 1945, his critical output slackened only slightly with the advent of his return to fiction writing and a guest editorship at the surrealist arts magazine *View*.

He seems to have been coached only slightly in his review writing by Thomson. "He chastised me once," Bowles later said. "Just tell 'em what happened, baby. That's all they want to know. Nobody cares about your opinion. Who are you?"[12] The statement jibes closely with Thomson's oft-stated critical philosophy (if not actual practice), which was to rely on description, not opinion-mongering, in writing a review. During the Thomson regime, even the headlines on reviews were noncommittal, factual. "He always said, 'You must consider what you're doing is reporting on an event, like a fire in the Bronx or something. You go, tell what you see, you don't say, 'I didn't like the color of the fire. I don't like the smell of the burning rubber,' " Bowles said.[13] This, of course, may have been a necessary admonishment for a group of composer-critics with little or no practical experience in journalism; they would have to be reminded that they were writing for a general circulation newspaper. At any rate, many of

Bowles's reviews managed to attain something close to this dispassionate reporting stance.

In February of 1943, only a few months after joining the staff of the *Herald Tribune,* Bowles's status as a critic for two publications got him into ethical hot water. Not surprisingly, the trouble was precipitated by a tight deadline and absent inspiration. Specifically, Bowles had resorted to rewriting material that had first appeared (or was about to appear) in *Modern Music* for a Sunday column in the *Herald Tribune.* From the letters preserved in Lederman's *Life and Death of a Small Magazine,* we can deduce that Lederman had discovered the offense only by happening upon the *Herald Tribune* column, not from Bowles himself.[14] "I didn't consult you about the film article for the *Herald Tribune,*" Bowles wrote Lederman, "because my intuition, which is generally accurate, warned me that you would object." She did.

According to Bowles, Thomson had given him forty-eight hours to come up with a Sunday column for January 31st.

> I racked my brains for a day to find a subject. . . . I told Virgil flatly that I couldn't think of anything at all, and twenty-four hours had already elapsed. He suggested the film business, and I countered with your hypothetical reaction, which he dismissed as utterly without foundation in fact. I confess, however, that his suggestion was to simply to rewrite the article [in *Modern Music*], which had already appeared, or was to appear within a day or so, and the device of including two new films was entirely my own idea.

Lederman concluded that the situation was unacceptable. "I think it's simpler to call off our present arrangements for the time being," by which she meant the writing of the film column. "I'll miss your column acutely, and so, I'm sure, will the readers of *Modern Music.*" In subsequent issues, Elliott Carter and Lawrence Morton assumed responsibilities for covering film music. Bowles would contribute only three more articles to the journal, two "In the Theatre" columns in 1944 and "In the Tropics," an account of his musical explorations in Cuba and Central America, in 1946. Oddly, Bowles took little advantage of the freedom granted by Lederman. Less than a year after their disagreement, and after just three additional essays on the subject, Bowles gave up writing about film music for the newspaper, too.

Bowles produced a small amount of music criticism for other periodicals. Shortly after the Lederman debacle, he wrote an article on current jazz records for the April 1943 issue of *Mademoiselle* (the popular women's magazine), which was largely a reworking of material found in another article, "The Jazz Ear," which appeared the same month in *View.* Published in New York from 1940 to 1947 and coedited by friend Charles-Henri Ford, *View* was a surrealist arts publication that would eventually play a significant part in Bowles's return to fiction writing. As a guest editor of the May 1945 issue of *View,* entitled "Tropical Americana," Bowles translated a number of mythical stories and anthropological texts, including "The Story of the Sage Earth Fish" and "The Fertile Serpent of Bat Mansion" from the ancient *Popol Vuh* of the Quiché people in Guatemala.

> Little by little the desire came to me to invent my own myths, adopting the point of view of the primitive mind. The only way I could devise for simulating that state was the old Surrealist method of abandoning conscious control and writing whatever words came from the pen. . . . It was through this unexpected little gate that I crept back into the land of fiction.[15]

The immediate result was the disturbing short story "The Scorpion," first published in *View.* But the method would serve him well for the rest of his life.

The criticism is a different animal, though, and always a pleasure to read. Thomson's influence is evident, but Bowles has a quieter voice, with few axes to grind. In keeping with the tone of the *Herald Tribune,* the reviews and columns assume a reader's interest, though not necessarily his expertise. They are gentlemanly. The critical apostrophe is rare (the review of an eighteen-year-old Eugene Istomin is an uncharacteristic glimpse of Bowles writing in the throes of enthusiasm); so, too, is the no-holds-barred put-down. His dismissals are quiet and measured. In its clarity and spareness, the writing is rarely showy, though Bowles resorts to the occasional colorful metaphor or slang word. (He calls Mahler's Second Symphony a "shocker.") Despite his clear agenda for American music of the Boulanger school (he was a composer in this line), as well as for non-German European moderns, Bowles seems to have been the best kind of critic, one who went to an event with a relatively open mind. In the end, he admired what worked, and it could sometimes be a close call—and while Josef Lhevinne's straightforward playing did, Yehudi Menuhin's dispassionate dispatch did not. Perhaps Bowles came closest to stating an aesthetic manifesto for performance in a review of pianist George Chavchavadze:

> Although his program was made up almost completely of straight Romantic music, there was no embarrassing abandon, no false poetry, and no falling into moods. The only poetry was that written into the music; and mood was created, sustained, held at arm's length rather than bathed in. This would be considered by many music lovers to be the indirect, rather than the straight approach. It is certainly the objective one, and for that the more moving, because it reflects a more evolved degree of civilization.[16]

Bowles's criticism covers a wide range of musical subjects, from jazz and pop to film and folk music, from traditional classical music to avant-garde. At the *Herald Tribune*—where Thomson attempted to broaden the range of music criticism and critics often took an anthropological interest in nonclassical music—Bowles fit right in, reviewing Frank Sinatra, the Trapp Family Singers, a child accordionist, a thereminist. He heard Stravinsky conduct his own works, Villa-Lobos, too, and first performances of Shostakovich, Prokofiev, Vaughan Williams, Thomson, Bernstein, Cage, Milhaud, and many others. To these reviews he brought a composer's ear for craftsmanship, a composer's personal taste and sense of expressive ends and means. He seems to have loathed Rachmaninoff above all other practitioners of his art, at least in print. (Out of a sense of self-preservation, perhaps, he declined to publish his distaste for Beethoven.) "The piece itself," he wrote of Rachmaninoff's Second Piano Concerto, "is couched in an unamusing, degenerate style whose sole point seems to be that of keeping the textures every moment at the highest possible degree of richness. Unfortunately that richness palls almost immediately, as greasiness does in cooking."

Though Bowles had avoided tutelage with the stern Nadia Boulanger, his music and his music criticism (through Copland and Thomson) show her influence. By definition, he abhorred the big statement, sentimentality, thick orchestrations. "The music came from the modern Italian school of Pizzetti and Respighi: grandiose, sugary, and gaudy," Bowles said of one piece by Villa-Lobos. He found the last movement of Copland's *A Lincoln Portrait*, which quotes Lincoln's speeches, the least palatable. Taste, for

Bowles, could have political consequences. He asserts that in the "Resurrection" Symphony, Mahler's "eloquence is employed almost exclusively to give tongue to a megalomaniacal passion for the grandiose. One has a suspicion that, given the proper circumstance, he might have qualified as a favorite with certain groups in the Third Reich, whose doctrine of glorification of the irrational conditions all esthetic manifestations of that country." He much preferred the trim music of Thomson to that of the overstuffed Mahler. Of Thomson's *Sonata de Chiesa,* he wrote that the "idiom is stark and dry, making concessions only to those who love their music naked and don't care how bony it is."

A critical infantryman at the *Herald Tribune,* Bowles wasn't invariably given the most glamorous assignments. Reading the entire run of his reviews, it sometimes seems as if for long spells he was relegated to a peculiar kind of critical hell, reviewing the concerts of wannabes, hopefuls, and has-beens attempting to make their names with a New York recital. Many of these reviews are brief, some as short as five or six sentences. One occasionally senses routine creeping into the writing, a feeling that the writer knows he doesn't have a lot to report and, in any case, hasn't much room to say it. Rare is the review, however, without at least one golden nugget of observation.

Given the room, Bowles showed himself to be a perceptive critic at even the most innocuous events. A review of the Goldman Band in Central Park sparkles with insight and good will. A dreary-sounding concert of new works performed by the Walden Quartet becomes a mini-disquisition on the academic style. His painstaking ethnomusicological studies, including articles on calypso, spirituals, and Mexican, Latin American, and North African music, add to his autobiography, as well as providing vivid examples of the evils of commercialization. Certainly few critics then or now would be capable of writing them. The film columns form an especially interesting subset. Led by the example of Copland, who had gone to Hollywood in 1939 to write a new kind of film music for *Our Town* and *Of Mice and Men* (both scores were nominated for Academy Awards), many American composers were engaged in writing for new mediums in expressly American and modern idioms. Bowles and Thomson had both written scores for documentaries, and Bowles's film columns—nuts-and-bolts looks at the entire soundtrack of a film—clearly delineate the dictums of the new aesthetic. The Max Steiners and Erich Wolfgang

Korngolds were the enemy; music as integral part of the cinematic drama, not merely aural cushioning, the goal.

The short fiction began pouring from his pen, though, and magazines such as *Harper's Bazaar, Horizon,* and *Partisan Review* were publishing it. Early in 1946, Bowles resigned from the *Herald Tribune.* At the time, he viewed it not as a divorce from music but a reengagement. "I'm not 'going in' for writing instead of music at all," he told the composer George Antheil. "On the contrary, I resigned this past winter from the *Herald Tribune* staff where I'd been working three years and a half, precisely because I wanted to write music instead of having to write about it."[17] He did indeed continue to compose, but the fiction slowly grew in importance. In 1949, when his first novel, *The Sheltering Sky,* was published, his reputation was sealed as the writer-who-once-composed.

At least one person remembered Bowles as a critic, though. In 1954, when Thomson finally left the *Herald Tribune,* he recommended Bowles for the job. Bowles never got the chance to turn him down—the position had been filled by the time Thomson got around to plugging for Bowles—but he no doubt would have. He later told Thomson: "I don't think I could have handled it, any more than I could have followed a career in composition. I lacked the musical training that you and Aaron had." And so, Paul Bowles the music critic became a chapter in the life, not the whole book.

Notes

1. See Jeffrey Miller, *Paul Bowles: A Descriptive Bibliography* (Santa Barbara, Calif.: Black Sparrow Press, 1986), for a complete list.
2. Millicent Dillon, *You Are Not I: A Portrait of Paul Bowles* (Berkeley: University of California Press, 1998), p. 250.
3. Gena Dagel Caponi, *Paul Bowles: Romantic Savage* (Carbondale: Southern Illinois University Press, 1994), pp. 93–94.
4. Quoted in *Conversations with Paul Bowles*, ed. Gena Dagel Caponi (Jackson: University Press of Mississippi, 1993), p. 7.
5. Paul Bowles, *Without Stopping: An Autobiography* (New York: G. P. Putnam's Sons, 1972), p. 122.
6. *In Touch: The Letters of Paul Bowles*, ed. Jeffrey Miller (New York: Farrar, Strauss and Giroux, 1994), p. 103; which article exactly Bowles is referring to is unclear, as the first article to appear in *Modern Music* under his own byline wasn't until 1935.
7. Minna Lederman, *The Life and Death of a Small Magazine* (Modern Music,

1924–1946) (Brooklyn: Institute for Studies in American Music, Conservatory of Music, Brooklyn College of the City University of New York, 1983), p. 7.

8. Quoted in Mark N. Grant, *Maestros of the Pen: A History of Classical Music Criticism in America* (Boston: Northeastern University Press, 1998), p. 189.

9. See Anthony Tommasini, *Virgil Thomson: Composer on the Aisle* (New York: W. W. Norton & Company, 1997), p. 375.

10. *Without Stopping,* p. 247.

11. *Romantic Savage,* p. 94.

12. *Conversations,* p. 197.

13. Paul Bowles to Irene Herrmann, June 1999.

14. Lederman, *Life and Death,* pp. 131–34.

15. *Without Stopping,* pp. 261–62.

16. *New York Herald Tribune,* 23 March 1943.

17. *In Touch,* pp. 173–74.

ARTICLES AND REVIEWS

......

1935–1939

Thomson's Mass and Other Choral Works

MAY–JUNE (1935), *MODERN MUSIC*

The Dessoff Choirs, consisting of the Adesdi Chorus (women's, sounding well) and the A Cappella Singers (mixed, singing well) gave their final and not very enjoyable performance at Town Hall on April 10, each chorus presenting works by two contemporary composers. The Adesdi gave the premiere of Virgil Thomson's Mass, commissioned by the League of Composers a year ago. The two vocal parts are simple and singable. The addition of percussion gave the music a real punch and clipped off as much as possible the tiny but annoying loose ends of sound left over between words by the singers, who obviously failed to get the idea of this matter-of-fact, hard-boiled piece. (The critics were right on one score: it is no more devout than any group of nuns who have just finished tidying up the chapel and who are looking forward to some rolls and coffee.)

In the Kyrie the accompaniment of cymbal and the alto's ostinato figure established the straightforward mood. At times the snare-drum's punctuation of phrases in the Credo evoked the similar drum remarks stuck in between strophes by the Saharan storytellers. And it was used very much in the same way and for the same reason: to keep up the interest by helping to unify a long and repetitious text without much sense, by distributing landmarks in the form of various rhythmic designs spread along the large melodic design. The trim opening motif that recurs at "Et resurrexit" and again at "Et unam sanctam" is a perfect example of Thomson's unique prosodic gift. It has humor and it is an excellent tune. Both the

Sanctus and Benedictus were very pretty, but I believe that since they were almost foolproof even for the Adesdi Chorus, they would have been better without the cymbal, which seemed to be playing just because it was there. Agnus Dei found us back with the ostinato, underlined by the bass drum and cymbal in slow regular beating, pianissimo at the outset and crescendo to the end. The Mass is serviceable and quasi-streamlined; it is better and more personal music than *Four Saints.* It is time for the musical public to lose its idea that Thomson strolls in the byways of music, or that he leans to the chichi or special.

Schoenberg's *Friede auf Erden,* sung by the A Cappella Singers, if not of chaotic conception, at least gave the impression of chaos with its unnecessarily complicated harmony and its wandering melodic line. The atonal idiom seems the least at home in the human larynx; there is a sense of strain apparent during the singing. The piece, while it sounded well at any given moment, was unconvincing and confused because it lacked harmonic contrast. There was nothing to tie it down, nor, if one cared to follow it, could one locate oneself at any point along the way. The tendency toward a tonic at the end may have been an extramusical idea; it seemed to have no organic reason, but perhaps it had. (It is difficult to judge the music of the epoch immediately preceding one's own.) The general effect was that of something disembodied and floating in space, which is quite apt for a peace hymn.

Hugo Herrmann's *Chorvariationen über die Sonnengesänge des Franciskus von Assisi* (!), sung by the Adesdi Chorus, was a bad piece, full of silly caressing harmonies smuggled in from France. Herrmann had found a little piano figure that tickled him, and so he used it at the beginning of each "variation," with the result that they all sounded exactly alike. Much of the central portion seemed to have been suggested by good old *Volksmelodien* from east of the Rhine, but the composer had camouflaged them by changing all the thirds to fourths. The piece smelled pseudo, and it was quite in keeping that the theme as well as all the variations (including a gigue, which was at least elegiac) should have been marked with the indication: *Tempo di Gregoriano*!

The Three Choruses by Jacques Pillois were shamelessly cheap and stupid. There was an antique finish on the *Cantique Béarnais (Nouste Damo),* but that was all. The other two were good radio music.

Recent Books: Anatomy of Jazz

MAY–JUNE (1939), *MODERN MUSIC*

Winthrop Sargeant's *Jazz, Hot and Hybrid* (Arrow Editions, 1938) covers a lot of ground. Most of this is new, and he ploughs it up thoroughly, indicating, however, on every hand whole areas of still virgin territory. The book has a way of convincing the reader by making him feel that he himself is carrying out the explorations and discoveries. Warily Sargeant accustoms one to the idea that notation is essentially inadequate to express musical ideas completely. Then patiently he takes our contemporary folk music to pieces so that we see what makes it go. He analyzes the component parts, and then establishes beyond a doubt that the controversy over jazz arises from the fact that its most salient features are wholly foreign to Western music.

Theories as to the White or Negro authorship of any particular melody do not concern him, since much cross-pollination has of necessity occurred between the two idioms and responsibility even for a given phrase cannot be determined. What he wants to show is that the Negro race in this country, through tradition and atavism, has added completely new elements to American music, and that these elements can be isolated and catalogued. The best means to settle the widely debated White or Black question, he says, is to listen to the actual performance rather than to read the written versions. Even the most careful notation by a trained musicologist will contain but a few of the elements present in the playing of jazz by Negroes or Whites (through imitation and tradition). One conclusion here is that polyrhythm, or "secondary rag," where the accents of the superimposed rhythm are spaced differently from those of the basic rhythm (as opposed to simple syncopation, where they are spaced similarly), existed long before the emergence of jazz or ragtime. This is not even specifically Negro; it is common to Western music. Not the presence of polyrhythm, but the kind it is, namely, three-over-four, stamps a phrase as Negroid. Many examples of Negro melody are quoted, and even some "White" tunes where the three-over-four device figures. This has become such an integral part of our national musical expression that we are likely to accuse the writer of seeing Negro influence even where it is absent. But actually the results of the marriage between the two cultures are everywhere and inescapable. It is important to recognize them: "The characteristic rhythmic patterns of hot jazz melody . . . depend for their effect upon a single rhythmic principle: the interruption of an established regular alternation of strong and weak rhythmic pulses. The interruption is accomplished by the shifting of recognizable, repeated melodic elements from strong to weak positions and vice versa. The elements so shifted in repetition may be dynamic accents, notes, groups of notes, phrases, rhythmic patterns, patterns of melodic movement, particular types of harmonic ornamentation; even tone-colors."

In the actual melodies, very little remains of the purely Negro. The early substitution of English for the native languages and the constant exposure to Western harmony have combined to recast the general contours of melody in a Western form. In vocal music there is undoubtedly more left of the African melodic line than in the instrumental passages; but even here in certain cases, as in "breaks" (where for an instant there is no harmonic background) or when the accompanying chords are held so long that improvisation may go ahead without regard to harmony, one may distinguish melody of purely Negroid inspiration. (Sargeant finds a distinct resemblance between the intonations of a hot trumpet solo and those of Negro speech in general.)

The material on the scalar structure is good, except that no mention appears of what might be called the "blue fifth," a surprising omission, since the tone is sprinkled plentifully through blues recordings where the more "primitive" scales are used. It is generally sung to begin a downward-moving phrase—accompanied by chords on the tonic or subdominant. And when the true fifth is used in contradistinction later, the accompanying chord is on the dominant.

"Progressional harmony, a principle of purely European origin, has been influenced in a very peculiar manner by the American Negro," says Sargeant. A kind of harmony exists in present-day West African music. Parallel thirds, for instance, are very common. More noteworthy are dominant seventh and ninth chords, which seem to be preferred to the simple triad. But these can scarcely be considered harmony in our sense, since for us the word implies harmonic progression, whereas in African music it is a static thing, used for effects of contrast with passages in unison.

Once transplanted to America, these seventh and ninth chords become part of a new and relatively involved chordal language which is harmony of the truest kind. The surprising progressions that make up "barbershop" harmony, by which term one can loosely designate jazz harmony, were evolved through banjo fingering, Sargeant suggests. And there seems to be no other explanation to account for the strange chromatic progressions of seventh chords in the music of hillbillies and other rural musicians. The advent of "barbershop" harmony on the printed page, he says, rather than the accredited rhythmical distinctions, marks the end of ragtime and the beginning of the jazz age.

As to the form of jazz, that is simple. It is determined by its one psychological purpose—to create a feeling of unrest followed by a sensation of relief. Since the duration of sections where the crucial elements fall on weak accents (thus effecting the first part of the purpose) can be prolonged almost indefinitely, it is obvious that the element of syncopation invades the field of musical form. This intertwining of psychological effect and rhythmical structure, according to the author, is the main characteristic that separates jazz from Western music. "The situation during the silent pulses is one that challenges the listener to hold his bearings. If he has any sort of rhythmic sense he will not be content to lose himself. If he does not feel the challenge, then he is one of those who will never understand the appeal of jazz." "When the players, dancers and audience alike are hanging desperately to their sense of rhythmic orientation on one hand and are violently disturbing it (or listening to it being disturbed) on the other, the result is jazz in its purest form." To Sargeant, jazz is akin to the architecture of the skyscraper. It has a beginning, but its end is something determined not by any system of esthetics or logic, only by practical limitations. It is not created with any thought of permanence, but rather to fit the needs of the moment. He compares the jazz musician to the Hindu *ustad,* who would surely consider his powers of musical imagination insulted if asked to learn to play a *gath* two times in exactly the same way.

Jazz, Hot and Hybrid is exciting to read. It should be the spark to touch off a whole series of books on subjects briefly indicated therein—Negro vocalization, West Indian and Caribbean Negro music, detailed analyses of the Negro rhythms and prosody of West Africa as compared to those of Negro music of the Western hemisphere. Sargeant himself points out that we need a comprehensive analysis of the collections of African tribal music already available in recordings here in the United States. His own volume is a masterful anatomy of jazz music. To those who may regard so painstaking a work as out of proportion to the value of its subject matter,

Sargeant says: "Jazz does not attempt to sound the profounder depths of human emotion, but it gives a meaningful account of some of its shallows."

Wilder Hobson's *American Jazz Music* (W. W. Norton, 1939) could have been pared down to half its size and inserted at the end of Sargeant's book as an appendix. The nonhistorical material is superficial and inadequate because Hobson attempts to explain jazz without actually showing that he knows what it is himself. His selective list of thirty records is satisfactory enough, but the enthusiastic descriptions are pretty dull. The larger part of the book is given over to a spirited and very readable history of the growth of jazz. Jazz musicians seem to be a strange nomadic tribe of talented and musically undisciplined people destined to produce at most times below their best capacity. As Hobson says, there will be good music only if those making it "feel well." The reader may wonder that there is any good swing music at all. That is one of the exciting things about folk-music—it is never guaranteed.

As a reference volume for those who need one, the *Yearbook of Swing*, by Paul Eduard Miller (Down Beat Publishing Company, 1939), can doubtless be of service. It also contains a history of jazz (but only from 1900 on); a list of the instrumental groups of the past four decades; an extensive biographical section, including most of the important vocal and instrumental performers; a list of records with the personnel of each recording; a rather frightening list of collectors' items with prices—often exaggerated, one hopes—that will scare away all but the true devotee (a good many of the records are quoted at $25); and finally an amusing glossary of contemporary swing terms, wherein the reader may learn that a "spook" is a white performer, a "warden" the secretary of the union, and a "woodpile" a xylophone. Anyone who wants a Grove's Dictionary of Twentieth-Century American Folk Music will find it fairly complete right here.

Negro and Non-Negro Music

OCTOBER–NOVEMBER (1939), *MODERN MUSIC*

Of the two evenings in which Negroes figured at ASCAP's Festival of American Music, no one could say with fairness that either offered more than a few bright flashes in a series of horrors. In both, the musical element wandered and lost itself in a sea of sentimentality, pretentiousness, banality, and just plain bad taste. It is important to note, however, that wherever there was good music, its value went just as far as the degree to which the truly Negro elements therein had been left alone and not subjected to whitening.

The program "devoted to compositions by our Negro Composer-Members" was excellent evidence of the effect chauvinism can have upon musical culture. The music was considered a thing apart because Negroes had written it, which would have been valid if the material had shown any connection with Negro music. In reality what one heard was not too good Radio-City-Music-Hall. For these particular composers it would certainly have been better if Ferde Grofé had never been born. The symphonic pieces were unsavory dishes served with utter disregard for the listener's receptive faculties. Thus William Grant Still conducted a long slow number, followed by the equally long and slow second movement of the *Afro-American Symphony,* by which time even the academic cuteness of the third movement was welcome.

The fact that a Negro writes or plays music is no guarantee that the result will be "Negro music." However, when Negro music is to be produced, it is a Negro who in most cases will give the best result. Juanita Hall led her group in a choral number whose form and content sprang directly from a Negro religious service. The piece was *Go Down, Death,* with text by the late James Weldon Johnson. I can think of no finer Negro choral number. Its vocal line is a carefully considered succession of solo and group speech, shouting, Negro-preacher recitativo and melody couched in true Negro prosody. There is also a quality of improvisation present, which gives the music tremendous spontaneity and strength. Parts of the ensemble speaking will call to mind effects in Milhaud's *Choéphores*, not because of any inherent resemblance, but simply because the field of comparison for this truly unexploited medium is so small. Its racial characteristics have been consciously retained and highlighted, instead of pared away to conform to "white" standards of harmony and sonority. The performance was dramatic and satisfying.

Louis Armstrong and his band also helped remind the audience that the real thing existed. Virtuosity on the drums seems more certain to stop the show these days than anything else, and Big Sidney Catlett did just that with some very beautiful sounds from his cymbals during a cadenza for traps. For the last hour and a half, the stage was full to capacity with several dozen composers who sang and played the popular tunes they had written during the past forty years or so. The very idea of such a program, in which serious composers, choral groups, swing bands, and Tin Pan Alley men are herded together into one evening of a series of eight concerts, simply because they belong to the same race, is pretty appalling.

The second time Negroes took part in the festival they stole the show completely. Appearing with Benny Goodman were Fletcher Henderson, Lionel Hampton, and an inspired young guitarist who, with Goodman and the rest of the band, produced the only music heard that evening. Paul Whiteman offered a saxophonist playing "Nola," florid banjo antics, impersonations, and a clowning male quartet, everything being performed in what was aptly called a decade ago "late Paramount Style." Fred Waring traveled the whole distance to vacuity, soothing the ear with chimes and celesta, inciting tenors to sing pure soprano and leading his smirking chorus and beatific brasses into ever more offensive harmonies, each of whose crescendos set the audience cheering out of pure nervousness. It was like the altar music for the temple of some monstrous Californian cult. Goodman was best when he kept his ornamentations as close to the Negro idiom as possible. The *One O'Clock Jump* had a powerful cumulative effect, although it lacked the purity of the original Basie arrangement. The exquisite pieces for quintet of electric guitar, vibraphone, piano, drums, and bass had a watchwork-like quality which was a joy to hear. But in certain rhapsodic numbers for the entire band, everything fell to pieces because there was no logical harmonic progression to take for granted beneath the fantastic improvisation and virtuoso-playing.

During the swing numbers, the audience attempted to keep time to the music by clapping hands on what it imagined to be the offbeat. It was astonishing that never once was there a unanimity of opinion about the rhythm. The hall seemed filled with continuous desultory applause. Said one Negro: "This could never happen at the Apollo!"

On the Film Front

OCTOBER–NOVEMBER (1939), *MODERN MUSIC*

The prevalent criterion of film music seems to be that quality is in direct ratio to imperceptibility. An unnoticeable score passes for competent when it doesn't detract from the spectator's interest in the film. We do not need to consider the basic fact that a musical soundtrack is three things: dialogue, sound effects, and music, perceived together and thus inseparable. But let us consider music alone (unfortunately still the composer's sole precinct). Why grant extra alibis to film music for the privilege of being dull?

What music is to good choreography, the visual action of a film should be to its soundtrack. Regardless of the music's form, the dance springing from it must have a recognizable pattern. And no matter what the vagaries of the film (including the restrictions imposed by the bugbear dialogue, which is usually scattered haphazardly), the music created to give an extra dimension to the final impression must have a logical design and a sense of direction.

If this is obvious, why do the best composers, after showing whatever resistance they can muster in one film, fall back upon formulas for music by the yard? This makes background music, which usually provides for one motif per situation, and at most underlines the general *Stimmung* of said situation. Such film scores may be amusing when frankly inspired by the old pit movie music, from which our present-day symphonic scores are really not far removed. But these same symphonic scores are by no means genre pieces. They purport to be satisfactory auditory counterparts of a visual art which has reached a technical level so much higher that the disparity is painful to perceive.

As to the music whose form consists of a block (phrase, measure, or even arpeggiated chord) known as A, a block known as B (same thing, slightly altered), a block of A, a block of B, and so on until the given scene changes—well, we've all done it under stress, but that in no way excuses its hack quality.

To ask that music be synchronized as exactly as sound effects is the same thing as asking that the execution of the dancer's steps and gestures exist in some sort of fixed relation to the beat of the music, and not that they should merely come to pass during a given section of it. Such matching of the two tracks presents a more delicate problem to the composer, and involves cutting a few frames of film here and there. It also presupposes a degree of cooperation between director and composer which appears practically utopian. (In the noncommercial film, of course, such things have been known to happen. Cocteau and Auric gave a good example of it, eight years ago, in *Le Sang d'un poète.*)

……

Honegger has done a score for Giono's *Harvest* which as music per se is not too bad. As one might expect, a few sections are better than what we get from the West Coast. The soundtrack is technically crude. It cuts into the musical sequences with sudden thuds, and stops the sound-effect passages just as peremptorily.

The music falls into two categories: cute and serious. The latter is very symphonic, sounds like Puccini, and definitely does not come off. The cute music consists of as good a solution of the carrousel problem as that in *Petrouchka,* and the scissor-grinder motif, in spite of being repetitious, works, because with its ratchets, castanets, sleigh-bells, and small woodblocks over an amusing brass score featuring slides on the trombone, piccolo squeaks, and archaic bassoon tunes, it achieves a state on the borderline between sound effect and music, without, of course, imitating actual sound effects (a fatal procedure). It is particularly here that one can see Honegger's sensitivity to motion that involves rhythmical disturbances.

In a way I suppose it is a pleasanter task, depending upon the nature of one's talent, to provide a score for a film which leaves great stretches of time without dialogue, where there is room to state *and* develop an idea. At any rate, Aaron Copland's score for *The City* is always good and often beautiful. Most of it is readily identifiable with later Copland; the Sunday motoring music for instance sounds like the *Outdoor Overture.* (There is also a note-for-note quotation of Debussy's *La Neige danse,* which comes in the disguise of traffic music occasionally, and works very well.) The themes have great charm and a pleasant elasticity, which makes them capable of being prolonged at will without sounding as though they were stalling for time. There is always vigorous rhythm, either implied or expressed—a powerful support in the case of *The City,* although no music, however healthy and inspired, could sustain the unfortunate final letdown of the picture. In places the soundtrack shows signs of hurry, both in the score and in the effects. It would have been better, for instance, not to continue the andante right through the automobile accident. The fourth time a certain Morris Dance theme returns, the listener's ear is pretty jaded. But the score is notable for its touches of beauty. There are spots where the music transcends the film in such a way that the action is a photographic accompaniment to the music. These few passages, in which visual and auditory elements merge, are the most poetic moments in any American film score.

It has been possible several times during the past season to hear at the Museum of Modern Art what is probably the earliest good movie music: the score by Satie for *Entr'acte.* A lone pianist down front plays this stately little piece, and it comes in the middle of a program of just plain movie accompaniments, but you will listen and be delighted. The use of the block system, reduced here to what amounts to a mere frieze of repeated patterns, gives the music organic form. Present also are Satie's usual wan elegance, his perverse humor and nostalgia.

ARTICLES AND REVIEWS

......

1940

From Spirituals to Swing

JANUARY–FEBRUARY (1940), *MODERN MUSIC*

"From Spirituals to Swing" is the name given to an enterprise which after two concerts (December 1938, December 1939) promises to become the institution for the presentation of American Folk Music to New Yorkers. The second annual affair—should one call it a festival?—took place Christmas Eve in a packed Carnegie Hall, under the aegis of the Theatre Arts Committee. The reaction of the audience left no doubt as to its success.

Styles ranged from the most primitive kind of folk manifestations to the blatantly circumspect devices of metropolitan swing. All participants, with the exception of Goodman and two of his men, were Negroes. It was fun to see, in the flesh, blues singers whose records one had been hearing for years; to watch, for instance, a typical male blues singer vocalize while accompanying himself on the guitar. This kind of bard is well represented in recordings, but opportunities to hear direct performances of such music are rare in the North. Leadbelly we know, but he is a very personal artist. The three well-publicized boogie-woogie pianists, Ammons, Lewis, and Johnson, performed together and separately. Boogie-woogie as a pianistic style by itself is poor entertainment; at its worst it is a virtuoso trick, at its best, accompaniment music of considerable charm. The same passages which, played alone, are devoid of any but a rhythmical interest that grows progressively fainter as one listens, acquire new significance when a melody appears to relieve the reiterated pattern of unchanging I, IV, and V chords.

Benny Goodman's *Sextet,* in whose performance rhythmical precision and technical mastery reach a new high, drew the greatest applause of the evening. But probably the one really astonishing number of the entire program was a strange little piece for harmonica called *The Fox Hunt* by "Sonny" Terry. His instrument provided the horns, while his falsetto voice made fox-calls and hound-bayings. This miniature of tortured reed-sounds and human-animal cries was sinister and unforgettable.

We need more opportunities to hear music of this sort. There are magnificent folk artists in our country. Let John Hammond find Blind Blake, Rube Lacy, Dobby Bragg, Peetie Wheatstraw, Iva Smith, Elzadie Robinson, Blind Percy and his Blind Band, Cow Cow Davenport, and Blind Lemon Jefferson (if they have not died of starvation!), and ship them here for another concert next December, or preferably sooner.

On the Film Front

JANUARY–FEBRUARY (1940), *MODERN MUSIC*

In the series of "nonfiction" films shown daily at the Museum of Modern Art, there have been a few with soundtracks of some interest. *The Song of Ceylon,* produced by the Ceylon Tea Propaganda Board, claims to be a "dialectic treatment" of the "influence of Western Civilization on native life." The subject matter called for a fancy score, which Walter Leigh, after consulting *El Amor Brujo* briefly, and the *Sacre* at greater length, successfully provided. There is masterly dubbing and blending of sounds throughout. The track is composed of bits of genuine "exotic" Leigh (mostly with use of skillful and rich-sounding percussion work); recordings of actual native music, street calls, and songs often superimposed upon the score itself; commentary in the Living Newspaper style and conversation in English and Hindustani relieved by sound effects, and a chorus which seems too obviously included by the producers to show they could afford the works. The gongs and bells record magnificently, and are used with wise restraint. But the soundtrack suffers from insensitive cutting.

The score Alex North and Earl Robinson did for *People of the Cumberland* has a few touches of interest, as for instance the banjo passage for the titles and credits, and the folk dances later in the film. Otherwise it is a routine job. I had expected something a good deal more lively and tasteful; this I suppose is another example of work done in a hurry.

Revueltas's music for *Redes* [The Wave] adds depth to both the lyrical and violent moments of the film. He has an unusual harmonic sense which often brings forth exciting stuff. (At other times it lapses into Scriabin.) There is a definite absence of melodic invention, which is not too much of a handicap in this case, except at the end of the film, when an excellent rowing theme comes forward, grows, and becomes finally a rhythmical background for an embarrassingly pompous and savorless tune. The fight music is exceptionally good; it sounds more like his passionate *Homenaje a García Lorca.* Revueltas deserves to be better known here.

······

Ernst Toch has written quite an adequate score for that old warhorse, *The Cat and the Canary.* The melodic material is practically nonexistent of course, since the subject matter calls rather for instrumental effects which can be combined with straight sound. In this case the two have been made practically indistinguishable. Most of the time one scarcely notices where a chromatic passage, let us say, on the bass clarinet, leaves off, and where a door squeaking commences. I think this is a dangerous practice. Unless the audience has some way of telling just what elements of the total sound are supposed to be heard by the actors, and what are addressed to it over the actors' heads, it is going to get all mixed up. For instance, whenever the chandeliers flickered there was a squeal which, although in retrospect I can't assign it to any particular instrument, seemed to be a part of the score. From references to what the actors were doing I was still unable to decide whether they heard this or not. Such ambiguities can be obviated by any of several formulas devised to clarify and keep separate the music, which is a commentary on the action, and the sound effects, which are the action itself. To play his horror theme, Toch uses what sounds like a theremin surrounded by high, muted violins. The effect is excellent, like a thin beam of light in a dense fog. The dissonant idiom is of course admirably suited to provide atmosphere music for unpleasant and dangerous situations. The little figure, taken up in turn by various solo instruments as the boat glides through the swamp river, is most successful and supports the contention that in films sparse instrumentation generally comes off best as far as actual sound goes.

The score by Kabalevsky for *Shors* is mostly made up of military figures in brass and symphonic marches. It has a good deal of the inevitable large male chorus. The rest of the soundtrack shows more imagination. The juxtaposition of shouts, horses' hoofbeats, mass cheering, cannon detonations, and general uproar seems carefully arranged. One device is particularly fortunate. The White general's palace headquarters are surrounded. He cowers in his office listening to the approaching din as the enemy army forces entrance to the building. He covers his ears. The soundtrack is cut. Complete silence for a few seconds. He uncovers them. Even louder hubbub. Again he shuts it out and again there is no sound. . . . Apart from the scores, which vary from film to film, the soundtracks of Soviet pictures are almost uniformly good. At least of those that reach foreign countries. The Russians have a beautiful sense of the incongruities inherent in reality. They seem to love sounds for their own sake. Sometimes they continue endlessly with even the most repetitious ones, unaided by music, if it suits their dramatic purpose. (Especially the noises made by trains, both puffing and whistling, the sound of marching feet and battle cries.) Anyone who has seen *Peasants* will remember the murder scene. The kulak regards his wife's body with increasing horror. Suddenly snatches of a wild Asiatic song are heard from far away. Someone is singing in a distant street of the village. Nothing changes in the kulak's countenance. Only the audience has heard the sound. The music has absolutely no bearing on any part of the film, save that it provides a moment of intense poetry with its suggestion of the violent contrast between life and death. This is one example in many. I mention it to show the kind of dramatic possibilities which lie in subtle handling of the soundtrack, a thing Hollywood has not yet begun to attempt.

Calypso—Music of the Antilles

MARCH–APRIL (1940), *MODERN MUSIC*

The music of Trinidad is beginning to enjoy a vogue here, but the musicologists have had nothing to do with it. For years tourists have come back with reports of the amusing songs heard there. Then they brought back records. Then the musicians themselves were brought up, and now the United States is the principal export market for calypso music. English lyrics in some of the songs stimulated interest, plus just enough similarity in the music to that of the rumba to make the lay listener feel he is not in completely unknown territory. There is also the indisputable fact that here is an excellent example of the ballad tradition manifesting itself before our eyes. The recording companies have recently sent equipment to the island itself. When I arrived in Port of Spain, a native walking on Frederick Street stopped me and said: "I suppose you would like to see the building where the Decca Company made the recordings last year."

Calypso is the Negro music of Trinidad. (The island population is made up of a few whites, a few mulattos, some Chinese, more Hindus, and an overwhelmingly pure-black majority.) Its exponents have various contentions as to the origin of this music, but there is general agreement that the idiom came into being in the earliest days of colonization and slavery. "True calypso" is still sung in patois, a dialect similar to the Haitian Creole, which contains a good percentage of its original African material. However, the tendency is away from this patois toward English. There is no doubt that calypso songs were used, like our spirituals here, as a clandestine means of spreading illegal knowledge among the slaves. The religion also, because of its animist nature, was kept fairly occult. These two factors—religious and social repression—are perhaps largely responsible for the excellent preservation of the African element in the music. The slave system was officially abolished in 1838, but it goes without saying that actual democracy has not yet arrived in Trinidad. Plenty of calypso songs today decry British colonial oppression and racial inequality, with the result that all the lyrics are now subject to strict censorship. There have been numerous confiscations of recordings.

The popular present-day calypso, like our swing (not our blues-singing), is an urban product, and enjoys about the same means of dissemination: it is played over the radio, made into records, given in park concerts, used to entertain at cafés and at dances. Lyric sheets are hawked on the street. There is also the annual tournament of calypso, a healthy phenomenon notably lacking in our swing scene.

Every February at Mardi Gras, all the musicians of the island come to Port of Spain in brilliant carnival costume. There each group sets up a tent, which is its own territory, and then proceeds to "invade" another group's tent. Upon entering, the leader, who is the vocalist of the invading band of troubadours, sings a war declaration challenging the leader of the other group to engage in a battle of song. The battle is one of extemporaneous dialogue between the two contestants. Polite insults are exchanged in verse. Wilmoth Houdini, probably the best-known calypsonian, explained it to me thus: "You have to sing in such a way as to tangle up your adversary. You can tell in a minute if he is really improvising, or only singing something he has made up beforehand. If he is doing that, it is your place to sing in such a way that when his turn comes to reply he *must* make it up on the spur of the moment in order to answer you. Singing is just like boxing. You use ring tactics all the way." Clever use of long words, rhyme, and melodic invention within the given limits of the form chosen by the challenger are elements considered by the public in selecting the winner. Each singer has a favorite key which best suits his (or her) voice and tastes, and the challenger makes it his business to choose a key as remote as possible from that one in order to "put him out." There must be no repetitions of verses, and the improvising continues until one of the opponents hesitates or stops entirely, at which point, if the other has not already denied him the privilege, he may cry "Bar!" Then begins a duet in which the singer on the defensive improvises a sixteen-line lyric on any subject, and the aggressor attempts to make himself heard above the melody by contriving a contrapuntal melody which takes advantage of each rest and long syllable to make itself heard. Here syncopation reaches its height, and the crowd is likely to cry: "Rusó!" which seems to be the "Olé!" of Trinidad. The rules of the contests are as complex as the fine points in bullfighting, and the public knows them all.*

The rustic calypso orchestra is composed pretty much of homemade instruments, of which the bamboo is outstanding. There are two types of bamboo execution. For the "cut-in," a fat bamboo trunk about four feet long, stopped at one end, is hit with a hard mallet. The other is the *foulaing,* and consists of a pair of eight-inch sections of trunk which are struck together. The *vira,* Trinidadian variation in metal of the Cuban notched-gourd *guiro,* the gin-bottle, either empty or tuned with water, the *cuatro,* oversized ukelele, and a small hand drum complete the group. This is by no means representative of the big-time bands of the towns, where the first addition is the flute, and then, as the process of urbanization goes on, the clarinet, trumpet, sax, violin, or piano. The orchestra may use any combination; there may be two pieces or ten. All sound fairly well, although

* In a regular band repertory, improvisation naturally does not play such an important part, although it is never absent.

the saxes are too heavy for the nervous accompanimental figures. Muted trumpet and clarinet over guitar and piano with percussion suit the idiom best. Even though the orchestra seldom provides more than an accompaniment to the vocal line, its ingenious ornamentations are always in evidence and form no small part of the music's charm.

......

The composers and orchestra leaders (generally identical) place no musical restrictions upon themselves. They tackle all the forms known to them with equal zest. Their repertories include rumbas from Cuba, fox-trots from the United States, pasillos and waltzes from the neighboring mainlands of South America, and even that polyglot old trouper, the tango. Most of the foreign pieces are unsuccessful. The rumbas are unsubtle, and not really rumbas at all; certainly no Cuban would claim them. Their fox-trots and tangos are laughable. Perhaps the Colombians and Venezuelans would not go so far as to complain that their pasillos (which term is corrupted into "paseo") are unrecognizable, even if the islanders do make them simpler and more deliberate than those I have heard in Colombia. The waltzes, incidentally, they play quite well, outlining with percussion the particular distortion of waltz rhythm consisting of a rapid 6/8 taken in three, with secondary accents on the second, third, fifth, and sixth eighths.

But their true understanding is reserved for the material of strictly local origin. This finds its expression in the form-categories of the *calypso-ballad,* the *leggo,* the *kalender,* and the *shouter.* Where a song does not fall under one of the indigenous or foreign subheadings, it remains just a calypso-ballad, and this general category embraces the majority of pieces.

The ballad's thematic material suggests purely European derivations: English and Spanish, and perhaps some French folk tunes and children's song-games. An intensive use of syncopative distortions and a tendency to rather urbane harmonic progressions make a relatively sophisticated product. The rhythm approximates that of the *biguine martiniquaise* played a little too slowly, and in general the rhythmical pattern is far less complex than that of the Cuban *son* with its stately frenzy. There are in general two basic melodic plans, called by the natives double- and single-tone calypso. Double-tone may be in major, in which case the four phrases of a refrain will be: 2A unresolved + B + A resolved, or a variation of it. If it is in minor, the third phrase will modulate rather complicatedly to the relative major, and the fourth will modulate back. Double-tone is the duller musically, because the melodic line is not short enough to have any hypnotic effect in its repetitions. The listener knows what is coming, but he always has to wait a little too long for it. On the other hand, the single-tone (two identical or two alternating strophes, one solo and one chorus, using simple I, V or I, IV, and V backgrounds in either major or minor) makes a different music (in sound rather like that of the Ibani in West Africa) and is much more successful. Being violently repetitive, it often stirs the soloist to lyrical improvisation and even the members of the chorus to occasional outbursts of frantic melodic variations and misplaced accents. This kind of calypso approaches an inspired *son* in its effect, but never in quality. The *son* is both purer and more evolved.

The *leggo* is a primitive form of single-tone calypso. Here the percussive element is much more evident; its African ancestry is clearly discernable. A plectrum instrument is sounded carelessly a few times to indicate the tonic and dominant, the soloist announces phrase number one, and then phrase number two, the chorus responds with number one, which henceforth is to be its private property, uttered with unchanging uniformity throughout the song. After two or three responses a police whistle is blown, the signal for the entrance of the battery of percussion. Then everything goes on together until there are no more words, at which point the piece stops suddenly. The percussionists are allowed less rhythmical variety than in the *son.*

The *shouter* is a translation into English of songs about performances of the *shango* and *bellé*, ritual dances of animism, dances dealing with mass hypnosis and secret-society songs which are survivals of African ritual. The relation is pretty distant by the time the *shouter* is made.

The *kalender* was evolved for a specific purpose: the accompaniment to jousts of club fighting. It is lusty and strident, sung to rhythm provided only by a powerful metallic battery which has long passages to play alone.

For the subject matter of the calypso's lyrics, let me quote a few of the several hundred titles of records available in the United States now: *The Devil Behind Me, The Lindbergh Baby, African War Call, Roosevelt Opens the World's Fair, Civil War in Spain, Ramon Navarro, Bastardy, Seven Skeletons Found in the Yard, The Strike, We Mourn the Loss of Sir Murchison Fletcher, The Horrors of War, Lavabo, The History of Man, The Rats, Exploiting, Why I Killed Winifred, Zingué Talala, Joe Louis, Workers' Appeal, The Shop-Closing Ordinance, Who Has Done the Best for Humanity?, Trinidad Loves to Play Carnival.*

Unfortunately the musicians of Trinidad are impressed by the tunes and effects of Tin Pan Alley, which they generally discover a few years late. Too often they scatter undigested bits of New York pap through their own music, or even make an old piece over to suit themselves, and certainly the calypso versions are no improvement on the originals.

Each exponent of calypso adopts an official *nom de guerre* before he organizes his group and leads it forth to its first battle. Thus the heroes of Trinidad call themselves variously the Tiger, Attila the Hun, the Executor, Lord Beginner, King Radio, the Growler, the Caresser. All these are managed by a gentleman from Madeira by the name of Eduardo Sa Gomes who, like the Baida Brothers in the world of Arab music, has a monopoly on calypso in the West Indies. Sa Gomes owns a network of stores throughout the Antilles and even in British Guyana, where he sells the records of the men he controls. In Jamaica, for instance, more calypso records are sold than in Trinidad; they are more popular than the native *mentor,* more popular in Guyana than the *badji* of Demerara, in Barbados more popular than the Brumley melodies. Mr. Sa Gomes has made a special point of seeing that the idiom becomes a favorite. Commercialism is no respecter of tradition. Calypso is fast becoming a kind of international Caribbean swing, reaching from Jamaica to the southernmost tip of the Antilles, a hybrid novelty for Pan-American consumption.

Here is one of the few gay folk musics of the world. It is a hybrid, true, but it has a certain quality of completeness. With the loss of insularity it faces, in its present form, the danger of disintegration. Let those who have a taste for shouters, leggos, kalenders, collect their records now—calypso may not be with us very long.

Excerpts from Calypso Lyrics

EDWARD THE VIII

It's love it's love alone
That caused King Edward to leave the throne,
We know Edward is noble and great
But love caused him to abdicate.
It's love it's love etc.

(Refrain repeats after each couplet)

Oh what a sad disappointment
Was endured by the British Government,
On the 10th of December we heard the talk
That he gave the throne to the Duke of York.
Am sorry my mother is going to grieve,
But I cannot help I am bound to leave.
Old Baldwin try to break down his plan;
He said come what may the American.
And if I can't get a boat to set me free
I'll walk to Miss Simpson across the sea.
He said my robes and crown is upon my mind,
But I cannot leave Miss Simpson behind.

JOHNNY TAKE MY WIFE

Verse I

After Johnny eat my food
After Johnny wear my clothes
After Johnny drink my rum
Look, Johnny turn round and take my wife.
Ah looka misery
Wherever I meet Johnny
People, people will be sorry to see
The grave for Johnny and the gallows for me.

Verse IV

I went in the house to get my gun
My wife see me coming and she start to run
But let me tell you where I lose my head
Mr. Johnny was hiding underneath the bed
Ah looka misery
Wherever I meet Johnny
People, people will be sorry to see
The grave for Johnny and the gallows for me.

HE HAD IT COMING

Chorus

He is stone cold dead in the market
Stone cold dead in the market
He is stone cold dead in the market
I ain kill nobody but my husband

Verse II
All of his family they're swearing to kill me
All of his family they're swearing to kill me
All of his family they're swearing to kill me
And if I kill him, he had it coming.
Now, he is stone cold dead in the market—Murder
He's stone cold dead in the market—the criminal
He's stone cold dead in the market
I ain kill nobody but my husband.

Verse IV
There is one thing that I am sure
He ain't going to beat me no more
So I tell you that I doesn't care
If I was to die in the electric chair.

HOT DOG, HOT DOGGIE

I must buy me a hot dogs stand
Now that hot dogs is in demand
Hot dog has really made its name
Through their Majesty with title and fame.

Verse I
With the King and Queen hot dog made a hit
So my friends, let me tell you this
At Hyde Park you people didn't know
That hot dogs came in and stole the show
Hot Dog, Hot Doggie
Hot Dog, Hot Doggie—Oh what a dog
At Hyde Park you people didn't know
Hot dogs came in and stole the show.

Verse II
King George did not use his knife and fork
He said I will do nothing of the sort
So he held hot dog in his hand
And face hot dog man to man.*

* Words and music for *Edward the VIII* are by Rufus Calendar; the other songs are by Wilmoth Houdini.

On the Film Front

MARCH–APRIL (1940), *MODERN MUSIC*

I am told that *The Fight for Life,* the de Kruif obstetrical epic, has the longest accompanimental film score ever written. Pare Lorentz (producing for the United States Film Survey, now in Hollywood) wanted drama made out of pathology, and so he subordinated everything to the music and got his drama. He familiarized Louis Gruenberg with the film material, Gruenberg wrote the score, Alexander Smallens and the Los Angeles Philharmonic recorded it as one big block of music without ever seeing a shot. Then Lorentz cut both film and music track and arranged commentary and dialogue in terms of the music. Result: a superb film, better than either *The Plow* or *The River.* Whatever imperfections the soundtrack may have are certainly not due to lack of intelligent handling, but rather to occasional insensitivity in the music itself: a tendency to oversentimentalize in conceiving thematic material.

There are two important motifs in the film: life-death suspense (giving birth) and repose (after delivery). Gruenberg solved the first problem by using Lorentz's suggestion of writing music around recorded heartbeats. (Auric used an actual recording of heartbeats in *Le Sang d'un poète* in 1930.) The recurrent theme for cello against varying arrangements of the same rhythmical pattern made by percussion, piano, and contrabassi pizzicati has a solemn and mysterious beauty (inseparable from its visual context, to be sure); it is a memorable bit of film music. In the second or lullaby theme, the composer throws subtlety to the four winds and gives us one of those sweet, callous cinema-dawn numbers which is meant to relieve the morbid tension of the birth scenes. But given the fact that all the babies are born into surroundings of the foulest poverty, the music is violently incongruous. There is no relief implied in anything one sees. It is one long and wonderfully harassing experience; the sentimentality hits a very sour note.

There is a soliloquy scene during which the young doctor, having lost his patient, walks alone down wet streets. Here we have a curious barrelhouse selection beginning with a slow piano solo, whose sound is in keeping with the mood of the sequence until the clarinets and trumpet begin to wail, and then it seems forced. The atmosphere music for the long, hot night of waiting is good; as a basis Gruenberg has used a Yucatecan song: *El Rosal enfermo.*

Lorentz likes to point up a scene with a fortissimo. He has a trick of suddenly turning up the controls to the blasting-point. Usually this summary treatment of the music is swell. Not inevitably. Sometimes it throws a weak musical moment into relief. There are no sound effects. The music and dialogue are independently audible at all times, yet there is no conflict in capturing the spectator's attention. A triumph of common sense and skill.

......

The credits of *La Marseillaise,* directed by Jean Renoir (last big picture under auspices of the Front Populaire) promise charming things: original score by Sauveplane and Kosma (writer of songs with Cocteau and Prévert), and period music by Lalande, Grétry, and Rameau among others. God knows what happened to it all. What one actually hears is several distant trumpet calls, a few marching songs heard above recorded symphonies, some drums and bagpipes once, chimes ringing for a good twenty minutes, and a lady playing the minuet from *Don Giovanni* on the harpsichord. There is also some nice shouting as the word "Fin" is projected.

Operas on the screen lose all the dignity that a stage presentation gives them, and for me the cinema loses all its own charm when it gets mixed up with opera. The relation of the picture of a spectacle to a real spectacle is perhaps less striking than that kind of relation can be with regard to anything else. The eye is hard put to find anything that can evoke sympathy in close-ups of human faces whose owners are busy trying to hit high notes. The mind is unpleasantly affected by the constant irrational juxtaposition of normal realistic cinema procedures and variations on purely formal opera conventions. The film version of *Louise* may not be so revolting as most others. Still, it's all nonsense. On the screen, Grace Moore's stock-in-trade pantomime is quite confounding. Gestures which probably would not be too excessive on the opera stage are monstrous when followed by the camera's eye at exaggeratedly close range. The film needs about ten times as much screen-adapting as it got and that, I dare say, goes for all the opera-films ever made.

The score for the new Disney wonder-film, *Pinocchio,* is of course deplorably flashy. Here we have Hollywood in all its gilt and plush horror, particularly noticeable when there is unusually fantastic subject material like this. Choruses of awestruck tenors and moralizing school-teacherish sopranos caroling horrid pseudo folk tunes. Glockenspiels, celestas, vibraharps, and God knows what. You know all about that kind of thing. It gets into Ravel every once in a while and then perpetrators Harline, Washington, and Smith bring it back to normal. And the normal level is very low indeed. The nausea music at the billiard table is quite nice and so is some of the ocean and undersea stuff. Rich and crackling sound effects often save the music from utter disgrace. One can either rage at the bad score for spoiling the film or completely disregard the matter of sound, which is probably wiser. The film is so tremendously good.

An actor, Fred Stewart, has made the score for *Men and Dust,* a short two-reeler about silicosis. Here was a problem of really limited funds. The entire soundtrack is of a piece with the film in its intelligent simplicity. One does not remember any music as such, but rather a constant sound of human voices, talking, singing, or humming. The idea of the possibility of human ascendancy over the deplorable conditions shown is thus made more vivid. There are four commentators who have different things to do, depending upon the timbre and kind of delivery needed for the occasion. Sometimes they chant in rhythm, and sometimes they merely repeat a sentence again and again with varying inflexions. (Once the command: "Get away from that dust!" is shouted as an accompaniment to a whole sequence of landscape shots.) There is an impressive little section during which Will Geer has time to render an entire song: "There Are Strange Things Happenin' in This Land." The eye sees a long panorama of flat land with the dismal chatpiles in the background. When the song ends, the action continues. The soundtrack is notable for its clarity and ingenuity rather than for any actual musical content. Good commentary by Sheldon Dick.

......

I suppose Alfred Newman is to be felicitated upon the scantiness of his music in *The Grapes of Wrath.* Apart from a folk-dance sequence called for by the script, a bit of guitar travel music, and the faint harmonium strains used for three scenes described below, there isn't any music at all. The only concession to what Hollywood considers popular taste is in the nondescript orchestral credits music. No orchestra was needed. The single instruments (banjo at one point during the credits, and harmonium) tell their tale perfectly. The crickets, birds, frogs, dogs, roosters, and distant train whistles do the rest. However, since there is so little music anyway, I think Zanuck might have gone the whole hog and tried none at all. Then in place of the sad harmonium tune in Ma Joad's head at these various points we could have heard, for instance, the wind rattling the panes or a shutter creaking when she burns her keepsakes; a far-off train whistle or the equally poignant sound of an automobile horn on the highway at the burial scene; an owl or a baying dog when Tom leaves his mother and goes off into the dark. Care would have had to be taken to make these effects credible, to keep them from seeming forced or arbitrary; nevertheless, it could have been done.

In reviewing *Of Mice and Men,* the *Times* movie critic found fault with the music played during the dog-shooting scene. His contention was that what he called the variation on *Hearts and Flowers* was not in keeping with the film. It is quite obvious even to the layman, if he listens to Copland's score, that there is not the slightest *musical* connection between the blatancy of that old tune and the sensitive music for this scene. What the critic really meant was something else. He objected to the *idea* of using music at all to foster emotion for such a patently sentimental episode. Such an objection is justifiable only if it is carried to its logical conclusion. In that case, the music would be suppressed throughout the film, which would be a perfectly valid thing to do esthetically. But if one is going to admit the hypothesis that music heightens dramatic effect, he has to accept the idea that pathos, as well as suspense, humor, and atmosphere, has the right to its musical crutch. The difficulty is that pathos music, of all accompanimental music, is the most accessible to ridicule. Hardboiled resistance to it is a part of every audience's receptive equipment.

I should say, after one hearing, that Copland has done an admirable dramatic score. The music always seems to be going somewhere. Even where it is just a filler-in, it doesn't sound like it. The dog-shooting scene, with its touching cadences ending in a single flute tone; the nervous tension of the fight, when the staccato chords flying about in space suddenly crystallize into one painful, endlessly spreading dissonance as Lennie catches his assailant's hand and starts to crush it; the amusing eating music with its porcine contrabassoon noises; the tragic texture of the final sequence—these places among a great many others in the score should be ample proof to producers that a good composer can write better music (yes, even movie music) than their Hollywood music men.

On the Film Front

MAY–JUNE (1940), *MODERN MUSIC*

There's not much to talk about this time. Franz Waxman's score for *Rebecca* is not even as good as Hitchcock's direction, which in this film is certainly no great shakes, considering his past record. Of course there was a lot of music to be written for the film, the first part of which has an almost constant background of strings. These lush sounds are a good deal in evidence throughout, and the ear is soon satiated. The passage where the harp clears the way for some whole-tone business was evidently meant to be a tonal tour de force. Occasionally a spot of dramatic interest appears, but in general the musical ideas lack imagination, a fault very noticeable, for instance, in the fanciful introduction to the film. Here you have a delicate passage where the utmost care should have been taken to establish the right mood to fit the particular kind of unreality in the sequence. Instead, thick scoring bogged everything down. I suppose this is not Waxman's fault. However, knowing the weakness of Hollywood arrangers for that kind of instrumentation, he would have done better not to use his leitmotif at that point. The ubiquitous melody with its lingering chromatics has a certain decadent charm, and technically the fading in and out of sound and music are more than satisfactory. The best musical moment seemed to me Miss Fontaine's entrance into the morning room. (Waxman's next picture is *Boom Town.)*

For the strangely futile antiwar film *Lights Out in Europe,* Werner Janssen has contributed a long, full, and varied score. If anything, it is too heterogeneous (and perhaps too long as well. Was it always necessary to continue with the music under the commentary?). The material is adequate but without distinction. The flow of sequences is often needlessly crude; the composer takes his film material too literally. Too often he wants a directly realistic accompaniment for each scene. He uses the first, obvious thing for a given shot as though that shot existed independently of its cinematic context. In a documentary film of feature length this approach can be fatal. What the listener gets is, for instance, a fanfare for brass followed immediately by a long vamp of double-bass pizzicati, broken into by thirty or so seconds of drum-beating, then a very symphonic snatch that sounds like Scriabin, leading into a pyramiding of flutter-tongue brasses, next a series of long agonizing dissonant chords without

it is difficult to find any conscious evocation of it in his later music. I am told that the earlier things such as *Colorines* were definitely Indianoid, and I should like another opportunity of hearing them. (Conductors please note.)

Revueltas knew the bases of music: the noises that accompany drunkenness and abandon. He had played in border bars and dives and movie houses in his youth. With this education his approach could only be healthy. He knew what music was for and what it was about. The younger composers, especially Galindo, Argote, and Contreras, felt this and admired him to the point of veneration. He represented to them the true revolutionary composer who in his work went straight toward the thing to be said, paying as little attention as possible to the means of saying it. Because he was musically a romantic, that thing to be said was usually an effect to be made rather than anything else. There is none of the preoccupation with form or conscious establishment of individual style that makes Chávez's music an intellectual product. With the instinct of the orator, he made his effects, barbaric and sentimental, after which he might have remarked with quiet pride: *He dicho.*

The way in which he so grandly disregarded the poverty and disease always present in his life perhaps helped to make him a great romantic figure. Whatever it was that did it, none who knew him escaped the conviction that here was someone who, if not a great composer, was all the same a great man who wrote music.

On the Film Front

NOVEMBER–DECEMBER (1940), *MODERN MUSIC*

Chapter one in the Story of How the Third Reich Conquered the World, known as *Feldzug in Polen,* has a score by one Herbert Windt. Herr Windt has obviously listened to lots of Sibelius with admiration, for the score is full of profound epic snorts and groans. Interest lies solely in the fact that it's fun to see what kind of soundtrack the Nazis make for an official propaganda vehicle. A kind of heroic relentlessness is obviously aimed at, and now and then almost achieved, but at these rare points it is the driving force of the film (made by army cameramen during the Polish campaign) which creates the illusion that the music has interest, never the music itself. The general effect is a succession of indigestible brassy sounds, often happily covered by noise of gunfire, explosions, and roaring motors. Amusingly enough, for sequences showing the Nazi army on the march, the music becomes typical villain music—the kind used for the wicked characters in Disney. Perhaps for the same reason: to terrify the children. There is an *Erlkönig* fate-motif, used only for map sequences showing Nazi victories and territorial expansion. You hear a good deal of *Erlkönig.* Technically the soundtrack is lousy.

The Long Voyage Home, with score by Richard Hageman, is the pure and good movie cruelly betrayed by the worthless score. You need a sensitive job for a film like this, which depends vitally for its effects upon the establishment and clinching of definite moods. There were numerous practically foolproof spots where any composer could have made himself at least innocuous. But Mr. Hageman apparently thought he could do better, and so he made himself offensive. The music starts out legitimately with *Blow the Man Down.* Then for a "native" scene laid in the West Indies, it does an incredible number which sounds very much like the Russian State Choir singing *Storm on the Volga.* With no shame for lack of transition, even from one bad thing to another, it plunges from that into super Herbert and thence into some whole-tone perversions of the shanty. Clouds of musical error keep rolling down across the beauty of the film. An example: after a touching death scene, one of the shipmates says: "Yank's gone." But what did Mr. Hageman use to punctuate that simple declaration? A Wagnerian brass comment, as jarring to the mood as the slamming of all the theatre's exit doors. The only pleasant spot musically was the scene near the end when the men go back aboard the *Glencairn* and an accordion plays some of that over-sweet music that has been forced on the orchestra in the rest of the film. At last one hears the idiom in its proper place, and it sounds all right. The only trouble here is that since the accordion was used as sound effect earlier, one is a little confused and automatically looks around the picture for someone to be shown playing it. Here it happens to be the score. The musical opportunities for effectiveness are not only muffed, but are turned into weak spots that hamper the film. Which, considering that we are given so few really good films like this one, is more than a misdemeanor on the part of the composer. The rest of the soundtrack is careful and accurate.

Two people named Espino and Tarin arranged a score for *Time in the*

Sun, the latest salvage from Eisenstein's Mexican material. They seemed unable to decide upon a single method, and so they put together some simulated Indian tunes and some popular songs. Even the few indifferently synchronized drums and rattles, helped out by an oboe (God knows why), sounded more like a bunch of drunks than like folklore. The harmonizations and vocal approach occasionally recalled the worst Hawaiian onslaughts. For the Tehuantepec sequence at least, they went ethnological and used the sandunga and a marimba. The carelessness accorded the soundtrack did much to make the film seem far less good than it was, although the footage offered us by Upton Sinclair certainly was better.

There is a sad story to be told about *Valley Town.* The film I saw will not be distributed, and in its place the public will be given an altered version hailing our forthcoming if still postponed entry into the present war. It is difficult to know just how Marc Blitzstein's score will sound when the revamped film is released. It is pretty certain that it will be less interesting. For there were among the portions suffering censorship two excellent innovations which, while they may not have been fully realized, nevertheless made the score important, I hope, as a pioneer. I refer to the soliloquy in the street: "What I wanna go home for?" (a step in the direction of something very desirable: actual and complete integration of score and commentary) and to the unbelievably heartrending song of the girl at the table. (She doesn't sing it, but it is her song insofar as it expresses in a stylized popular idiom what is passing in her mind. One feels it might be the kind of song she would dream if she heard music in her sleep.) Both these passages are of course a carrying over into cinema of aspects of the *Cradle* technic. The song is the more moving and the less successful. For even while I was being greatly upset by the emotional strength of the scene, I was conscious of a certain esthetic cheating going on somewhere. The gigantic close-ups of a miserable human face; the dogged insistence with which the film follows the unbearably pathetic business through to the end; and particularly the ascribing to the wife of a steelworker a song which in 1940 is still of a subtlety that limits its intelligibility to the sophisticated, politically or otherwise (even though the song a few years hence might easily be as generally understandable as *Father, Dear Father, Come Home with Me Now),* all these things turn out to be the old tearjerking technique using new material. Perhaps there is no better method. Still, there can be variations. At any rate, this scene, which balanced delicately on the brink of gross sentimentality, managed to remain dramatically effective. The piano is brilliantly used in the traditional "second movement" of social documentaries: mechanization of industry. Blitzstein writes a machine sequence which is superior to most composers' handling of the section: there is a basis of actual harmonic progression which makes for more sense than the usual list of rhythmical noises.

It is difficult to describe certain film scores without making lists of their ingredients. When a unifying element such as personal style or at least some sort of arbitrary esthetic is lacking, there is left a chain of disparate units which can be appraised only in inventory fashion, and in a rather long compound sentence. Anyway, the perfectly agreeable score by Ernst Toch for *The Ghost Breakers* was a succession of richly orchestrated diminished sevenths, bassoon squawks, string glissandi, clickings, and echoes of passages from *Prométhée* as well as from Schmitt's *Dionysiaques*. The effects were good, and I suppose that's all the director wanted. Improbable music and terrible dubbing where the heroine plays the organ tune that opens the secret door.

Power and the Land has a score by Douglas Moore, and the music is in the Unmistakably American School. It is bright and tuneful, inclined to the pastoral, and well coordinated with the film. Film music should not be heard. The spectator should only be conscious of its presence. If it suddenly is heard, the reason is likely to be that its insistence upon one thing has made the spectator cease to be conscious of it. There is then a reaction which makes him not only hear it very much but also become conscious of having heard it for the past ten minutes. Music constantly played can eventually lessen its own effect. One becomes conscious somewhere along in this film that the music is very much there. This is not a defect in the music's quality; it is a problem that often appears in the making of documentary films, particularly in those where the film is all cut when the composer is called in, and where the music is supposed to provide the emotional drive or the clarity that the picture and commentary probably lack. The director wants to pep up every scene and thinks that perhaps continuous music can do it. Certainly continuous symphonic music can't. *Power and the Land* is overladen with intricate music. It is all good music and pleasant music; there is just too much of it. There is a passage of commentary recited in strict tempo to the score. One can take it or leave it depending on whether he likes the way it sounds. It embarrassed me. I liked best the water faucet and shower scenes: a charming little divertissement of brass and violin glissandi.

The score of *Children Must Learn,* a short documentary, is a companion piece to last year's *Men and Dust,* and is also by Fred Stewart. All music is provided by voices and guitar. This device for turning out a soundtrack on a shoestring has many more possibilities than Mr. Stewart has as yet utilized. Songs are used here with satirical intent, to point up the action. I prefer the passages of humming. A certain perceptory confusion is bred by the introduction of sung words. The eye sees the interior of a Kentucky mountain shack with its forlorn inhabitants enacting their daily existence. The ear hears a chorus of voices singing a mountain ballad. But the desired unity of effect is not there because the imagination is troubled by an overwhelming sensation of proximity to the unseen singers.

There is nothing remarkable in Aaron Copland's score for *Our Town,* save perhaps that it managed to make a suspiciously arty film generally acceptable. The usual impeccable Copland taste and high musical integrity are of course ever-present, although the music turns out to be practically unnoticeable. The noncommittal themes are carefully suited to the subject matter and conscientiously worked out. He achieves a simple "home-folk" quality admirably, and without ever bordering on the vulgar. Toward the end of the film Copland had the task of writing music for a long scene full of maudlin pathos. Even here he did not compromise, though that lasting high note eventually grows monotonous. One feels at a certain point that it should grow either louder or softer. The burial music is as touching as one could wish. Other excellent spots are the deathbed scene with its flute and the night scene of the drunken choirmaster. If it were fair to compare fictional with documentary films as to the possibilities offered the composer, I should say that I much prefer *The City.*

ARTICLES AND REVIEWS

......

1941

On the Film Front

JANUARY–FEBRUARY (1941), *MODERN MUSIC*

Aside from *Fantasia*'s esthetic implications, the most important of which is having been called Nazi (not too ridiculous a term, in fact, since this kind of mindless super-slick kitsch is the perfect Fascist entertainment), it has a very real value in containing the best synchronization that has yet been made. Mention of *Fantasia* properly speaking doesn't belong here, since this column concerns itself primarily with soundtracks containing new music made for pictures. And *Fantasia* is a sight track made for music that we all know perfectly well. Nevertheless, "thrilling Fantasound" actually makes all other soundtracks one has ever heard seem feeble and mechanical in comparison. The night I went, something happened to the sound equipment and there were occasional roars followed by violent silences. Still I was able to discern the overwhelming superiority of the sound to anything I had heard before. The upper registers at last come through strong and clear without whirring. The various smaller percussive instruments stand out beautifully. Sometimes there is an illusion of reality, as in the tuning up or the solo female voice in *Ave Maria.* Often reality is improved upon, as in the *Sacre* (of whose mutilation Stravinsky is stated to have approved, although God knows why).

Antheil has written an unpretentious little score for *Angels over Broadway.* It's of the generally screwy variety, with Viennese waltz relief. When it's screwy it's full of small string glissandi or bumping bassoons, generally playing one slightly square theme which one hears a good many times.

Antheil, having dealt in dissonances longer than his confrères, handles this kind of thing better than most of them. When it's sentimental, on the other hand, it sounds a bit like bridge music between two themes of a pas de deux: neutral, rather pretty, climaxless. And here Antheil also has the edge on many other Hollywood men, because his tunes are a little less expected in their tournure, a little more inventive. Once in a while one is startled by hearing Richard Strauss or Scriabin. (Why do I keep hearing Scriabin in the movies? He must have written some good film music somewhere.) The beginning is the same old Hollywood favorite: a piece of stale Herbert with Ravel sauce, garnished with harps. The end is a little less unsavory but musically senseless. A detail: a little piece is playing. The hero is in a lunchroom, walks toward the cash register. The music rises in pitch and intensity. His money is taken, the sale is rung up. The music reaches its climax, stops as the drawer opens and the register rings. The bell sounds for a second alone, then the music picks up.

The general impression left with the listener by Roy Harris's score for *One Tenth of a Nation* is satisfactory. It is more difficult to be sure about any one section. The worthy music therein always has charm and always sounds well. It provides a proper setting for a wholly engrossing subject: the lack of educational facilities for American Negroes. Even that famous ineffable sadness that never really lets up anywhere in Harris's music is not inappropriate here. I don't even reproach the composer with having chosen not to include one Negroism in his score, even if he did decide to use folk music and had to get it in the British Isles. The film was made by Whites for Whites; it is without ethnographic overtones. And since it was only a sociological plea to the White population, its creators were esthetically free to use whatever idioms they thought most effective, provided that each element was completely subservient to the discipline essential in a propaganda film. But it seems to me that Harris rather arbitrarily steals the whole show. His music isn't functional. It is complex, and tends to be descriptive rather than evocative. A good deal of it would be better over the radio, with a few words of commentary first to explain it, such as: *Children Running down a Country Road,* or *Fishing in the River.* It is essentially concert music, and the musical line is often too long to be of service. The best sections are those where the composer had an opportunity to do some of his well-known "noble" mood music. Here the effect is touching and most successful. In other places the result is confusing; one feels that the show is a piece of rather nice music for which some pictorial sequences have been conceived as an added item of interest. There is one really bad moment: the end. It sounds quite accidental, like the ending of a record in the middle of a movement. Completely unsatisfactory. The recording is superb, although the piano is very much in evidence.

Escape evidently was a studio job, as its score went unsigned. Little wonder about that, although it was not much worse than the usual Hollywood thing. Short and very lush symphonic comments make up a good amount of the music. There was also a dull score for *The Merry Wives,* a dull film from Czechoslovakia, and a far better than average score by Richard Addinsell (of *Come of Age)* for a British film whose title, plot, and players I have already forgotten. The music was careful and sensible.

Dance Memorial to Revueltas

MARCH–APRIL (1941), *MODERN MUSIC*

Anna Sokolow's evening of dance dedicated to Revueltas turned out to contain only three pieces by the Mexican composer. Then, although *Homenaje a García Lorca* was played the way it should have been, by the orchestra hired for the purpose, *El Renacuajo paseador* turned out to be Alex North playing the piano alone, with the rest of the men sitting around watching. That, for a final number, sent me away disappointed. I had been looking forward with enormous interest to hearing *El Renacuajo.* I still hope to hear it some day. *Homenaje a García Lorca* is a daintily passionate piece. I think it comes off musically, but I wonder if it does so in any way Revueltas imagined. The line is florid and makes for a kind of sensuous decoration. The timbres are rich-sounding and on the "exotic" side; figures get going in a hard-to-stop fashion which he himself once called *estilo ruso.* The themes (to refute Virgil Thomson's statement that there are no Indians around in Revueltas's music) borrow in good measure from mestizo-influenced indigenous material. Conscious Mexicanisms are particularly noticeable in the rhythmic structure of the melodies. The title gives me pause. Is this charming little piece meant to be a hymn in praise of the murdered poet? Or an elegy lamenting the fact of his death? Or a musical summation of his character and works? Or is it just a Mexican suite Revueltas was writing at the moment, which he suddenly desired to dedicate to Lorca's memory? I vote for the last. In any case, the literary reference obscures the complete and immediate comprehension of the music which could be had if the listener were handed a more noncommittal title. Not very well played. The *Canciones para niñas* are not what you might expect from the title, that is, not for little girls at all, although they have considerable charm. Like most chamber music, these songs for piano and voice are not very danceable. Miss Sokolow is to be congratulated, however, on having brought even this much Revueltas to New York.

On the Film Front

MARCH–APRIL (1941), *MODERN MUSIC*

Louis Gruenberg has turned out a score for *So Ends Our Night* which, if less good than that for *The Fight for Life,* is so only because the film is less important and less interesting. Being a straight, even if very good, Hollywood product, it offers fewer opportunities for a composer to exercise his art. Nevertheless it is a first-class score. The thematic material is generally straightforward, simple, and rather distinguished, and the effect eschews corn as much as possible. Gruenberg gets nice dark moods with his strings and uses them a good deal. Also the orchestration does not suffer from overstuffing; he lets us hear single instruments and thin sounds occasionally. This is not to say that in certain suspenseful spots there is not too much symphony, nor that the love themes are not at times excessively lovely. But the score is pretty much of a pleasure for the listener. The beginning of the hospital scene is particularly sensitive and right. The high spot for most people will probably be the night train ride with the locomotive whispering, "Marie, Marie, Marie," above the blended train sounds and train music. It makes a beautiful piece. There are some poetic soliloquies with feeble music played behind them. This doesn't work very well, combined as it is with the down-to-earth treatment of the subject-matter in the rest of the film.

Miklós Rózsa, who did another grandiose Midwayesque score for *Four*

Feathers, wrote the music for *The Thief of Bagdad.* This one is a piece with its predecessor. It fits the Maxfield Parrish–like sets (in glorious Technicolor) with their Ludwig Baumann canopies and carpets. Practically ceaseless, the score gets off to a terrible start with a male chorus lamenting in fourths. Then there is an incredibly lousy song which Sabu manages to help a bit with his musically innocent little voice. Everything hopes desperately to be "Oriental"; you know what that means: fake Hindu, fake Jewish, fake Chinese, fake Balinese—anything that the composer imagines might suggest the atmosphere of Iraq. Wonder and magic are not present. Music renders the picture static because the sound is just what comes out of your radio during one of the more expensive commercial programs. It is hard to be breathless over events pointed up with music which may at any minute fade and give way to a wise-crack or a quiz. Poverty of invention everywhere. When the fatuous music already billowing out of the orchestra seemed insufficient to the makers, they simply added that damned lady-choir without which Hollywood has decided no film involving fantasy can be made. The ladies hum. There are also devices like this: a jazz-whistle (the kind acrobats swing to in vaudeville) to accompany fruit hurtling through the air, a xylophone ascending the diatonic scale step by step for a shot of Sabu running upstairs. Except for the complexity of sonorities and superior recording one might think the job was one of the old Riesenfeld scores of the pre-100-percent-all-talking, all-singing era.

The new Soviet film, *University of Life,* is a less excellent sequel to *The Childhood of Maxim Gorky.* There is a skimpy score by Lev Schwartz, and what there is is not very good. Surprising lack of feeling for the musical needs of the drama. That is, surprising in a Russian film. The hero walks down a quiet village lane at night and disappears from view. There is a shot, and presently he staggers back into sight. This is dramatic in itself, but not when the sound of the shot is followed by a huge Tchaikovskian theme played by a full symphony. Not even if the theme were good. And then why should a good sequence wherein Gorky first feels the nobility in the performance of physical labor be rendered hopelessly commonplace by injection of a long paraphrase on the "Song of the Volga Boatmen"? Otherwise the soundtrack is effective; it is made up of those elements which have given charm to countless Soviet sound films: frequent but judicious use, behind and between bits of dialogue, of boat whistles, train whistles, dogs barking, street cries, and folk music rendered by barrel organs, accordions, guitars, harmonicas, the human voice unaccompanied, and (less fortunately) by choruses. There is an exciting passage for barge whistles which echo beautifully across the river.

......

It's not difficult to do. Hollywood merely needs a good record library and a few people who know a little about geography. It makes all the difference in the world to the picture. Just take *Pepe le Moko,* for instance, and try to imagine what a horror it would have been to the ear if it had been subjected to general Hollywood practices. God knows Vincent Scotto's Puccini interludes featuring Cui's oboe are bad enough when they occur (Scotto wrote the score for *The Baker's Wife*), but the picture would have been a total loss if we had had nothing but those. But the film is not ruined even by such indescribably cheap symphonic moments. It is saved by the inclusion of the work of Sidi Mohammed Yguerbuchen, an Algerian composer, who if he did not actually write the native music (one has no way of knowing) at least decided which recordings and which native pieces were to be used. It is certainly due to him that we have the exquisite background for the streets of Algiers's Casbah: a great brouhaha of native horns, Kabyle flutes and drums, together with sad lost wisps of bal musette tunes on the accordion. There are Sud-Oranais pieces played on the strange chalumeau-like instrument that sounds like the human voices of the same region; and actual *Touchiats algérois*, wonderful and ridiculous bastard numbers from the Casbah's cafes. (Piano four octaves with embellishments, flute, drum, and tambourine.) What is particularly fortunate about this track is the fact that the ever-present music in the street scenes makes for greater realism: life in the Casbah *is* one long soundtrack like this.

There are two remarkable moments: the murder scene using the mechanical piano with drum accompaniment (although René Clair used much the same device years ago, it seems to me) and Frehel's song, where she sings to one of her own records on a wavering and scrapey gramophone. These two identical voices, sometimes falling one on top of the other and sometimes being an immediate echo one of the other, become the Past and the Present, giving the scene great dramatic force which is due in no way to the visual images.

On Mexico's Popular Music

MAY–JUNE (1941), *MODERN MUSIC*

There exists a state of great confusion about the factors that differentiate the various forms of Mexican popular music, even in the minds of Mexican musicians.* The best a non-Mexican can do, outside of serious musicological research, is to record the confusion by stating what is known. No one has yet done the work which will enable future listeners to know they are hearing a *Son* and not a *Huapango*. The name "Son" has been applied to practically everything, even in the few recent musicological books brought out in Mexico, and terms are used loosely and with complete interchangeability. (There is also the custom of calling various dances in different regions by the names of the Spanish ancestors from which they may have in part developed: one hears *Fandango* used in connection with the playing of *Sones, Huapangos* are called *Rondeñas, Malagueñas*, and so on.)

Last year Chávez pointed out that this state of confusion must come to an end. The trouble is that the music may come to an end before the confusion does. The really fine Mexican music is naturally intensely regional. Talent scouts from Mexico City radio stations are fast destroying the local cultures by carrying away the best musicians from their villages. They teach them the monstrous bastard kitsch which now passes for music all over Central America (Cuba, Argentina, and Hollywood all in one dish) and then allow them, in their program of broadcast horrors, to perform one or two of their own already damaged native songs. This is true particularly of players of *Huapangos,* whose collective rhythmical devices are so delicate that Blas Galindo, the young Indian composer, assures me a week of radio work is sufficient to ruin a group forever.

There are two types of *Huapango*: the *Huasteco* and the *Veracruzano.* They are both in 3/4 or 6/8 and lack the frantic repetitiousness of most Mexican music. Both have in common an extremely successful exploitation of contretemps: the voices go along, seemingly unaware of each other or of the rhythmical variations in the accompanying bass. The *Huasteco* is the simpler of the two, the disparity in rhythm between the melody and accompaniment is less, and the melodies themselves are less involved and

* The word "popular" is used in the strict sense as opposed to commercial music, which unfortunately is quite another thing.

less soaring. Often the second chorus is in the supertonic instead of a related key, the choruses thereafter alternating between tonic and supertonic; doubtless this is a guitaristic device.

The *Veracruzano* probably has the distinction of being the most complicated folk music in the country. There is no doubt in my mind that certain ones I have heard have Negro influence, a thing made noticeable in the rhythms of the counterpoint invented particularly by the harpist. Certain Negroisms in the singers' intonations can be detected as well. The music however remains overwhelmingly Spanish, but not like any folk music one can hear in Spain today. The hands of the performers being occupied in playing their guitars and harp, the singers' feet often take over the job of making the rhythm more incisive, of emphasizing certain offbeats for the sake of variety, which the clapping hands do in Andalusía. Sometimes at the end of a chorus comes a *desplante* during which the dancers, if any, rest or sing falsetto allusions of a challenging or insulting nature regarding each other's defects. (This happens in the *Fandango* in Spain.) Along the Gulf Coast, yearly regional contests are held. Participants are usually fishermen, some of whom have attained an unbelievable proficiency not only in the pure technic of their instruments, but also in the art of melodic and rhythmical improvisation. In 1937, Gerónimo Baqueiro Fóster brought back from the region of Alvarado two such men to his home in Mexico City, where I heard them. Their improvisatory genius and their ability to sustain not alone interest but prolonged excitement in the listener was comparable only to that of the best swing men. There seemed to be no end to their contrapuntal inventions. Two voices, four hands, and four feet managed successfully to contrive more complications than one would have thought humanly possible.

The *Son* (to be kept absolutely apart from the Cuban *Son,* of course) is still the most mysterious of the forms. One writer claims the *Huapango* is a variety of *Son,* another that the *Son* is part of the *Jarabe*; no one can give its particular characteristics. (Galindo is preparing a thesis on the *Son* proper, the first work of its kind.) Although *Sones* of a degenerate and indifferent sort can be heard pretty generally, actually good *Sones* are extremely rare, their point of origin being restricted to the region of Jalisco and Michoacan. The interest of the piece lies completely in its rhythmical complication; the more complex and varied the accompaniment, the purer the *Son.* The easiest distinguishing feature is the so-called alternate

6/8 and 3/4 meter, proper to the *Son* alone. Galindo prefers to consider the entire piece as being in 6/8, and gives me the following examples of rhythms from his native Jalisco. The lower notes represent the percussive section, as played by the guitarron and sometimes drum, the middle notes are the harmony section carried by guitars and jaranas—small guitars, from which the Yucatecan dance takes its name, also called vihuelas, depending upon the region—and the top line is that of the instrumental melody played by violins. The vocal line is sung above and apart from this fundamental accompaniment (see Fig. 1).

The tempo is far more frantic than that of the *Huapango,* and certainly the rhythms are much more indigenous, making the consequent general effect nearer the primitive side. *Sones* and the Mariachi orchestras that play them are inseparable. (Revueltas once told me that during Maximilian's time these little instrumental groups were called in to assist at weddings, which were then known, by a current snobbism, as *mariages*; but since the Mexicans' French pronunciation was far from perfect, the orchestras came to be known as Mariachis. It may be a legend.) There is no fixed recipe for the composition of a Mariachi. A fairly classical arrangement of instruments would be: violins, harp, jaranas, guitars, and guitarrones (enormous guitars played pizzicato on a single string). Vicente T. Mendoza, Mexico's foremost musicologist, gives the following list as comprising a typical group in Guerrero: two violins playing in thirds (participating only between choruses), two vihuelas, whose players sing as well in the form of responses to the principal singer or go along with him in thirds, and a drummer who plays a cylindrical-shaped instrument with two different sticks, one short and soft for the membrane and the other long and hard for the rim. The drummer is the principal singer. In cities a trumpet is often added and there are generally more of each kind of instrument.

Two forms whose interest lies principally in their lyrics are the *Canción Ranchera,* or Mexican *lied,* which comes in two varieties, amorous and zoological, and the *Corrido,* an endless saga, differing from the former in that its choruses are generally shorter and repeated practically forever or at least until the tale is told. The *Corrido* may be military, religious, criminological (these are called *Tragedias* in the north of Mexico) or may deal with the less heroic things of life, such as adultery, deception, jealousy, ridicule; or just important events like the installation of electricity in a town, or the inauguration of a new bus line. It is not a localized phenomenon, although

Figure 1.

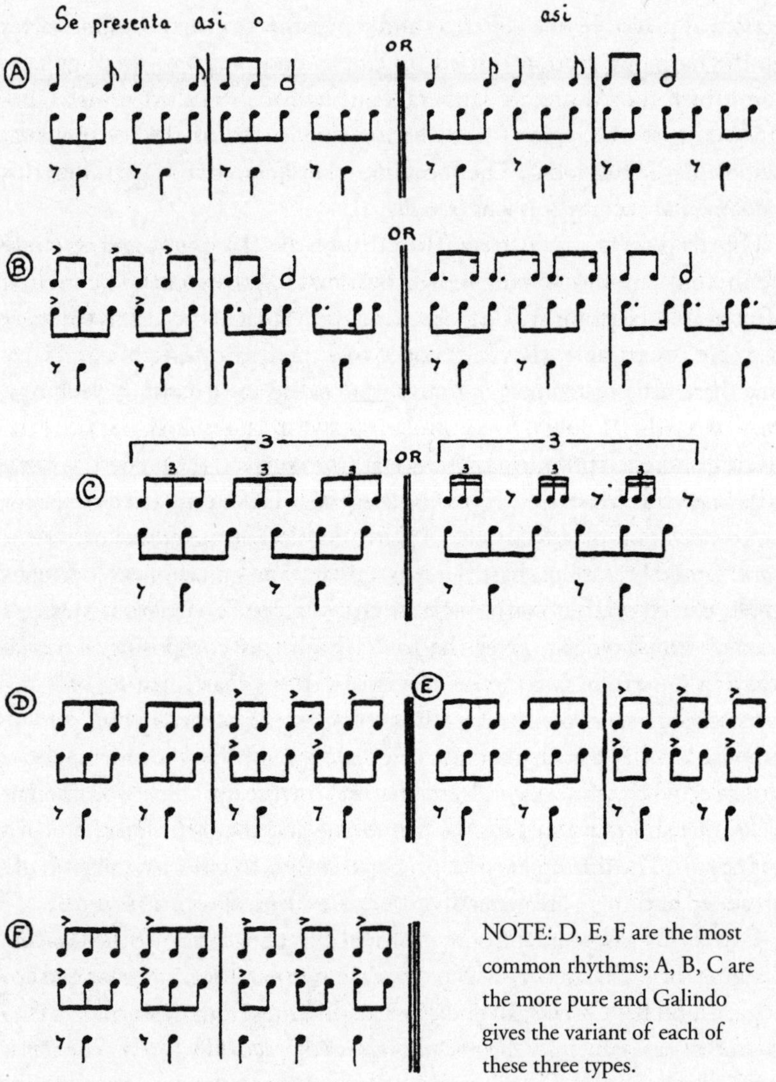

Se presenta asi o asi

OR

(A)

OR

(B)

OR

(C)

(D)

(E)

(F)

NOTE: D, E, F are the most common rhythms; A, B, C are the more pure and Galindo gives the variant of each of these three types.

the region richest in *Corridos,* as well as in a good many other musical manifestations both indigenous and transplanted, is the state of Michoacan. The meter is generally ternary, although like the *Canción Ranchera,* it may be binary. Occasional measures of 7/8 and 2/8 appear. A good deal of study has been done by Mendoza, tracing the development and metamorphosis of the old Spanish *Romance* and the *Corrido Andaluz* into the *Corrido.* It is certain that a great many of the songs are practically identical even after three centuries or so, although the tessitura of the *Corrido* is definitely greater. An interesting note is that practically 60 percent of all *Corridos* end on the mediant of the scale. *Corridos,* like *Sones,* are rendered by Mariachis or by anyone with a guitar who feels like singing about something in particular.

Mendoza has the following to say of the *Corrido*: "In cases where there exist irregularities of form, whether in the number of syllables which make up the line or in the number of lines which form the chorus, there frequently appear *estribillos*" (the *estribillo* is that part of any song which can be considered as a refrain—a recurrent theme, as in a rondo), "interspersed, perhaps as exclamations, as spoken words, or as phrases which break up the symmetry of the literary or musical forms. In some cases these *estribillos* develop in such a way that they are not simply one or two lines but constitute independent verses of four or more lines, sometimes having a different meter from the *Corrido* proper. The purpose is to achieve more rhythmical variety or greater emphasis, and it does give the form an extraordinary liberty. In this way, the *Corrido* acquires a wealth of forms, meters and rhythms, developing as time goes on into a true work of art." He adds that if one will trace the history of one individual *Corrido* from its earliest rudimentary state up to its most complex form, he will at the same time have followed the historical development of Mexican music.

The *Jarabe* is primarily a dance form, and is usually a suite (rather like the classical suite) of short pieces played in rigorously fixed sequence, leaving a certain leeway at one point in the choice of a section (as between the *Sarabande* and the *Gigue*). There is no doubt that the *Jarabe* (originally *Sarao*) was brought over whole from Spain in the form of *Seguidillas, Zambras, Fandangos,* and *Jarabes Gitanos.* All these are *danzas zapateadas* (shoe or tap dances), which arrived in New Spain in their pure state but were gradually molded, sometimes even consciously, by means of straight ridicule, by those to whom they were brought, into something quite different. The melodies are lively, nearly always in major, with a good deal of changing of key, not only to the relative dominant and subdominant, but also to the related keys of these in turn. The meter may also change between sections, although it may remain one of 3/4 or 6/8 all the way through. The *Jarabe Tapatio* of Querétaro (which Saldívar suggests should be called the Official *Jarabe*) includes both binary and ternary meters. Another, more vulgar *Jarabe Tapatio,* the best-known outside Mexico, uses in turn sections in 6/8, 3/4, 2/4, and 2/8.

All this music certainly started out Spanish and ended up Mexican, and the two sound very little alike. Most Mexican forms are Spanish melody-types encased in indigenous rhythms, but that is not all that is different. Mexican music is insistent, childlike, impersonal, and lacks, except in rare cases, just those qualities of subtlety, hauteur, and brilliance which characterize the music of Spain. Listen any evening in the Plaza Garibaldi to the simultaneous playing of six or seven groups of ordinary Mariachis. The rhythms are unpredictable but earthbound. Nothing could be much farther from the hard, circumspect precisions of Andalusía or Asturias. But the great differences lie not primarily in the melodies, nor in the harmonic progressions, nor yet in the rhythms, but rather in a whole mass of innumerable details affecting all these things, details which when combined make a result distinct from the original music. What remains is as much a direct product, I think, of the climate and topography as of the civilization these have helped to engender. The voice and intonation of the Indian and mestizo are not the same as those of the Spaniard. Guitar technic is very different. The Indian taste for falsetto singing and whooping helps to carry the music in the opposite direction from Spain.

The interest for the foreign musician certainly does not lie in the music proper or its text, be it ever so authentic and touching, but rather in the special charm inherent in the playing of each kind of performing *conjunto.* The same piece rendered by a group of Mariachis in Guadalajara will sound very different in Cordoba, when given by a Veracruzano harpist and guitarrist (and will probably be unrecognizable if played by a rural Indian band anywhere.)

Here is a whole national music dying before it has been made known to the cultured world. Even the strictly indigenous music may survive longer than this popular mestizo, because it is more protected from degeneration through contact. There are no recordings available of good Mexican popular music. Men like Daniel Castañedas, Mendoza, Fóster, Luis Sandi,

Ruben M. Campos, and Saldívar have initiated in the last ten years a study which should be carried on tenfold in the years to come if the musical heritage of four centuries is not to be lost.

Letter from Mexico

NOVEMBER–DECEMBER (1941), *MODERN MUSIC*

Mexico City, November 1

The composer's opportunity to live solely from the music he writes, rare enough in the United States, is reduced to all but zero here in Mexico. Due to the absence of any royalty-collecting organization, even famous songwriters like Augustin Lara, Dominguez, Tata Nacho, Ruiz, and Marroquin are compelled to be constantly on the lookout for small radio jobs of arranging programs and accompanying singers. Lara receives a monthly stipend from XEW, the most important station, for writing and playing whatever music is required, but it can't matter very much to him if a song is a hit here, or in Cuba or the United States, since in any case he won't receive a centavo beyond his salary and those infinitesimal publisher's rights. (Practically all the serious composers are given pittances by the government for teaching classes or playing in the Orquesta Sinfónica.) During the past few months a local ASCAP, called the Sindicato de Autores, Compositores, y Editores de Música, has been formed, with the object of trying to persuade the officials of film and radio (even more commercial here than in the United States) that the inauguration of the system of *pequeño derecho* would not be amiss. Of course the officials scream injustice and regimentation. The composers have yet to receive their first royalty check, but they seem confident of success. The Sindicato would also make obligatory the drawing up of contracts for film and popular music, a procedure which might tend to protect the composers' interests, although not necessarily, as some of the film companies are fly-by-night outfits with which a contract is perfectly useless, since it has on occasion proven impossible for composers to collect even with names on dotted lines.

The Mexican radio is of such a technical and esthetic poverty as to make practically any American program, commercial or sustaining, seem the acme of good taste and talent. There are no professional arrangers anywhere, and the job is taken on in spare time by instrumentalists who know enough about how to put notes on paper to be able to make some parts. Scores are not bothered with. An arrangement costs from two to three dollars. Rehearsals are often considered superfluous, and when a one-hour commercial program is given a two-hour maximum rehearsal period, half the musicians are likely not to appear. Naturally composers want to have as little as possible to do with the radio.

So far there have been practically no cinema composers in Mexico who have turned out actual scores. The norm has consisted of untalented arrangements of standard tripe. Only two Mexicans have substantial lists of integrated film scores to their credit. One is Revueltas, who began with *Redes* and continued with a long list of documentaries and several feature films, the most important of which are *La Noche de los mayas, Bajo el signo de la muerte, Los de abajo,* and *Que viene mi marido!* The other man is Raul Lavista, who at the moment has a virtual monopoly on grade-A Mexican films (if indeed such can be said to exist). Lavista believes in Hollywood, has the greatest admiration for Max Steiner, and explains that the film people here have always preferred his music to that of Revueltas because he knew how to make concessions to popular taste, a thing Revueltas refused to do. The music for his four most recent films: *Viviré otra vez; El Hijo de cruz diabolo; Ay, qué tiempos; Señor Don Simon!* and *La Casa del rencor,* is decidedly nonexperimental and completely competent. He has to do all his own orchestration, as well as rehearse dancers and singers, conduct at recordings, and write lyrics if needed. The average price paid for an hour's score is the equivalent of five hundred dollars. Since feature films are made here on budgets comparable to those provided for short documentaries in the United States, practically no time is allotted for rehearsals. Fortunately the musicians are from the Orquesta Sinfónica, which eliminates some of the headaches. Deservedly or not, Lavista now receives the same credits and publicity accorded to the director of the film, a state of affairs inconceivable in Hollywood!

......

One event of the past symphonic season was the new Stravinsky symphony, which, even though the composer conducted, proved a balancing job a bit too difficult for the orchestra. Instruments supposed to pick up the line unnoticed would blurt boorishly in, apparently unaware that they were destroying the extremely delicate fabric. However, the reception was favorable. The other event was the good old-fashioned *succès de scandale* provoked by the world premiere of Copland's *Short Symphony.* The critics of the three large dailies were divided. One simply announced he considered it shameful that Chávez would stoop to conduct such a piece publicly just because it happened to be dedicated to him. Later I questioned this gentleman as to why he had so heartily hated the piece. "Copland is a Jew," he replied, "and I never review Jewish music. Not even Ravel."

The Lener Quartet and Irma Gonzalez gave Virgil Thomson's *Stabat Mater* what was probably its best performance to date, in spite of Señorita Gonzalez's unrecognizable French. Chávez conducted Revueltas's *Janitzio,* to which I took an Indian from Noxtepec, in the mountains of Guerrero. His comment was: "How beautiful! It sounds just like a *cantina.*" A few nights ago a little orchestra with a long name, La Orquesta de Camera de la Sección Cultural por Radio (part of the at present much-beleaguered Secretaria de Educación Publica), played two Revueltas pieces. In spite of the uniformly bad execution, *8 × Radio* sounded well, perhaps because it is a pastiche of the kind of folk music one is accustomed to hear rendered with extremely indifferent technic. *Planos,* a larger orchestral piece arranged for nine instruments, was less happy. The vengeful dissonances came out watered and senseless, and the ostinato passages, which should have force, lacked dynamics and became monotonous.

The Revueltas family is not eager to have the work of its most illustrious member made known to the world at large. Victor had agreed to make an album consisting of *Homenaje a García Lorca* and the orchestral version of *Siete Canciones* with text by Lorca, the men had been rehearsed and everything was set, but the family refused permission. They were adamant also in not allowing Steinbeck and Kline to use Revueltas music for *The Forgotten Village* when it was suggested that a score be pieced together out of sections of various orchestral works. I have even heard it said that Koussevitzky had to forego playing a certain piece of Revueltas because he was unable to obtain the family's sanction.

The Orquesta Sinfónica offered a prize this year for the best new work by a Mexican composer. Prize: one hundred dollars. Conditions: ink score, and parts furnished by composer. Result: no entries.

ARTICLES AND REVIEWS

......

1942

Films and Theatre

NOVEMBER–DECEMBER (1942), *MODERN MUSIC*

The World at War is one of the better propaganda pictures and has one of the better soundtracks. The copy I saw (in upper New York State) suffered from frequent cuts, so that sometimes it was impossible to understand even the commentary. However, the logic of its sequences seemed straight enough. Naturally it is a task to make background music for a conversation between a group of dive-bombers and several anti-aircraft guns. The sound effect carries the day nearly every time, as against the music. The important thing would therefore seem to be to write music which sounds so much like the noises covering it that the ear will not find it too easy to detect any disparity between the two: protective tonal coloring. Anything to avoid that symphonic strain over which suddenly spreads a curtain of motor noises as the planes rise into the sky. (This I admit to be one valid dramatic solution to the problem, but by no means the only one.) Gail Kubik has done a good job, but one feels he was not in on the scenario or the cutting. But then, how often *is* the composer? Does the director or compiler, outside of musical pictures, ever work from an integrated scenario, as precise as an opera score, with every word of the dialogue or commentary set to a definite measure of the score? That is obviously often the only way to make a good soundtrack, and it is just as obvious that no one but the composer wants to do it. However *The World at War* was made, it is pretty choppy. This is unfortunate, because the musical material is of the straightforward, hard-hitting variety, with good basic rhythms guaranteed to catch immediately the interest in any given sequence. The trouble is one is often let down when the rhythm is drowned by noises or when it is simply cut off by the commentary. What seem to be actual newsreel soundtracks are interspersed without esthetic casualties. The Japanese baseball game is charming. There is a funeral march for Pearl Harbor. The paraphrasing of Brahms while the Nazis sleep along the roads of France struck me as the best bit.

If it were my function to comment upon extramusical messages conveyed by films, I could be indignant at greater length than I can here about the *Battle of Midway.* Considered as a film used for propaganda purposes by a great nation at war, it is lamentably ineffective. Aside from the expected technical defects inevitable in a document made during the heat of battle (defects which incidentally might have been turned into virtues by more awareness in the cutting room) the film is as trite and depressing a bit of flag-waving as one could hope to see, even in time of war. It is unfortunate that John Ford had access only to a color camera, because the resulting hues are those of a Kodachrome reproduction in a copy of the *National Geographic Magazine,* vintage of 1925. There are no screen credits for the music, for which someone must be grateful, for if the film is operetta-like, chauvinistic, and infantile in its approach to the war, the music catches up with it in lack of planning, silliness, and bad taste. Thus we get things like a sky of bomb-puffs painted by Tanguy, with the *Star-Spangled Banner* flanked by the humming of motors. We also have *Onward, Christian Soldiers* (but wouldn't a purely Aryan army appreciate it more than ours?) When there is no place for commentary or motors, a sudden sweet symphonic bit is interpolated for an instant and then ruthlessly truncated for a new five-second airplane-motor passage. Each sequence resembles what goes on musically during the captions in a newsreel, the difference being that the newsreel themes have cadences. If we are in this war for any purpose at all, it is to rid the world of its irrational ideological heritage. Nothing in this dangerous film suggests that the struggle involves anything more than the rapid annihilation of the present political enemies of the United States of America.

The much-touted *Mrs. Miniver* is another picture full of the noises of war. It is difficult for most of us to know, as yet, how near to or how far from reality all these sounds are, that we take so much for granted in present-day movies. We can only accept or question the word of technicians and war initiates. As to their esthetic value, however, aside from direct functions, such as the growing or diminishing volume of airplane motors serving as a kind of gauge to the imminence of death or the emotional impact of explosions used as punctuation for a scene, it seems to me that such noises have yet to be put successfully to use through incorporation into the dramatic and musical fabric. Here these sounds are quite mellow in tone, and sometimes even seem neither dubbed nor like a percussion section. The score by Herbert Stothart has the regular overstuffed, plush tonality of Hollywood. Part of the monotony of the American film comes from the leveling influence of music which provides the same luxurious ambiance for all kinds of scenes. The Ravel instrumental cloak always offers expensive-sounding comfort, especially when it is used to cover musical comedy tunes. And why, whenever a cat is shown on the screen, must the soundtrack carry a very unfeline—or if feline in sound, untimely—meow?

This Is the Enemy, from the Lenfilm Studies, is a collection of shorts about the Nazis, and each section is the work of a different director. Some have considerable interest one way and another, but never musically. It is badly recorded; marching scenes are shown to music in marked waltz meter. In the Yugoslavian sequence there is one good passage for cello, trumpet, and snare-drum.

On the other hand, *Soviet Border,* a less recent Lenfilm production, besides being adult, has a score. It is by Pushkov, and is pretty well mitred into the dialogue and sound effects. In general, the musical background is scanty, a characteristic which has come to be associated with a good film score. And there are grateful, dramatic silences. As usual, the Russians break into spontaneous and harmonized singing. One of these songs, used as a leitmotif, sounds very much like the *Lied der Einbeitsfront* of Eisler but isn't. There is another one which is reminiscent of our own colonial *Peter Grey.* Pushkov's favorite chord seems to be the diminished third, and he is also fond of elaborate trumpet fanfares. A Mongolian plays a nice piece on an indigenous violin.

Jacare, Frank Buck's newest object lesson in nature for the kiddies, is all about caimans in the Amazon, and he has a score by Miklós Rózsa, specialist in exoticisms, which runs throughout the seventy minutes of the film. The never-stopping symphonic score is indispensable in films like this, without continuity of plot, or even the verisimilitude which is the sine qua non of documentary films. A travel theme, which is used for going up the river into caiman-land and back down again on the return trip, combines the vamp of *Dardanella,* an Augustin Lara tune, the orchestration of *Boléro,* and a rumba rhythm section with maracas and claves. Along the way there are animal leitmotifs which are used as literal musical underlining for their visual counterparts: a bass sax tune for peccaries, a string meow-piece for a jaguar, piccolos and oboes playing minor seconds and ninths for monkeys, and so on. In fights between beasts of different species this system leads to thematic complications, which are solved by adding augmented triads ascending the whole-tone scale in the brass section. It is unfortunate that the commentator's diction has the precision of a grammar-school child reciting a badly learned lesson; it is often impossible to understand.

Sol Kaplan has the screen credits for *Tales of Manhattan.* The score is a Californian commodity of the kind whose output must be one-a-day. It begins with lots of harp-vomit, which is probably not the composer's fault since that dish seems to be a permanent one on the American cinema menu. The Sherry-Netherlands is shown to a special arrangement of *An American in Paris.* There is a love scene with some solo violin-playing, a comedy scene with animated cartoon music, and nice *Salomé* memories for the best bit of the picture: when Ginger Rogers decides to capture Henry Fonda. There is also Charles Laughton playing the part of a composer who conducts his *Bacchanale Moderne* in (Grauman's) Carnegie Hall, but the role's very conception is as much an insult to the profession as the subsequent Negro sequence is to that race. Here the Hall Johnson choir makes some pleasant sounds, pitted against a very insistent wind machine. At the last minute Paul Robeson strikes an attitude, and the whole thing becomes a musical, with palm-out hand-waving and other devotional gestures. You even have Chinese music in this amazing film, but I mean the good old Chinky-Chinky kind with the winds playing appoggiaturas in fourths. I think the harp-vomit is the worst, though, and it's certainly not restricted to *Tales of Manhattan.*

Ballet, like opera and acrobatics, needs to be seen in the flesh. It is a nonrealistic, virtuoso action, and it must look prodigious to look true. Nothing, except perhaps factual recordings of events, can really be prodigious in the cinema because the cinema is a medium which lends an air of complete realism to even the most unlikely fantasy. So you have your dancer, who needs the formal frame of the stage, fished out of fantasy and plunked into realism. Close-ups of his grimacings and gesticulations are a further insult. (Thus Massine, in the filmed version of *Gaité Parisienne,* looks just like Eddie Cantor.) Dance figures are cut into or prolonged at will. The familiar tension between musicians and dancers, one of the principal problems in ballet (and how beautiful it is when satisfyingly solved) is gone. In its place is an invisible orchestra, mechanically synchronized. One feels that each downbeat has been blooped in the soundtrack and made to fit a foot touching the floor. There is also the question of the ballet score's having been written with the fact in mind that the audience sees the entire ballet from one vantage-point. In the film that changes every few seconds (it would be just as bad if it didn't, probably much worse) while the music, made clumsy by the visual hopping about, lumbers on. It is like watching someone try to fit a Mercator's projection of the world around a globe.

In the Theatre

There really is nothing to say about the *Rosalinda* of the New Opera Company. God only knows why the critics liked it. Perhaps *they* thought the brash production fitting to *Fledermaus,* or the cheap, tinselly costumes humorous in the right way, or the slick Broadway orchestration an improvement on the original. But even they could not possibly have liked the acting. Miss Virginia MacWatters as Adele did most of the good singing. Her diction enabled you to get the full force of the English lyrics. These in general were completely repulsive, as witness the text of the theme song and third-act finale:

> Oh, Jiminy, oh, Jiminy!
> What joy to be forever free.
> Oh, Jiminy! Sweet Liberty,
> We sing in praise of thee!

Balanchine's choreography was well-nigh indistinguishable from the rush of the crowd on the stage packed with people. In the drunk ballet one could at least see what was going on. Because of the crudely coy performances, and probably also because of the typical Straussian lack of harmonic variety, all the songs had a tendency to sound alike. The playful period sets by Oliver Smith and the melodies were more or less of a piece: they were gay and diverting. The rest of the production hadn't the distinction of an old-time vaudeville act.

Massine put Revueltas at a disadvantage in *Don Domingo,* the ballet he pieced together for the Ballet Theatre out of old scores by that Mexican composer. The impression given was one of not very competent collage. Practically all of Revueltas is genre music, which, more than any other kind of music, has to be left alone in its context if it is to retain its meaning. Here practically nothing was left untampered with long enough to establish a mood. The dissonances, which make sense when the music is played in its original form, seem unable to vindicate themselves; they remain naughty-boy harmonies. Inasmuch as Revueltas is never strong melodically, relying rather for his power on cumulative emotional impact, it is impossible to present scraps of his music without losing most of the flavor. In *Don Domingo* the barbarous splendor of the orchestration becomes noisy chaos. One notable exception is the dream, which is set to the *Duelo* from *Homenaje a García Lorca.* This pas de deux is the most moving passage because the music is sufficiently repetitious and mood-making. The fact that the ballet at this point abandons its quasi-ethnographical approach in favor of pure fantasy also has something to do with it. The folklore in *Don Domingo* has the quality of a tourist poster. It is a little too exact to be so fake. Practically all the instrumentation is Revueltas's. Dorati reorchestrated *Duelo* and *Baile* from *Homenaje,* and finished *Troka.* The rest of the score is made up of parts of *Janitzio, Caminos,* and *La Coronela.* The inclusion of a dismemberment of Revueltas's last work, itself a ballet, I consider a shameless procedure. If at some distant time in the future someone wants to compile a posthumous Stravinsky ballet, it might be considered legitimate if parts of the *Symphony for Wind Instruments,* the *Capriccio,* the *Dumbarton Oaks Concerto,* and a magnified version of the *Octet* were strung together to provide a score (although the result would be esthetically worthless). But if the compiler added one page of *Petrouchka,* his action would be, as far as I am concerned, unethical and lousy. *La Coronela* is a very good ballet in its own right. Why should anyone break it up in order to make an inferior one?

Spanish Work Is Performed at Cosmopolitan

NOVEMBER 20 (1942), *NEW YORK HERALD TRIBUNE*

La Leyenda del beso, Spanish zarzuela, book by Enrique Reoyo, Antonio Paso Jr., and Silva Aramburu; music by Soutullo y Vert, presented last night at the Cosmopolitan Opera House with the following cast:

Amapola	Maria Robles
Amapola	Pilar Arroyo
Ulita	Mary Reid
Charito	Nina Zabal
Margot	Margarita Conti
Ketty	Natalia Farge
Coral	Ana Elina Barea
Estrella	Virginia Sanchez
Clavellina	Mildred Cardozo
Violeta	Beatris Garcia
Mario	Carlos Morelli
Ivan	Fausto Alvares
Goron	Nestor Pardo
Cristobal	Enrique Gonzalez
Alesko	Luis Orta
Ernesto	Pablo Galvis
Alfonso	Joaquin Fernandez
Señor Juan	Alejandro Elliot
Gurko	Antonio Iveas

Conductor, Pedro Sanjuan. Chorus director, Bernabe Solis.
Stage manager, Hernando Silva. Dance arrangements by Loja Bravo.

The Spanish zarzuela is an amorphous combination of elements from forms as unlike each other as grand opera, musical comedy, and vaudeville. In Spain all this is doubtless integrated by the powerful Spanish personality. Spaniards have the gift of making everything they do seem very precise and expressive.

In last night's production of *La Leyenda del beso* there was very little Spanish personality. Since a zarzuela given in New York is of necessity a genre piece, and the Spanish dramatic tradition at its best might easily be taken for plain ham acting by the New York public (accustomed to the ethnological approach to art manifestations of that country), great care should have been taken to do all the directorial, musical, and scenic manicuring possible. The whole thing should have been forced into a genre frame. As it was, the piece became a not very diverting succession of love duets, choral numbers, and spoken dialogues, performed before a sadder set than the Metropolitan ever saw.

Carlos Morelli, as the jovial host, seemed to have a good deal of pitch trouble. Maria Robles was a pale gypsy with an even paler voice, Nestor Pardo and Pilar Arroyo made a pleasing duo, and came through both musically and as characters. Enrique Gonzalez was a convincing bumpkin, and created his role beautifully with the repeated use of one restrained ballet-like gesture.

Most of the dialogue and humor was of the rural "carpa," or tent-show, variety, with violent asides to the audience from downstage—a particularly welcome device in a piece where everything, especially the acting, ought to be highly formalized. The general impression, however, was that an Italian company was giving a show in Spanish, and there was an Italian approach to all the singing as well as to the use of popular Spanish music. In Madrid, even with the same cast, the result would probably have been much happier.

Aitken, Pianist, Is Heard in Bach-Debussy Concert

DECEMBER 1 (1942), *NEW YORK HERALD TRIBUNE*

Webster Aitken, pianist, played last night at the New York Times Hall in a program devoted to works by Bach and Debussy. It was unfortunate that an abundance of draperies around the stage prevented the sounds coming from the piano from being brilliant. Also, the pianist worked with extreme reticence. It was a gray, stifled concert. The playing had a distraught, almost unconscious quality. One felt Mr. Aitken to be so continually immersed in treating with the details of each separate figure that there was no past or future for any phrase; the line appeared never to be envisaged.

The Bach numbers (the Toccata in F-sharp Minor and the Partita in E Minor) were attacked with a nervousness which, with its resultant unpredictable, capricious effects on the playing, left the spectator seeking vainly some special, subtle point that it seemed the artist must be making. The agitation never broke through into activity.

Debussy fared somewhat better. Mr. Aitken obviously loves to make the suitable liquid sounds indicated in pieces like *Poissons d'or* and *Cloches à travers les feuilles,* and he made such sounds very creditably. His arrival at *L'Isle joyeuse* was attended by hand-crossing difficulties; at the same time the piece came off best because he stayed with it all the way through. The entire evening's playing, however, was singularly inexpressive. Mr. Aitken's conception did not have the necessary power to warrant his style's being so impersonal.

Kirkpatrick Is Heard in Harpsichord Recital

DECEMBER 3 (1942), *NEW YORK HERALD TRIBUNE*

Last night at Carnegie Chamber Music Hall, Ralph Kirkpatrick, harpsichordist, gave the first in a series of four Bach recitals. It is difficult not to be inordinately enthusiastic over such a concert, if only because it involves the harpsichord itself, that antidote to the poison sounds of our era's daily life. It is the instrument which allows every note of every voice of a piece of contrapuntal writing to be heard with complete clarity; remote and recessed as a voice may sound, it is never hidden. In any case, there was no reason to inhibit one's enthusiasm last night, as Mr. Kirkpatrick performed with style, feeling, and accuracy.

The Sarabande of the Partita no. 2 in C Minor was played with a peculiar halting gait, almost imperceptible, but which enhanced its mysteriousness and made it sound like the uneven ticking of a clock's pendulum. It was the Sarabande again in the Partita no. 1 in B-flat Major that contained some most impressive playing, with its thin fabric of sound, behind which silence seemed to form a part of the music itself.

The instrument used last night by Mr. Kirkpatrick lacked the incisive upper register that one is accustomed to hear in the harpsichord. From where the reviewer sat, two unwelcome noises often marred the rendition: the loud wooden sounds of the instrument's action and the apparently unconscious humming of the performer.

N.B.C. Symphony Plays Two Works by Americans

DECEMBER 7 (1942), *NEW YORK HERALD TRIBUNE*

Leopold Stokowski conducted the broadcast of the N. B. C. Symphony Orchestra late yesterday afternoon in a program including his own arrangements of Bach and works by contemporary American composers and Wagner. It was a badly chosen program, and (probably because the best music as well as the best execution came at the beginning) one which had a depressing effect on the listener.

Mr. Stokowski's sonorous Bach orchestrations all resemble each other in the fact that they manage to make the music sound quite unmoving and not very much like Bach. In the Chorale-Prelude, "Wirglauben all' an einen Gott," the quality was slightly impaired by a leaden woodwind section; this cleared up presently and the piece reached a bright climactic ending. The Adagio from the Toccata, Adagio, and Fugue in C finished with an unfortunate single vibraphone note, a fitting preparation for the unbelievable vulgarities which immediately followed.

The two American works were the "Exile" Symphony, by Alan Hovhaness, and the Symphonic Rumba, by Paul Lavalle. Both abounded in material of the sort that is generally conceded to be "exotic" when used in film scores. The "Exile" was music for an extremely long sequence of monkeys chattering in the jungle, as done for the more spectacular Hollywood animal pictures. Miklós Rózsa gets better results, however, because film orchestration is cleverer. The Symphonic Rumba was a five-minute trip to Cugat-land with Ravel, whose main musical connection with Cuba was the addition of claves, guiro, bongo, and maracas to the percussion section. These pieces were exotic in one sense, to be sure: They remained outside the precinct of music.

When Mr. Toscanini plays unforgivably bad modern Italian music, one consoles oneself with the thought that contemporary Italy is musically decadent, but there is no alleviation to the disappointment one feels upon hearing two so empty and unmusical American works played on the same program.

Emanuel List Offers Schubert Song Recital

DECEMBER 8 (1942), *NEW YORK HERALD TRIBUNE*

Emanuel List, basso, sang last night at the New York Times Hall in a Schubert program whose principal number was the *Winterreise* cycle, complete in its twenty-four parts.

One would have liked to concentrate on following the melodic line in its leisurely lyrical voyage through the suite of songs, but the myriad tonal ambiguities prevented it; the rendition was by no means close enough to the kind that would have permitted that kind of listening. For instance, at the beginnings of phrases there was sometimes a difference of as much as a minor third between the tone the voice hit and the tone it had to slide to. Also, unaccented syllables were often robbed of their pitch, and there was a sharp, acid quality in forte passages which suggested a muscular tightness in the throat. The correctness of pitch was in inverse ratio to the volume of voice used. This applied to all registers.

Mr. List's performance last night was patronizing to his audience. Apparently he assumed that Schubert lacks sufficient expressive quality to be put over without byplay. He dramatized the mood according to his fancy. He sang this somber piece as though its sentiments were light and quite pleasant—as though Schubert hadn't really meant to make all this gloom and was really only fooling. Thus there was a constant incongruity between the written music and the sounds one heard professing to represent it. Purely lyrical music such as this needs no histrionics in its performance. The mood was implicit, and could have been had by simple stating of the material.

Sometimes in serene passages the delivery was distinguished for a fleeting moment. It was not until the cycle's epilogue, "Der Leiermann," that one heard what one had hoped to hear: an entire song given with the voice subdued and thus enough under control to sing the actual notes written.

Vronsky-Babin Team Heard in Carnegie Hall

DECEMBER 9 (1942), *NEW YORK HERALD TRIBUNE*

Last night at Carnegie Hall, Vitya Vronsky and Victor Babin presented a two-piano program consisting mainly of music by living composers. Miss Vronsky and Mr. Babin make a pleasant team and they play unspectacularly with verve and shine. Last night's performance nearly always showed an ample measure of simultaneity. The artists seemed to realize that if two pianos cannot be twice as interesting as one, an effort at least must be made to see that the duo compensates in brilliancy and technical feats for what is lost in personality projections. There were no attempts at causing tones to sing, no personal intrusions to get in the way of clear, shining playing.

In the vivace of the Sonata in C Minor for Two Claviers and Pedal, no. 2 (arranged by Mr. Babin), there were some nebulous passages of runs which made atmosphere rather than Bach: the pianists had not yet warmed up. The Duettino Concertante after Mozart by Busoni was far more successful. It went off with lightning virtuosity. The endless Rachmaninoff Symphonic Dances (op. 45) was a thick piece, full of obtuse, arbitrary key relationships. The composer's deficient harmonic sense was very much in evidence in this static parade of chords stuffed with carelessly chosen false notes. Miss Vronsky and Mr. Babin did all that could be done to put across the tasteless, floppy material.

Stravinsky's Tango and *Circus Polka* were also made up of harmony whose interest lay in its false notes, but here they were all in focus. The two pianists took these uninhibited pieces a bit cautiously, never opening up on them as one would have liked. Perhaps they were saving their fire for the Milhaud *Scaramouche,* which really sounded the way two pianos should, making noises that no other combination can. This was the best writing for the medium, with its battery of bright, cold treble notes like xylophones, its four hands, each busy with different figures, its constant expressive effervescence. They played it superbly: one wished it had been three times as long.

Grace Moore Sings Tosca at Metropolitan

DECEMBER 21 (1942), *NEW YORK HERALD TRIBUNE*

Tosca, opera in three acts by Giacomo Puccini, book by Victorién Sardou, Luigi Illica and Giuseppe Giacoss, first performance of the season at the Metropolitan Opera House Saturday night, with the following cast:

Floria Tosca	Grace Moore
Mario Cavaradossi	Charles Kullman
Baron Scarpia	Lawrence Tibbett
Cesare Angelotti	Walter Olltaki
The Sacristan	Salvatore Baccaloni
Spoletta	Alesio de Paolis
Sciarrone	George Cehanovsky

Conductor, Cesare Sodero; stage director, Lothar Wallerstein; chorus master, Giacomo Spadoni; scenic designer, Joseph Novak.

On Saturday evening, Miss Moore's portrayal of *Tosca* sounded better than it looked. It is true that at times one could see her lips moving mutely without hearing anything but the orchestra. But when the vocal line went into a higher register, passion and tenderness were in the voice. The role was convincingly sung, but the persuasiveness relied solely upon the voice for its strength. Miss Moore's gestures and postures detracted immeasurably from her portrayal. Always there was too much swaying of the torso, too much stiff striding about.

In the tenser minutes of the second act, her bodily movements became so dramatically unsure, so twitching, that one was in spite of oneself reminded of the way the characters jump in an ancient film. One did not mind the excessiveness of her posturing so much as its lack of gracefulness and elegance. "Vissi d'arte" was sung with sonorous tone and much dramatizing. The audience was appreciative.

Mr. Tibbett's Scarpia was polished, if not perhaps the complete embodiment of egocentricity and malevolence that would have made his amorous activities seem really repulsive. His voice sounded curtained, muffled all evening, notably at the first act finale, when he had to compete with loud orchestra and chorus.

At this point, incidentally, the ostinato of chimes that were more than a quarter-tone flat was anything but helpful to the effectiveness of the music. These are not supposed to be sound-effect chimes; the entire structure of the passage is based upon the succession of harmonies placed above the two alternating tones.

Mr. Kullman was pleasant as Cavaradossi. His intense and excited portrayal, explosive articulation, and sometimes querulous voice made for an exaggeratedly romantic characterization, but he was a sympathetic figure.

Salvatore Baccaloni's voice and acting created an excellent sacristan; moreover, his diction was the best of the evening. A good many of the choirboys (ladies wearing silly wigs) looked like Harpo Marx. Their prancing around Mr. Baccaloni made neither a beautiful nor an amusing spectacle. Mr. Sodero made the orchestra sound uniformly well.

North African Music I

DECEMBER 27 (1942), *NEW YORK HERALD TRIBUNE*

From Agadir on the Atlantic across to the shores of Chott Djerid in Tunisia there are a lot of Americans just now. It is safe to assume that, if they stay there very long, they are going to hear a good deal of the music of these parts in spite of themselves, and even without paying visits to cafés and *quartiers réservés*. While they probably won't return knowing all the stanzas to the popular Tunisian, Algerian, or Moroccan songs of the epoch, still it is quite conceivable that among the musical by-products of the war will figure a song or so about North Africa. Something like "Fathma from Fez," perhaps?

If one moves either coastwise around or inland across this part of the continent, one finds a varied supply of music. First of all, the Arabs have been more successful in imposing their religion and language than they have their music upon the native Hamitic Berbers. The Berber influence sticks through strongly in many songs whose words are in Arabic. Berbers are everywhere: It is Berber terrain, just as Mexico is Indian terrain, and a proportional amount of influence per century has been exerted and resisted. In urban zones the Berbers live as Arabs: in the remote country they live more or less as they did before the Arabs arrived.

If we go on the assumption that the present Arabic music is found where pure Arabic is spoken, we have to conclude that the true Arabic music of today is that of Egypt and Syria. By this token the material heard in northwestern Africa would not be strictly Arabic, although it abounds in examples of traditional Arabic vocalization, executed with wide variations.

The pieces with the greatest, and those with the smallest amount, of Arabic influence, are both to be found, strangely enough, in the same country: Morocco. This region's contact with Europe has been that of conqueror: in its decline it has been comparatively unmolested by industrial Europe. By virtue of this, also because it once had colonies in Mauretania and Senegal, and thus has a fair amount of admixture of Negro culture, it is richer in musical variety and interest than Algeria and Tunisia. In the latter countries there is plenty of music, but in Morocco music is inescapable.

Everywhere in Moroccan streets is found the *rhaita*—in Spain it still exists and is called *gaita*—the perfect outdoor instrument, an oboe of a stridency that permits it to be heard miles away, yet capable of executing the subtlest melodic figures. A special performing technique has been devised which permits the elongation of a phrase at will; gills are pierced in the neck of the player through which he draws air. Thus his cheeks can remain constantly inflated. The *rhaita* is used especially for wedding and circumcision processions, where it alternates with sung strophes, the whole being accompanied by the ubiquitous jar-shaped drum called the *darboukha*. There are also *rhaita* corps in the army bands, which play in between bugle tunes during parades; here no particular performing skill is required.

Outside the walls of the cities there is a continuous side-show of Negro Gnaoua cultists who torture themselves to rhythms supplied by large bronze castanets, magicians divining secrets from the earth through reed flutes, storytellers, snake charmers, performing and nonperforming mendicants, all of whom use music in their trade. And, most important, there are the Chleuh dancers.

These itinerant showmen, usually between the ages of eight and twenty, come down from the Atlas Mountains and circulate through the cities of central and southern Morocco. The Chleuhs have absorbed a minimum of Arabic culture; however, they seem at one time or another to have listened seriously to West African Negro music. The antiphonal element, so much a part of Negro song everywhere, is always present in their singing, as well as the tendency to drop the vocal line at the end of a phrase, in a heavily accented slur, to as much as an octave below. The word "guttural" is insufficient in describing the Chleuh articulation. It is really uvular; even when a word begins with a vowel sound, the Chleuh feels impelled to send the vowel sound off with a "rh." The vocalization has its family ties with the South: it employs an excessively rapid tremolo not unlike that of the goat. This combined with Arabic ornamentations makes for a lively idiom. The scale is usually pentatonic but the intervals vary.

Instruments are primitive violins, often made from tortoise shells, strung with twisted horsehairs covered with resin. These are bowed, and the resultant grating noise follows closely the vocal line and seems to have the quality the singers strive to attain; it surely has been a modifying factor in determining the vocal tradition. There is also a plucked mandolin *(djimbri)* so tight that players can dance at the same time. It sounds like a loud banjo with paper between the strings. For percussion the Chleuhs like the piercing sound of the metal insides of an automobile wheel, or a piece of hollow pipe struck rapidly with small steel mallets. The smaller boys wear tiny cymbals attached to their fingers, which they play like castanets.

In 1931, I assisted at some evening music classes in Fez. It was so much fun that each year thereafter, on arriving in that city I made inquiries about them, but they seemed to have been disbanded for lack of pupils. That year there were about thirty, most of them at least middle-aged. I was the only nonparticipant in the music-making, which was led by an ancient gentleman playing a magnificent old rebab. Most of the men were playing modern violins whose guts had been replaced by silk strings, and they played them cello-wise, resting them on the floor against their folded legs.

There were lutes, tambourines, and drums; no wind instruments. Everyone sang. Some pieces lasted as long as seventy minutes, and it was all in strict unison with complex basic rhythms.

This was classical Fassi music; they insist on calling it *musique andalouse,* considering it a trophy of war brought back from Granada. It is only in the more vulgar Fassi social-gathering music that the amazing improvisatory talents of these people become apparent. The result is a vocal and instrumental polyphony unlike anything else in the world. And while this peculiar music has very little to do with anything that can be heard in Spain today, yet Niño Marchena, probably the greatest male singer of *cante jondo,* used to visit Fez each year, stay in the recesses of the native medina, and spend his nights stretched out on a mattress listening to what the Fassi claim is the only real Andalusian music extant.

All of this betrays local influence. The only purely Arabic music one hears in North Africa, apart from the muezzin and what one can overhear coming from the inside the mosques, is in cafés and homes furnished with gramophones. These instruments, most of them equipped with lovely morning glory–shaped tin horns, are objects of great chic and can be rented by the hour or day for festive or family use. The proper music to play on them is that recorded in and imported from Egypt, Cairo being the cultural center of the Islamic world. In great favor still are the creations of Professor Abd el Wahab and Mlle. Ol Kalchoum. Flamenco records are popular, French music-hall songs fairly so, American swing not at all. Records of *musique andalouse* are unprocurable. Even the popular Fassi songs have fallen into disrepute. They are old-fashioned, you will be told at the record shops.

Modern Works Presented in Concert Here

DECEMBER 28 (1942), *NEW YORK HERALD TRIBUNE*

League of Composers presenting program of birthday works for its twentieth anniversary at the Museum of Modern Art, last night, with the following program:

Praeludium Salutatiorum	Arthur Shepherd
Six Portraits for Harpsichord	Virgil Thomson
Rye Septet with Voice	Lazare Saminsky

Quintet for Wind Instruments	Douglas Moore
Three Pieces for Piano	Roy Harris
Concertino	Bernard Wagenaar

Assisting artists: Maria Maximovitch, soprano; Ralph Kirkpatrick, harpsichord; Johanna Harris, piano; Vivian Pine, piano; Misha Muscanto, violin; Joseph Vieland, viola; Rudolph Sims, cello; Mortimer Rapfogel, flute; Engelbert Brenner, oboe; Alex Williams, clarinet; Simon Kovar, bassoon; Richard C. Moore, horn.

Last night's affair at the Museum of Modern Art was announced as a program of birthday works. There seemed to be little good feeling or high spirits at the party. With the exceptions of Virgil Thomson and Douglas Moore, the composers called upon to bestow presents on the League of Composers for its twentieth birthday showed a solid front of gloom and misery. The prevailing idiom was the accustomed noncommittal gray one, wherein whatever attempts at gaiety were made appeared as forced as the smile on the lips of the condemned.

Ralph Kirkpatrick played Mr. Thomson's six portraits on the harpsichord with a flair for the dramatic. The pieces came under two categories: people from Paris and people from here. The Paris group somehow seemed more describable on this instrument than the American. The little pieces gave the impression of having come from nowhere, and moved airily in and out of the focus of consonance like breezes through a pagoda. They were perverse, sinister, mincing, imperative, and lyrical one after the other, and always carefully expressive.

Mr. Moore's *Quintet* had a mind of its own, which it sometimes made a point of not making up. The first movement was sprightly, the second hesitant, inconclusive. The third was playful, and in spite of its tongue-in-the-cheek attitude, was the most successful for being the most compact. Nowhere were there tonal ambiguities; the composer had used well-tried harmonic recipes.

The *Rye Septet with Voice* of Mr. Saminsky had two short vocal passages sung pleasantly by Miss Maximovitch, whose full strong voice contrasted strangely with the tortured idiom of the piece. The music was forbidding and could have been even starker if the composer had not allowed himself so wide a latitude in the choice of tonal juxtapositions: it was a self-indulgent atonality.

The first of the Roy Harris piano pieces used the Copland pounding technique, but lacked the harmonic interest that one is accustomed to hearing with it. The second seemed empty and over-sentimental. Significantly or not, it was called *Contemplation.* The third had the greatest amount of constructive skill, but all three, like most piano music by important contemporary composers, gave the impression of being sketches of orchestral ideas left undressed and presented that way.

Bernard Wagenaar's *Concertino* was a thorough and well-organized piece, if a somewhat somber one with which to end an evening. Tonalities circumspect, style sincere and intransigent, mood bleak.

Arthur Shepherd's *Praeludium Salutatiorum* was in one long, severe movement, by turns sonorous and thin. The composer directed.

ARTICLES AND REVIEWS

......

1943

Films and Theatre

JANUARY–FEBRUARY (1943), *MODERN MUSIC*

Although *In Which We Serve* is a good picture, there is no doubt that a better score would have made it a more finished one. It is something of a mystery why, with so many more important elements here, Noel Coward should have been so eager to risk spoiling things by writing his own score. For he must be aware that however many facets of dramatic ability there are to his personality, serious musical composition does not figure among them. The score is of negligible value. Its thematic and harmonic material is undistinguished; few men in Hollywood would turn up with such a corny leitmotif. An opportunity to write some important film music was completely thrown away in the case of the recurrent flashbacks. A group of men struggling in the sea after being torpedoed recall moments of their respective lives; there follows a series of water-logged memories which make up the greater part of the film. The sinister repetitious phrase (like a cracked gramophone record, or the final sinking into anesthesia) was effective in the episodes which began with the losing of consciousness. But the music here was as prosaic as elsewhere. A harp glissando now and then, to bear out the water theme. The music track was very bad technically: it buzzed and rasped. That may have been beyond Mr. Coward's control. But the ineffective score was not. Where were Britten, Walton, Addinsell?

It is too much to have to describe in detail the inanities of another Baghdad picture. This one had chaotic symphonic sounds every minute of the time it ran. The music came from the Russians generally, with Borodin and Rimsky-Korsakov leading. The stomach dances were a little better than usual, and there was actually no harmony at certain moments. The sets, costumes and dialogue were all early Beverly Hills. The title was *Arabian Nights,* and Frank Skinner signed the score.

Spring Song is an amusing Soviet version of the familiar musician-movie theme of the die-hard classicist who is finally converted to popular light music. The same old plea is made for music "the public" can enjoy, but in more sophisticated terms than usual. The film has a score by Kabalevsky, and contains some tuneful songs and some others with satirical patter which is perhaps funny. I don't know Russian. There is one lovely scene which I fear would never have occurred to Hollywood. A composer is trying to collect on a song which a singer has commissioned. The singer offers him fifty. Her husband says reprovingly: "Pay him the hundred, darling. After all, he's a composer."

In *Paratroops,* a nine-minute short distributed by OWI, Gail Kubik has as many minutes of music. (No screen credit.) The idiom, symphonic, dramatic, is Hollywood; the harmonic texture and treatment of melody are more distinguished. There is the same fault as exists in other documentaries: our composers and scriptwriters don't get together until dubbing day. I wanted to hear the music, which went very well with the picture. I also wanted (although less ardently) to understand the commentary. Of course they coincided every instant, and one had to sacrifice one or the other. It seems to me that knowing beforehand one is going to have to supply so many hundred feet of music over which words are going to be (even though not intelligibly) pronounced, one might attempt to devise really subservient music: a sort which would never try to get its hooks into the spectator's attention. A cruel thing to ask of a composer, since it would be difficult to make suites later from his film music. Naturally this is not the ideal solution; on the contrary it is a compromise with the existing unsatisfactory setup. But it is a compromise which would involve the abandonment of constant symphonic sounds. This in itself would be a godsend. And it might also involve the development of better music for documentaries.

In the Theatre

The Pirate had a terrible book, excellent sets and some music by Herbert Kingsley. It is difficult to say just how much music there was, as most of it was played backstage, and the sounds from that place were on the borderline of the inaudible. One often had the sensation that a stagehand was playing with a radio back there, so indistinguishable were melodies, tonalities, even rhythms. Of course that may have been the calculated effect. In a whimsical production one never knows what may have been considered intriguing at rehearsals. However, there were several audible numbers. One was a fanfare played before the curtain rose in each act. I thought Mr. Kingsley might have written us three fanfares instead of insisting that we learn every note of that one, but no matter. It sounded like the brass accompaniment to the best-known record of Niña de los Peines singing a *saeta.* (Or an Egyptian military band.) It was all right. There were Negroes in the cast, and so there were, I believe, choral numbers. Or, the sound might have been made by wind-machines. Certainly there was no sign of any kind of Negro music. The rhythms one heard were sotto voce and nonsyncopated. Even if the added atmosphere which would have been created by any sort of adaptation of Negro music was not wanted in the production, at least the score would thereby have taken on a stylistic unity. Perhaps even such unity was not aimed at.

A pleasant flute piece accompanied Miss Fontanne's reading scene. It broke down into backstage sounds. The noisy parade in act 1, scene 2 was the big number of the show. It had verve and color, included a barrel organ. The ballet for celesta and double bass I liked. There were several little musical punctuations used to represent the actors' interior states—comments from an instrumental chorus. (Or like vaudeville trapeze music, underlining the moment when the acrobat nearly misses and falls.) In the last act a song was sung. It was on the edge of being popular music but lacked harmonic push. There was plenty of variety and some charm in the score. However, its effectiveness was constantly minimized. It all came out the small end of the megaphone. And I should have liked a little auditory suggestion of Trinidad, Martinique, or Barbados. Mr. Kingsley allowed the sets to provide all the ambiance. In fact, they completely stole the show.

Something new in *Schrecklichkeit* was the New Opera's *Pique Dame.* The English version made forced and exasperatingly bad prosody. I wonder if it is possible to make a distinguished and functional opera translation into English. In this the sense was damaged by use of silly English words and phrases, and the sound of the vocal line was marred by wrong accents which were given prominence. Example: second syllable of the words "listen" and "secret." Add to this a performance whose diction had so low a general standard that even in a sequence where the hero read aloud a letter, it was impossible to get more than every tenth word. There was no stylistic unity in the decors. The gaga troupe ranted in front of sets whose projected cloud-effects twitched; their gestures were caricatures of the operatic tradition. The direction brought the entire chorus wandering pointedly across the stage to sing a few lines which might better have been sung offstage. One had the recurrent impression that the first scene was meant to be outside a lunatic asylum during the noon rest hour, and that all the gentlemen parading before the footlights thought they were Napoleon the First.

On the other hand, *Macbeth,* besides being simpler, more singable, and a better opera than *Pique Dame,* enjoyed the advantages of a good production. For one thing, it was given with the original untranslated libretto, which was an astonishing device for the New Opera to try—Verdi in Italian! Then, it had good sets, effective direction and one superb characterization by Regina Resnick. This was really Lady Macbeth; Miss Resnick never forgot she was working in the theatre. She merely happened to be singing instead of speaking her lines, and she sang them beautifully. It was clear she did not consider an opera an animated concert in which one moves about, wears a costume, and takes just a few more liberties with the music than as if one had to stand still. She made no bones about stealing the show. This was a good idea, as it comes off better that way, at least up through the sleepwalking scene.

Joseph Wood's prize-winning one-act opera, *The Mother,* was given for the first time at the Juilliard School, jointly with the first New York stage production of Randall Thompson's *Solomon and Balkis,* also a one-acter. The best thing about *The Mother* was the orchestration, which also seemed to be what had interested the composer most. The piece was like an instrumental tone-poem with vocal accompaniment. In form it was a series of static tableaux. What dramatic quality it had was made by the orchestra rather than by the vocal line, which was usually a secondary consideration. There were one or two tunes which seemed to have been allowed to grow naturally, but one felt the greater part of the melodic material to have been formulated by adherence to preconceived theories about prosody. Any given tone appeared to have been chosen more with an eye to its general pitch location than to its effect on the line's logic or its strategic harmonic value. There was rough handling of word accents, too. The libretto was embarrassingly ingenuous.

Randall Thompson's *Solomon and Balkis,* commissioned by both the League of Composers and the Columbia Broadcasting System, was a competently written little opera whose argument presupposed that polygamy necessarily makes for humorous dramatic material. Even if this were true, the element of humor is not a thing that can be developed in song. One understands it instantaneously if it is there, and no amount of verbal elaboration can possibly sharpen its impact. Not being made of satire, the exposition always seemed to be explaining something quite obvious. One found oneself hearing and understanding the words and rather wishing one couldn't. However, a simple harmonic structure and singable vocal line kept things moving. Instruments did not get in the way of voices, and the melodies were not forced. With some other subject matter the piece could have been extremely enjoyable.

At the High School of Music and Art, the students, after doing a bit of unsuccessful rewriting of the end, presented the Copland-Denby *Second Hurricane* in its first functional New York performance. It is a spirited, poetic work. In spite of its apparent delicateness, it is pure sinew, made to stand up under rough treatment. The kids went at it with gusto, and enunciated superbly. It was too bad there was no direction to help them know what to do with their bodies while they were supposed to be "acting natural." The less moving around a character was allowed to do, the better his performance was. But the music more than made up for production weaknesses. It is Copland's most lyrical work, and contains, too, some of his most nervously exciting passages.

Recent Books

JANUARY–FEBRUARY (1943), *MODERN MUSIC*

In *The Real Jazz* by Hugues Panassié (Smith and Durrell), you can learn, if you are interested, that Hot Lips Page used to play the trumpet in Bennie Moten's Band, or that Jack Teagarden was the trombonist in the Mound City Blue Blowers' recording of *Tailspin Blues.* I was most interested, but that's because fifteen years ago I played nothing but Bennie Moten and the Blue Blowers on my phonograph. Otherwise, all but the first four chapters of this book would have been pretty annoying. Only the reader who shares at least some of the author's boundless enthusiasm for jazz and blind admiration for its more talented exponents will have the patience to go through the volume.

The book is really two. The first four chapters are a fairly accurate and complete account of the nature and development of jazz. The next twelve are simply Mr. Panassié's personal reactions to all the important (and many unimportant) interpreters of it, with a chapter devoted to each instrument, plus one to singers, one to arrangers and one to recordings. (Throughout the book there are innumerable references to records, most of which are now unobtainable.) In these chapters of summaries occur most of the examples of imprecise overwriting for which other jazz books have been justifiably censured. By being scattered casually through the text, expressions like "greatest," "prodigious," "dazzling," "beautiful," "above all possible praise," "tremendous," "unforgettable," "monumental," "limitless," "vast, grandiose," "magnificent flights," "massive," "sublime," "breath of genius," to pick out a few, greatly weaken the force of its argument.

For the book has a polemical element: it is a defense of jazz against those who are left indifferent enough by it to fail to recognize the difference between the true and the false.

The public's failure to distinguish the one from the other, he believes, is destroying the art form. He deplores the commercialization of jazz during the past twenty years, and attributes it to various factors: the end of the era of prosperity, the evil influence upon the Negroes of the white man's radio, the Negroes' own inferiority complex regarding White culture, and most of all the jazzmen's acquisition of an "artistic conscience." This was forced upon them, of course, by just such people as Mr. Panassié. The cascade of hyperbolical praise in the form of ecstatic magazine articles and books, which appeared about the time commercial "swing" took the public's fancy, was certainly not designed to keep jazz pure and humble. On the contrary, every performer whose talent ranged from mediocre up was encouraged to think of himself as possessed of a truly personal style.

At the end of the book there is an eighty-nine-page appendix which lists recordings by exactly one hundred and fifty musicians. I quote the text apropos of this list: "For each of the great jazz musicians I have chosen a certain number of records . . . which are typical of his style, in order that the reader . . . may know and study the musical personality of each musician." It is manifestly impossible that there should be that many instrumentalists (only seven of the total are vocalists) worthy of such minute consideration.

In the expository section of the book we get a story whose synopsis is roughly as follows. The Negro church service, whose musical keystone was the Protestant hymns they had been given to sing, first of all underwent certain modal changes dictated doubtless by unconscious observance of tradition.* A musical style emerged, incorporating these scalar changes with the original harmonic base of the songs, the accents on the offbeats (handclapping, tambourines, and drums are still used in church). For secular use, new and profane words supplanted the sacred text; the musical material remained the same. This is already the blues, purely vocal, with rhythmical accompaniment. Next a solo instrumentalist—probably a cornetist, trombonist, or clarinetist—interpolated responses based on the singer's vocal inflections. This approximation of Negro vocalization was the most important factor in determining the instrumental style which was to characterize jazz playing. In New Orleans the procedure was applied in bands which used collective improvisation in the playing of adaptations of ragtime, polkas, quadrilles, and marches. The melodic instruments played on the strong beat, with the weak beats still taken care of by the percussion.

The new art moved northward, was adopted by some Whites who understood it and by many more who perverted it. Here the piano and saxophone made their appearance. At this point Mr. Panassié offers his apologies for having stressed in his earlier writings the importance of the so-called "Chicago style," which he now ostensibly considers only a transitory phase. The rest of the story is the sad one about the degree to which each individual and performing organization has accepted or withstood commercialization. The author sees little hope for the future. Although he upholds the present trend toward larger orchestras, thus indicting the snobbish preference of today's swing fans for small groups, which, he claims, lack good men, he believes the ability to read music weakens the

* Here Mr. Panassié assumes that the alterations are fixed and consist only of the ambiguous third and seventh tones of the scale. In the deep South I have been present at entire services where the scale comprised only the tonic, the mediant, the dominant, and a tone halfway between the last two mentioned: a partially sharped subdominant.

musician's ear, and that in turn damages the improvisatory faculty. He fears jazz is doomed to undergo a paralyzing further transformation which will rob it of all its spontaneity and beauty.

There are shrewd remarks and valid observations as well as exaggerations and misstatements. On the credit side we have things like: "When a Negro sings the blues, it is not to give way to his sadness, it is rather to free himself of it." "Most improvised interpretations are more beautiful at the end than at the beginning" (because of the interchange of inspiration between each player and the others). "Music with an unchanging tempo is more natural and is a direct reflection of life." (This is true of art music as well as folk music.)

On the debit side we have Mr. Panassié's assumption that music, any kind of music, is a universal language. "No previous education is required in order for the notes to signify what they were intended to signify." Ridiculous, of course. He claims that the record gives us "at the same time both the interpretation and the musical score itself." He says that the Negro's instinctive marking of offbeats in keeping time to jazz "would be enough in itself to explain the white man's lack of understanding of jazz." Perhaps he means the European's lack of understanding; plenty of Americans, regardless of their racial antecedents, mark the weak beats. Apropos of the "eternal weakness" of written music as opposed to the oral tradition and improvisation, he writes: "At best, musical writing can only be a memorandum to suggest the ideas of the composer." Composers like to think of notation as something a little more solid and complete.

There are too many signs of the priestly attitude: "One cannot define it (swing) for him (the listener), just as one cannot describe the idea of the diversity of colors to a blind man." This pontifical air is likely to try the patience of the analytical reader, whether he is a swing fan or not. Duke Ellington came nearer to a definition when he said: "You can't write swing because swing is the emotional element in the audience."

North African Music II

JANUARY 3 (1943), *NEW YORK HERALD TRIBUNE*

It has always been impossible to buy recordings of North African music other than in the record shops of the regions producing the particular kind of music desired. Records of Kabyle music are found only in the coast towns of northern Algiers, whereas Chleuh music is not sold at all in Tangier and Rabat, but only farther south. Interest is particularly centered on local stars, who sing songs of local significance.

It is amusing to note that while the average colonial Spaniard in Spanish Morocco accepts the Hebrew and Gypsy exoticisms of Flamenco singing, he is shocked by similar vocalizations sung in Arabic by the Riffians and Moors; and the Arabic-speaking public finds the music of the Chleuhs pure cacophony. Doubtless the Chleuhs themselves would likewise consider barbarous, if they could hear them now, the sounds produced by their Negro neighbors to the south; yet the interrelations are multiple among these four musics, none of which can be called primitive.

Really primitive music sounds more or less alike the world over. There is uncomplicated rhythm, a scale of few intervals, a tendency to short phrases and repetition, and a straight, unadorned and childlike vocalization. It is only when the primitive music has had some commerce with the music of a more evolved culture that it develops interesting symptoms. Then some one, or more than one, of these characteristics moves from simple to less simple. The various musics of North Africa have had lengthy contacts with the Arabic or the Negro schools, or both, and these two schools are highly developed systems of musical expression. The contact with Europe has not yet begun to make itself felt much here, save in the large cities like Algiers and Tunis, where occasionally, in a low-life song, a rudimentary harmonic basis is suggested.

In the Algerian Sahara there are towns where one can hear Sudanese *tam-tams* (ceremonies whose musical accompaniment is purely percussive). Only three days' journey by car south of Algiers I heard, accompanying the violent dancing of an unorthodox religious cult, an eight-piece orchestra of drums whose diameter ranged from approximately four feet down to three inches, in the case of the ceramic drums played with the fingers. The players were Berbers, the rhythms unmistakably Negroid. (At the same time the Tuaregs, another branch of the old Berber family, who live much farther to the south and are in constant touch with the West Sudanese metropolis Timbuktu, have no directly traceable Negroisms in their music. Tuareg songs are primitive, but sometimes the vocal lines shows definite signs of connections with Anglo-Egyptian Sudan and Ethiopia; doubtless this parentage is far more ancient than the commercial relations of recent centuries with West Africa.)

In Algeria, and perhaps in all North Africa, the easiest local music for a European or American to enjoy is the Kabyle shepherds' flute music, which sounds rather like Debussy without the ninth chords. The citizens of Algiers know the idiom. One can hear them playing at it before the feast of Qurban, among the hills back of the city, where they go in the afternoons, each leading his lamb, to play while the lambs graze and fatten.

Any time of the year, in the evening, visiting Kabyles from the mountains frequent the Casbah cafés, and play solos between puffs on the kif-pipe. The music, like the corresponding present-day Greek clarino music, demands a virtuoso technique; however, it is much higher in register and more intense, and uses traditional Arabic modes.

In the Casbah dives in Algiers there are groups composed of piano (no harmony involved—just melody in two or three octaves, with ornamentations), flute and drums. The relatively commonplace rhythms of the drums predominate, and the result is rather ridiculous: an Arabic counterpart of backroom jive.

In the Sud-Oranais (southwestern Algeria) there are ballads wherein the human voice attains a maximum or incisive but self-contained raucousness (as opposed to the frenzied croaking of the Eastern Sudanese and Ethiopians). This quality is made to contrast with the incessant soft quivering of reed flutes which follow each tiny twist of the vocal line. The flutes rarely play beyond the range of a tritone, and the register is low, the highest tone being approximately middle C. This is the favorite instrument of the nocturnal camel guardians, who often sit alone all night among the camels, playing the same few grave, soporific phrases. The Algerians are partial to all-night concerts also in the *hammam,* which serves as steam-bath, clubhouse, and inn.

Isaac Stern, Violinist, Heard in Carnegie Hall

JANUARY 9 (1943), *NEW YORK HERALD TRIBUNE*

Isaac Stern, violinist, played last night at Carnegie Hall in a program of Bach, Mozart, Brahms, Wieniawski, and Szymanowski. Mr. Stern is a musician of fine sensibility and superb technique. His tone quality last night was usually caressing, vibrant and intimate, and his manner of giving the musical message of a piece sincere and direct.

The Bach Sonata no. 1 in G Minor for unaccompanied violin showed the artist's extraordinary technical control. The intonation of the Fugue was of an almost mathematical accuracy, without, however, any sacrificing of the piece's line, which retained its clarity throughout. Mr. Stern used few *sforzandi* in playing the double stops, so that the movement sounded less agitated than it usually does. The bowing and phrasing in the Presto were managed with skillful ease.

The selection of Szymanowski's Concerto no. 2, op. 61, for a showpiece was unfortunate. (One hopes it was not chosen for its beauty.) Mr. Stern ran its gamut of tricks and came out unscathed, but the piece is so lacking in stylistic unity that even technical mastery and intelligent interpretation could scarcely make it sound at one with itself. It is full of alternating tenseness and looseness induced more by hubbub than by harmonic sequences. Its tempestuous passages are at variance with the emotional atmosphere of their immediate context; they resemble little tantrums.

The closing pages were the most notable, with the repeated use of open strings, and the rapid bowed phrases ending in *pizzicati* by the left hand. It sounded rather like the music they play on the *hardangerfelen,* the fiddle used for folk dancing in Norway. Mr. Stern's handling of the difficult double-stop work was admirable.

Alexander Zakin assisted at the piano. As is usual in violin and vocal recitals, the accompanying figures were much too loud. Often the sound of the violin was all but lost.

Koussevitzky Conducts Three Russian Works

JANUARY 10 (1943), *NEW YORK HERALD TRIBUNE*

Boston Symphony Orchestra, Serge Koussevitzky conducting. Second matinee concert of its Carnegie Hall series, yesterday afternoon, with the following program:

"Classical" Symphony, op. 25	Prokofieff
Symphony no. 6	Shostakovich
Symphony no. 4 in F Minor, op. 36	Tchaikovsky

It would be difficult to try to picture to oneself a better example of collaborative virtuosity than yesterday's concert by the Boston Symphony Orchestra. Each of these three Russian pieces received the utmost in fine playing under Dr. Koussevitzky's benevolent vigilance. The orchestral sound at any given moment had the rare breathing quality that makes music come alive: the orchestra functioned like a completely integrated human personality. Delicacy did not preclude aggressiveness, nor firmness conflict with tenderness.

It was illuminating to see the Shostakovich Sixth in close contact with its musical forebears. The emotional atmosphere of its first movement comes in good part out of Tchaikovsky, but there is in the writing neither the clarity nor the charm of that composer.

Parts of the second and third movements seem heavily influenced by Prokofieff, the "Classical" Symphony in particular; but whereas the latter tightly knit little piece leads a life of its own, motivated wholly by its delicate harmonic impetus and phrasal badinage, the Shostakovich work is insensitive, heavy-handed clowning.

The two brash and brilliant last movements do not balance the endless first; they are simply another piece. The unusual orchestral effects are not so unusual that they justify a work's being written around them. The whole symphony is nervous without being taut; it is not relaxed enough in spirit to warrant being so loosely constructed. It has the esthetic of the billboard rather than of the canvas. The perfect performance it received yesterday merely made clearer the essential superficiality of its conception. One was saddened to see such pains expended on a callous work incapable, as it were, of appreciating them.

The unfolding of the Tchaikovsky Fourth was magnificent. In the second movement the tempo was kept up to allay the latent saccharine tendencies. The dramatic contour of the pizzicato passages in the third movement was admirable; the distinct dynamic levels established for notes holding the same position in rhythmical figures were rigorously observed. Other examples of beautiful playing were the opening brass fanfare in the first movement of the same work, and the perfect trills of the violin line in the larghetto of the "Classical" Symphony.

On Film Music

JANUARY 17 (1943), *NEW YORK HERALD TRIBUNE*

The cinema has generally been conceded to be potentially an art, which means that in certain rare pictures ideological and technical elements of exceptionally high quality have been fused to make an esthetically valid product. But the music written for most of even these very rare exhibits has been unsatisfactory. Music is invited to be present at the films more in the capacity of an eccentric celebrity whose presence may add prestige to the party than of the caterer whose unseen but careful assistance helps keep it running smoothly. That is the tradition, and the movies are nothing if not conservative.

So there is no cause for jubilation. What may a few years back have seemed a slow progress toward some sort of acceptable criterion of film music turns out to have been only the careful improvement of a technique. And the more competent technique has merely fortified the original conception. That is, if the composer uses a greater number and variety of instruments, unusual combinations, recherché sound effects, dissonant passages, and paraphrases of or quotations from famous melodies and orchestrations, he does so in order to make a richer, more padded and luxurious-sounding symphonic score in which to encase his film. He has not asked himself whether he wants a luxurious-sounding score; nor indeed whether he wants a symphonic score at all. He probably doesn't, but if *they* expect it, and he is the composer, there is nothing much to do but show them he can provide the desired commodity as well as the next man.

The manifest purpose of film music is to line the finished picture with lush, heavily instrumental sound, like the quilted satin walls of Hollywood interiors. The music is a bit of honorific display which pleases no one (except probably the producers), but which the public is being educated to consider a sine qua non of filmmaking. Of course if one is passively enough inclined to take an optimistic view, one may consider the phenomenon just one more fantastic ingredient of the perverse myth being created for the world and posterity in southern California.

From the point of view of the man who is writing the score for a new film, he cannot use the picture as a fortuitous occasion to bring out themes or other material ideas he has been wanting to show the public. A film is never an excuse to write music, any more than it is an excuse to use a camera. The picture's the thing, always, even in films (like many of Disney's) which are built around the music. The composer's job is to translate directly his personal reactions to any given sequence into musical (or purely auditory) terms. It would be ideal, of course, if he were given the liberty of working with dialogue or commentary—if the problem of film music were recognized for what it is: a form close to opera, wherein words and music are combined and juxtaposed with precision to make an auditory version of the visual action. That would be asking for a revolution. And film music's function is apparently destined, at least for a while yet, to go on being that of trained dog and trapeze music, in which the act and the sound simply begin and end together, with special effects to point up tricks, somersaults, and gags.

This being the case, it is up to the composer to distill what he feels to be the emotional essence of a given scene and express it in musical terms which are tough and neutral enough to allow for turning up and down of volume, intrusions of dialogue and sound, and both cutting and repetition. He must write a piece about the entire sequence, rather than underline its details as they appear. He will not be able to make a passage about heroes more heroic by fitting its action to a militant anthem, nor a love scene more poignant by adding the most touching love theme ever written, unless first of all he heeds the pronouncement made by the great Russian director Pudovkin. "Music in sound film must never be the accompaniment; it must retain its own line." (As a matter of fact, the really moving scene is often the one without any music. What the music does, far too many times, is to point out and magnify the emotional falsenesses or tritenesses of the scene it is supposed to build up.)

The composer provides an auditory stage for events to happen in, and the characters he considers first are voices and sounds rather than faces and situations. He has got to be interested in what his music is going to sound like along with the dialogue and sound effects. It is more important for him to coordinate his work with the rest of the soundtrack than with the visual part of the production. There must be no confusion in the impressions conveyed through the same sense organ.

Not only is film music usually too thick; it is practically always too long. There is too much of it. In fictional films they use it in places where the normal sounds ensuing from the action would be sufficient. In documentaries it is often put everywhere, those responsible apparently not wishing to take any chances on the persuasive power of the commentator's voice alone. Then they increase the volume while he catches his breath, and turn it down again when he begins the next sentence, regardless of musical phrasings, cadences, orchestral innuendos, and other details that might interest musicians.

In French and Russian films, the dramatic possibilities of silence have been pretty well exploited. Here we are afraid our audience's attention may waver if the tradition of impressive music is not upheld, especially in a film's big moments. And, of course, the synonym for "big" *is* "expensive." So we weigh down each of these expensive moments as heavily as we can, to make certain that everybody realizes it is a big scene.

A pleasant exception—with its resultant difficulties—to this unfortunate rule is the battle scene in the new film *Commandos Strike at Dawn* (score by Louis Gruenberg). Here dramatic power is intensified by using no music or dialogue at all. One hears only roars of explosions, cracking of guns, whizzing of bullets and rattling of earth and debris on the soldiers' helmets. When the battle is over and music suddenly takes over the soundtrack, the force goes out of the visual scene like a light going off. The spectator has to readjust his perceptive faculties very quickly to retain the same degree of interest. If there had been music through the whole scene, no such trouble would have arisen; but the sequence would have had infinitely less punch. Actually there was no need to bring music back at this point, but if there had been, it should have been cautiously, imperceptibly introduced not to strike a false note after such a burst of realism.

There is no insoluble problem. Music merely needs to be treated with the same consideration accorded the lights on the set. One neither overlights nor underlights, and certainly one never considers lighting a luxury. If music is necessary in a film—and a little usually is—pains should be taken to discover exactly where it is needed, and what is essential at that spot. Perhaps the trouble comes from the American mistake of considering the fine arts, and music in particular, a form of decoration rather than a system of thought.

Duke Ellington in Recital for Russian Relief

JANUARY 25 (1943), *NEW YORK HERALD TRIBUNE*

Twentieth Anniversary Concert of Duke Ellington and his orchestra, for Russian War Relief, at Carnegie Hall Saturday night with the following artists:

Duke Ellington, pianist-leader; Johnny Hodges, alto saxophone; Otto Hardwicke, alto saxophone; Chauncey Haughton, tenor saxophone and clarinet; Ben Webster, tenor saxophone; Harry Carney, barytone saxophone; Rex Stewart, cornet and trumpet; Ray Nance, trumpet and violin; Harold Baker, trumpet; Wallace Jones, trumpet; Joe Nanton, trombone; Juan Tisol, trombone; Lawrence Brown, trombone; Bonny Greer, drums; Fred Guy, guitar; Alvin Raglin, bass; Billy Strayhorn, assistant arranger; Betty Roche, vocalist.

Duke Ellington is the only jazz musician whose programs have enough musical interest to be judged by the same standards one applies to art music. He is the composer of many of the finest popular melodies of the last fifteen years, and he is the pianist, arranger, and conductor of what has consistently been and still is the greatest jazz orchestra in the country. His conscious search for harmonies, rhythms, and sonorities hitherto unused in jazz has been eminently successful because he has a musically creative intelligence which has protected him from the pitfalls of commercialization. His greatest achievement is to have been able to invent tirelessly and incorporate his discoveries into the medium without his music's losing the flavor, directness, and dignity of early jazz.

Precisely because of all these things, one expected more from the important number on Saturday evening's program, *Black, Brown and Beige* (a tone parallel to the history of the Negro in America). It lasted the better part of an hour and contained enough bright ideas for several short pieces. But, presented as one number, it was formless and meaningless. In spite of Mr. Ellington's ideological comments before each "movement," nothing emerged but a gaudy potpourri of tutti dance passages and solo virtuoso work. (The dance parts used some pretty corny riffs, too.) There were countless unprovoked modulations, a passage in 5/4, paraphrases on well-known tunes that were as trite as the tunes themselves, and recurrent climaxes that impeded the piece's progress. Between dance numbers there were "symphonic" bridges played out of tempo. This dangerous tendency to tamper with the tempo within a piece showed itself far too many times during the evening. If there is no regular beat, there can be no syncopation, and thus no tension, no jazz. The whole attempt to fuse jazz as a form with art music should be discouraged. The two exist at such different distances from the listener's faculties of comprehension that he cannot get them both clearly into focus at the same time. One might say they operate on different wavelengths; it is impossible to tune them in simultaneously.

Fortunately, there were other things on the program. The arrangements, barring tempo changes, were, of course, excellent. Such numbers as *Rockin' in Rhythm, Ko Ko,* and *Black Beauty* showed the band in all its glory. The instrumental give and take was never hysterical and the rhythms never jumpy or breathless. The saxes often played in unison, which eliminated the thick-sounding choir these instruments form in so many bands.

There was Jimmy Hodges, whose perfect, smooth alto sax playing reached a high at the end of *Don't Get Around Much Any More.* Rex Stewart did some superb musical clowning in a piece whose figures were based on the familiar noises made by a beginner on the cornet. Perhaps the most impressive solo playing was by Joe Nanton, who made his trombone sound like a protesting wild beast. He has always supplied more atmosphere for the band than any other one man.

The audience was so vociferous in its approval both during and after numbers that one could never hear the cadences.

On Film Music

JANUARY 31 (1943), *NEW YORK HERALD TRIBUNE*

Good movie scores are scarce these days. Not that one expects every film to have music and soundtracks as extensive and important as *Le Sang d'un poète* and *Son of Mongolia.* But occasionally it would be nice to see a good film with some music that is really about the same thing the film is about, and that says what the film says just as clearly and just as simply.

Aaron Copland is en route to Hollywood to write a score for Lillian Hellman's picture about the Soviet Union, *The North Star.* If the music for this is as good as his two previous Hollywood jobs, *Our Town* and *Of Mice and Men,* everyone ought to be fairly well satisfied.

One cannot mention *The City,* which is Copland's best film score, together with the other two, since the film enjoyed the unfair advantage of being a documentary, and documentaries almost invariably offer more opportunities to the composer for getting in some interesting music. Witness the difference between Louis Gruenberg's excellent work in *The Fight for Life* and what he has done in his most recent film score, for *Commandos Strike at Dawn.* The only notable thing besides the intelligent suppression of music for the battle is the execution scene. Here the idea consists in increasing the volume for suspense until the instant of firing; then instead of the expected sudden silence we have the more realistic and effective device of a rapid and tremulous *morendo*.

It is surprising that Noel Coward had the temerity to compose his own score for *In Which We Serve*. Writing the pleasant British ditties for a Coward play is quite a different thing from providing the musical continuity and background for a long dramatic film. This requires considerably more experience in musical composition, and at the very least enough talent for improvising to keep the harmonic line from bogging down into repetitiousness. Besides being dramatically ineffective, the score is musically more hackneyed than even our less well-made Hollywood products. This is especially reprehensible when one considers the wealth of opportunities offered by the flashback. Ostensibly Mr. Coward was too much occupied with directing and acting to give these things much thought. This is quite natural, but there are other composers in England who could have helped him.

Arabian Nights had a score by Frank Skinner which went on from beginning to end without any appreciable break. I suppose they wanted the constant music to reinforce the legendary and epic quality; in that case, frequent use of single instruments would have been more expressive than the symphonic hubbub that was kept up behind sound and dialogue. And why does Near Eastern music always, always have to sound like what one or two Russians had to say on that subject? There are plenty of other ways of creating the atmosphere of that part of the world besides rewriting Cui's *Orientale*.

It is too bad that Dimitri Tiomkin did not use his imagination a little more in doing the score for *Shadow of a Doubt*, since Alfred Hitchcock had used his sufficiently to make the film most of the things *Suspicion* should have been and wasn't. Especially at the beginning, he had a chance to write some dramatic music. The shots of the American city from across the desolate dump heaps, the sad little streets, and the sordid rooming-house bedroom with its window shade drawn suggested something less heroic and more sinister than the large symphonic number that went with them. One would have thought Mr. Tiomkin had been asked to write a tone poem on the hidden beauties of poverty. The very excellence of the direction in its insistence on drab detail brought home the basic disparity between the atmospheric essence of the film and that of the music, and made of this passage a classic example of audio-visual incongruity.

However, accepting the fact that the score never transgresses the limits of tradition, and that the musical material is commonplace, one can discover in it certain pleasant qualities. For instance, the sound of the orchestra is often kept in the background, so that it is scarcely audible. The piano is used effectively to set an agitated mood. The tragic element in an apparently harmless scene is not too noticeably suggested. The electric guitar makes a noise like an inhuman voice screaming the leitmotif as the hero is mangled by a locomotive. And to go with the (at last) believable sets, dialogue has been provided which occasionally sounds true because it uses in a really natural manner the confusion of simultaneous conversation.

Bate Is Soloist in Own Work at Carnegie Hall

FEBRUARY 1 (1943), *NEW YORK HERALD TRIBUNE*

Philharmonic-Symphony Orchestra, Bruno Walter conductor, in popular (students') concert Saturday night at Carnegie Hall, with Stanley Bate as solo pianist, in the following program:

Overture to "Egmont," op. 84 — Beethoven

Concertante for Piano and String Orchestra — Bate
1. Allegro risoluto alla toccata
2. Andante sostenuto
3. Andante maestoso; Allegro vivaca alla tarantella

Symphonie fantastique, op. 14A — Berlioz
1. Dreams, Passions
2. A Ball
3. Scene in the Meadows
4. March to the Scaffold
5. Dream of a Witches' Sabbath

When the English become objective in the arts, they are likely to do it with an air which implies that the process hurts them more than it does you. Mr. Stanley Bate merely gave the impression that the noncommittal quality of his piece, its careful keeping away from the dangerous ground of emotional expression, was for the common good. Mr. Bate's Concertante for Piano and String Orchestra was not really "astringent," as he claimed in Saturday night's program notes. It was a lean, angular piece which, although it had been scrubbed clean of every suspicion of subjectivity, was not free from a carefully formalized sentimentality.

The writing for strings was on the massive side, that for piano largely percussive in its effect, and the sonorous balance between the two was well considered. It is true that the sound of the strings often got a bit skinny; this is to be expected in a large ensemble whose flesh and blood of brass and woodwinds is absent, unless special care is taken to circumvent it. There were times when one felt that the conception called out for more solid and penetrating sound. It seemed to forget that its means of expression was one which demands restraint and subtlety in handling and, above all, one which must not be used to say certain things.

The first movement had a lot to do and was busy and energetic about it. A preference for intervals of the fourth both in the line and the harmony helped the music maintain its impartial air, giving it immunity, as it were, from modal choices. The Brahmsian second movement had a pleasant, subdued theme which eventually decided to express itself by putting on some unbecoming false notes. In spite of this, the mood was not broken, and one was satisfied, even though one had no illusion of being taken into the composer's confidence. The last movement began in a spirit of slightly sour English jollity, evinced, one felt now and then, at the point of a gun. Soon nobility came along and predicted the piece's end, which when it arrived was a little grand and out of character. Mr. Bate's hard touch made a proper contrast to the softness of the strings. The piece made a good impression. It was alive without being obstreperous, intelligent without being cerebral, cautious without being precious.

Mr. Walter also conducted the Overture to "Egmont" of Beethoven and the Berlioz *Symphonie fantastique*. Rarely has the Philharmonic sounded as coordinated and complete.

Jeanette Savran Heard in Carnegie Hall Recital

FEBRUARY 3 (1943), *NEW YORK HERALD TRIBUNE*

Jeanette Savran, young American pianist, gave her first New York recital last night at Carnegie Hall, the program consisting of the Bach Toccata and Fugue in D Minor and various nineteenth- and twentieth-century pieces. Miss Savran is a pianist of surprising force and considerable precision. Several times last night she showed herself capable of brilliant playing. In such pieces as the Chopin Etudes, where the message of the music could more or less be communicated by simple and correct playing of the notes (and she played them all), she was especially competent. Again, in Ravel's *Ondine,* her playing had the subdued languor and feeling for staticity that makes the piece the shimmering curtain of sound that it should be.

In those numbers which offered more leeway for interpretation, the Chopin Nocturne op. 48, no. 2, in F-sharp Minor, and the Ballade, op. 47, in A-flat Major, the conception seemed to spend its emotions and ideas as it went along; it failed to accumulate the necessary impetus to give the playing dramatic sense. Thus, in retrospect, each piece lacked flow. There was plenty of shading but little expression. This was also true of the Beethoven Sonata "Appassionata," which was adamant throughout.

Of the three movements from Stravinsky's *Petrouchka,* the "Danse russe" and "Chez Petrouchka" were sharp, glassy and, except for some minor sacrifices of tempo in the former, extremely well presented. "La Semaine grasse," however, required more physical power than even Miss Savran possessed, although she put up a good fight. The arrangement is such that it is hard in any case to tell false notes. The performance of the whole *Petrouchka* suite was fun to witness, because it seemed to interest the artist most of all the numbers, and the playing was consequently more lively.

Stanley Need, Pianist, Gives Town Hall Recital

FEBRUARY 4 (1943), *NEW YORK HERALD TRIBUNE*

Stanley Need, pianist, appeared last night at Town Hall, playing in a program which with the exception of one piece consisted wholly of nineteenth-century music.

This is rather a stiff test for a performer. Such a program requires more active effort and understanding on his part, since in the playing of Romantic music competent technique takes one less of the distance toward the successful transmission of the music message than in the playing of older or newer music.

Mr. Need appeared too much occupied with the mechanics of execution to devote himself wholeheartedly to the music.

The program opened with a forceful rendition of the Bach Chromatic Fantasy and Fugue, and continued with the Sonata "Appassionata" of Beethoven, in which the artist exhibited a good sense of the musical geography of the piece. A continued feeling of being definitely situated during the course of any number transfers itself to the listener and is the strongest factor in holding his interest.

Four selections from Chopin (the B-flat Minor Scherzo, D-flat Nocturne, G Minor Ballade, and C Minor Etude, op. 25, no. 12) were played in a literal and summary fashion. Here particularly the adequate technique failed to compensate for the absence of expression, the feeling one had that the music remained undigested. The last half of the program was devoted to the works of Liszt, and included his transcription of Schubert's Impromptu, op. 90, no. 3, his Fantasia quasi Sonata ("Après une lecture de Dante"), and his Twelfth Hungarian Rhapsody. The Fantasia, after one has extracted the few harmonic innovations, remains a welter of sound and fury. The playing was stolid and phlegmatic.

Percussionists in Concert Led by John Cage

FEBRUARY 8 (1943), *NEW YORK HERALD TRIBUNE*

A program of percussion music, last night at the Museum of Modern Art, directed by John Cage, presented by the League of Composers in association with the Museum of Modern Art. Assisting artist, Ruth Stuber Jeanne, marimba. Ensemble: Mary Anthony, Xenia Cage, David Campbell, Jean Campbell, Arthur Christie, Merce Cunningham, Renata Garve, Molly Howe, Cecil Kitcat, Helen Lanfer, Edward McLean, and Joan Palmer.

The concert was good for the hearing; it was an ear massage. Fourteen persons, 125 instruments, and about fifty sticks to hit them with. When things were not beaten or tapped they were shaken, rubbed, pulled, or immersed in water. There was an ominous audio-frequency oscillator, recorded sounds went on and off, and both thunder sheet and marimbula were equipped with electric pickups.

In percussion music so far there has been very little development other than rhythmical and that pertaining to the general sonorous architecture. Such things as melody and harmony, which involve the use of definite and related pitch, have been largely ignored. Henry Cowell's *Ostinato Pianissimo*, by virtue of the inclusion of a certain amount of both of these, proved to be more immediately enjoyable than some of the other numbers.

In the *Imaginary Landscape No. 3* of John Cage, the use of electrical instruments reminded one of Varèse's *Equatorial*, but the sonorous texture seemed better integrated. During the pieces by Roldan and Ardévol, one noticed the absence of a sustained sound; one thought of the human voice, perhaps because the music sounded very much like a complicated accompaniment to a "son" and one expected the arrival of a sound with some sort of carrying power.

In most of the music, the Oriental and African elements dominated. The effects quite clearly, if not consciously, strove to approximate those of the ritual music of the far parts of the world. Even the figures used by Mr. Cage in his delicate *Amores* for piano transformed with screws and clips were reminiscent of Bali, and often the passages of ensemble work were suggestive of the gamelan music of that same island.

Sometimes the level of excitement reached was below the obviously prodigious amount of energy expended to attain it. The complicated rhythmical juxtapositions then sounded neither complex nor simple, but desultory and accidental. But there were few of these dry spots. The music's principal aim was to achieve a maximum of sonorous effect, and the composers involved were adept at it.

It is not so much in themselves that concentrated manifestations like last night's are important, but rather, being in their very intensity the detonators of ideas, they indicate possible directions for Occidental art music to take.

Dushkin Gives Violin Recital in Town Hall

FEBRUARY 9 (1943), *NEW YORK HERALD TRIBUNE*

Samuel Dushkin, violinist, in recital at Town Hall last night. The program:

Sonata in D Major	Leclair
Suite of Waltzes	Mozart

Suite Italienne	Stravinsky
Pieces from the Partita in E Major	Bach
Danse pastorale, Rigaudon	Ravel
Two Hungarian Dances, nos. 1 and 4	Brahms
Two Dance Pieces	Revueltas
Habañera	Pittaluga
Spanish Dance from *La Vida breve*	de Falla
Short Story	Gershwin
Russian dance from *Petrouchka*	Stravinsky

Samuel Dushkin, violinist, played last night at Town Hall in a recital which formed the second program of a series on three centuries of music for the violin. The music ranged from Bach to Stravinsky and Revueltas, and even included a piece by Gershwin, intended, no doubt, as a friendly gesture to the New York public. But the same spirit of compromise that induced Mr. Dushkin to play this worthless bit from the great popular songwriter's pen also made him put in a lot of other numbers just about as uninteresting, thus ruining the second half of his program.

Mr. Dushkin is a strange and gifted artist, a better musician than technician. His intonation is often completely reprehensible, and his tone production pretty faulty. His unbuttoned, tousled style is astonishing in its unevenness; it combines beautifully articulated phrases with smears, exquisite refinement of sound with improper squeaks. Yet with his air of treating each piece as a separate, individual being, and of playing the music as if he had established complete communication with that entity, he manages to make what is in the music come alive. Each piece has its own existence, and thus it is a pleasure to listen.

The Leclair Sonata in D Major, the Suite of Waltzes by Mozart, transcribed by Mr. Dushkin and Mr. Erich Itor Kahn, whose excellent accompanimental work was of great aid to the program—these were both fresh and thoroughly enjoyable works played with sensitive imagination. The *Suite Italienne* of Stravinsky, much of which is taken from that composer's ballet *Pulcinella,* is one of the loveliest works for violin written in this century. Mr. Dushkin presented it with healthy impetuosity. The volume levels he kept distinct; this gave it a dramatic, orchestrated flavor.

It would be pleasant to report that the remainder of the program was as enjoyable. The four parts of the Bach Partita in E Major for unaccompanied violin were not strongly put forth. There was loose tonality in the double-stop passages, and a little too much inadvertent touching of open strings. The result was an uncertain and wavering quality. From here on, the program went along a downward course. Ravel, Brahms, Revueltas, Pittaluga, Falla, Gershwin, and Stravinsky were briefly represented, without very much coming to light save flashes of technical virtuosity. The numbers were all too fragmentary to kindle more than momentary interest.

Barbirolli Back as Conductor of Philharmonic

FEBRUARY 12 (1943), *NEW YORK HERALD TRIBUNE*

The Philharmonic-Symphony Orchestra, John Barbirolli conducting, last night at Carnegie Hall, in the following program:

Overture to *L'Italiana in Algeri*	Rossini
Marco Takes a Walk, Variations for Orchestra, op. 25	Taylor
Descobrimento do Brasil, Suite no. 1	Villa-Lobos
Symphony in A Major, no. 7, op. 92	Beethoven

This was the first concert of the season's series by Mr. Barbirolli, still the Philharmonic-Symphony's titular conductor. There was not much careful or sensitive sound-making. The playing, with the exception of the opening Rossini Overture to *L'Italiana in Algeri,* was stolid and inexpressive; what expression there was seemed due more to a surface observance of dynamics rather than to a completely realized feeling for their necessity.

Deems Taylor's orchestral variations, *Marco Takes a Walk,* was an ingratiating little piece which might have been attractive if it had not been quite so cute. The whimsical programmatic thesis was more amusing than the musical realization of it. This is usually the case when the literary conception offers the dangerous possibility of following every nonmusical idea literally in the music, even to the using of sound effects. Here there were too many temple blocks for horses' hoofbeats, the harmonies were soft and boneless, and there was always a too-ready relationship of tonalities. There was scarcely to be found a true melody; instead the line followed a course of unctuous diplomacy in its cautious eschewing of notes which could possibly cause any dissonance. The music was neither sophisticated nor ingenuous; it was suburban.

The two movements of the Villa-Lobos work, *Descobrimento do Brasil,* were even less rewarding to the listener. The music came from the modern Italian exotic, over-orchestrated school of Pizzetti and Respighi:

grandiose, sugared, and gaudy. In the Introduction there was a pleasing pastoral section for flute, bassoon, and viola which made one even more prone to place much of the blame for the blatancy of the number on its glided and pretentious instrumentation. In the subsequent "Alegria na Horta," a dance about gaiety in an orchard, the featured theme had a childish ugliness. At times the piece sounded like the music of Ferde Grofé in the predictableness of its phrasal tournure. It is hard to find any rationalization that can help one accept the bad taste of one's own epoch.

Kipnis, as Boris Godunov, Heard in Opera Matinee

FEBRUARY 14 (1943), *NEW YORK HERALD TRIBUNE*

Moussorgsky's *Boris Godunov* was given yesterday afternoon at the Metropolitan Opera House, with Alexander Kipnis taking the role of Boris for the first time this season. It would be hard to conceive a more impressive Boris than Mr. Kipnis. The delineation was magnificent, the voice rich and powerful, piercing the occasional heavy brass accompaniment with no strain or difficulty. In the last scene, the adjuration to the Tzarevitch was sung with a vibrant tenderness.

Yesterday's performance was Norman Cordon's first appearance in the role of Varlaam. This was another fortunate assignment; the voice was strong, the diction clear, and the part played with complete aplomb. René Maison made a good Dimitri, although in the garden scene the delivery had a tendency to be too dramatic. Thus the voice sounded querulous. His poses were a bit static here. Kerstin Thorborg as Marina was excellent vocally, particularly at the end of the garden scene.

The strange effect gained by Kipnis's singing of his role in Russian, against the Italian of the rest of the cast, was not so disturbing as it might appear. This was due solely, however, to the masterly interpretation he gave to his part. George Szell conducted: the score sounded superb.

210th Children's Concert Played by Philharmonic

FEBRUARY 14 (1943), *NEW YORK HERALD TRIBUNE*

Rudolph Ganz conducted the Philharmonic-Symphony Orchestra yesterday at Carnegie Hall in the 210th concert of the Young People's Series.

The educational part of the program was devoted to introducing the various instruments of the orchestra to the young audience. It was amusing to note that the sight and sound of the double bass caused a mild sensation. When the bassoon's turn came to be exhibited, one very young lady was heard to say in a loud voice: "Mama, I want a bassoon!"

Actually the demonstration of the instruments appeared to absorb the audience's attention far more than the music on the program, with two exceptions: the *Percussional Mêlée* written by Mr. Ganz especially for his youthful listeners (and whose inclusion of cuckoos and nightingales delighted them), and the First Movement from Lalo's *Symphonie espagnole* for violin and orchestra, played by Master Kenneth Gordon. This young man's performance was amazingly proficient: his playing abounded in sureness of technique and style.

The rest of the program was made up of the Overture to *Ruslan and Ludmila,* by Glinka, the Third and Fourth Movements of Haydn's Symphony in G Major, no. 13, Bolzoni's Minuet for String Orchestra, La Violette's "Masquerade" for flute, oboe, clarinet, and bassoon, the Bach-Abert Chorale for Brasses, and Johann Strauss's "Emperor" Waltz.

Symphony by Franck Played by Philharmonic

FEBRUARY 15 (1943), *NEW YORK HERALD TRIBUNE*

John Barbirolli conducted the Philharmonic-Symphony Orchestra Saturday night at Carnegie Hall in a program that included the Overture to Nicolai's *The Merry Wives of Windsor,* the Franck Symphony in D Minor, Respighi's symphonic poem *The Fountains of Rome,* Chasins's *Parade,* and Weinberger's Polka and Fugue from *Schwanda.*

This is the sort of program that Mr. Barbirolli does quite well. With the exception of the Franck, the pieces were of the kind in which the instrumental effect supplies whatever life the music has. The Franck Symphony is really complete in its opening movement, the other two being anticlimactic emotional prolongations of the first. The playing of this first movement began with feeling and intensity. Presently this was somewhat dissipated by the feeling of disjointedness made by the careless leaving open of the places where brass and wind passages meet those for strings.

The Chasins *Parade* inspired Mr. Barbirolli to execute a graceful ballet as he conducted it. It was a singularly static piece emotionally and evoked memories of the march from *Babes in Toyland.* It was dedicated to the defenders of Corregidor. The first part of *The Fountains of Rome* was taken at a rapid tempo, which made no difference at all in the way it sounded, except that it was over much more quickly than usual.

The same program was played yesterday afternoon.

Estrella Gives Piano Concert at Town Hall

FEBRUARY 18 (1943), *NEW YORK HERALD TRIBUNE*

Arnaldo Estrella, Brazilian pianist, at Town Hall yesterday afternoon, in the following program:

Sonata in D Minor	Cimarosa
Sonata in F Major	Cimarosa
Sonata no. 23 in F Minor ("Appassionata")	Beethoven
Rhapsody in G Minor	Brahms
Intermezzo in E-flat Minor	Brahms
Waltz in A-flat Major	Chopin
Ballade in F Minor	Chopin
Almeria	Albéniz
Feux d'artifice	Debussy
Study	Lorenzo-Fernandez
Toccata	Camargo Guarnieri
Alma Brasileira	Villa-Lobos
Impressoes Seresteiras	Villa-Lobos

The program yesterday afternoon at Town Hall took a long while to warm up. It was not until he reached the section of the program wherein was represented the music of his own country that Mr. Estrella gave the impression of functioning fully.

The Brazilian pieces provided him with an opportunity to become really interested in what he was doing, and this naturally gave the playing a personal element that had been largely lacking before.

A good solo performance is a complete delivery of the message. Faithful following of the notation helps a good deal in effecting this, but it is not the deciding factor. When the message in the music is completely understood and felt by the performer, it automatically takes on the inflection necessary to its intelligible expression.

One felt during the playing of the first part of the program that Mr. Estrella was substituting external inflections learned by rote. His romanticism in Chopin was objective and cerebral. This made the job of putting across such a piece as the Ballade in F Minor much more difficult. The Brahms Intermezzo in E-flat Minor came off better: the pattern of sonorities seemed well plotted. The Chopin Waltz in A-flat Major was curt and clean, if a bit hasty with the runs in the upper register.

One felt from hearing these pieces that Mr. Estrella was essentially a pianist of delicate sensibility, a bit too self-contained, and without enough physical force to do complete justice to such music.

But when he arrived home in Brazil he struck a flame at last. Knowing the folk tunes from which all these Brazilian pieces, with the exception of the Guarnieri Toccata, had manifestly sprung, and having a definite feeling for their Afro-Latin rhythms, he was able to get completely underneath them, as it were, and juggle them about as he liked. Here he indulged his flair for technical precision and brilliance and achieved some excellent effects, particularly in middle-register passages, where he used a nice, powdery-tone quality.

Most of the Brazilian numbers (there were eight, including the encores) sound rather alike. One thinks of Gottschalk mostly, expressed in terms of the French impressionists and Albéniz. The music is full of virtuoso effects, and at the same time utterly ingenuous. Only the Guarnieri Toccata was harmonically and formally evolved enough to awaken the kind of interest contemporary music should. The encores included *Na Corda da Viola; Pisa, Pisa, Pisa; Mulata;* and *A Marc en Cheu* of Villa-Lobos and *Dansa de Negros* of Fructuoso Vianna.

Oscar Ziegler Offers Town Hall Piano Recital

FEBRUARY 23 (1943), *NEW YORK HERALD TRIBUNE*

Oscar Ziegler, pianist, made his first New York appearance in four years last night at Town Hall. His program, which consisted of only five works, proved far more rewarding than the conventional list of "classic" numbers and virtuoso pieces that go to make up most piano programs.

Mr. Ziegler made a point of simplicity in his method of presentation. He began to play the second he was seated upon the bench, and disappeared from the stage as soon as he had struck the last note of each piece.

This demeanor was of a piece with his studious, direct, and careful interpretation of the music. The playing had no sparkle or flutter about it; the artist had apparently no desire to profit by effect-making. He seemed more intent upon displaying the anatomy of each piece, and this he accomplished by letting every note be heard at all times.

The Bach Chromatic Fantasy and Fugue seemed particularly to profit by Mr. Ziegler's elaborate caution. There was not the shadow of an attitude in the literal way he took it. It was an authoritative and personal version which allowed of no ambiguity as to his view of the meaning of music. The ending was beautifully clear and decisive.

In the Mozart B-flat Major Sonata (K. 315c), the excessive carefulness made the second movement almost sluggish in its forward course. The simplicity became exaggerated, but one could not truthfully call it objectionable.

It is doubtful, however, whether the same technical approach can be used with complete success in such a piece as the Symphonic Variations of Schumann. Here certain of the variations seemed to call out for a little more subjectivity in the interpretation and a little more variety in the tone quality, which remained pretty dry throughout.

Mr. Ziegler also played a strange and charming Toccata by Michelangelo Rossi, of the early seventeenth century, and the Beethoven Sonata in C Minor, op. 111.

Serenade Given At the Museum Of Modern Art

MARCH 4 (1943), *NEW YORK HERALD TRIBUNE*

The First Serenade, a concert of chamber music presented by the president and trustees of the Museum of Modern Art at the Museum of Modern Art Tuesday evening, with the following artists: René le Roy, flute; Frank Brieff, viola; Carlos Salzedo, harp; the Britt String Ensemble: Remo Bolognini, Edwin Ideler, Conrad Held, Gerald Kunz, Horace Britt; the Chamber Music Guild Quartet: Elly Bontempo, Bernard Ocko, Lucien Laport Kirach, Eir Lifachery; the St. Cecilia Club, conducted by Virgil

Thomson and Hugh Ross; Janet Fairbanks, soprano soloist; in the following program:

String Quintet in G Minor (K. 316)	Mozart
Sonata for Flute, Viola, and Harp	Debussy
Choruses from the *Medea* of Euripides	Virgil Thomson
Piano Quartet	Bohuslav Martinu
A la Musique	Chabrier

Why was the first Serenade concert so pleasurable? Perhaps because it brought to New York faint memories of its brilliant Parisian forebears, the delectable Concerts de la Sérénade of the now-distant recent past; and memories of the elegant, aware, and active public which attended the concerts. But without taking into account this connection, it was evident Tuesday evening that the audience went away from the Museum of Modern Art in a happy frame of mind. The concert had a carefully chosen program of first-rate works and distinguished performers to interpret them, and was given a neat, disciplined visual presentation. There was also a public present which appreciated the pains that had been taken in its behalf.

The outstanding performance of the evening was given by Messrs. Le Roy, Brieff, and Salzedo in a magnificent playing of the Debussy Sonata for Flute, Viola, and Harp. The piece is at the same time one of the loveliest and most direct of the composer's works. The three artists lived and breathed it, passing the little flame of the music back and forth among them without ever letting it go out. It is true that sometimes the harp seemed a bit strident for the hushed sustained notes, which it almost blotted out, but otherwise the three instruments made an angelic ensemble upon which it would be difficult to imagine any improvement.

Martinu's Piano Quartet, played for the first time, is another proof, if more is needed, that contemporary composers have no need to wander out over the morasses of atonality in order to write original-sounding new music. Completely diatonic in implication, the work is a fresh and vigorous example of neoclassical writing, and not even too contrapuntal. For instance, the opening section of the second movement, for strings alone, has a course plotted largely by vertical considerations. The piece has a sunlit yet solemn pastoral quality. Its decorum is not precious and is not disturbed by unexpected turnings and solutions, nor even by the threats of obstreperousness which arise now and then. Elly Bontempo played the piano part with style and precision. The strings sometimes produced an abrasive quality in agitato passages, but not enough to mar the sound seriously.

The St. Cecilia Club gave Virgil Thomson's *Medea Choruses* its first public performance, and the composer conducted. It is an effective piece, with a clear vocal line, economical and dramatic. The sonorities are varied, and there is a strong kinship to Negro spirituals in the melodies.

The concert ended at a very late hour with the lilting *A la Musique* of Chabrier, the sentiment of whose text was particularly applicable to the occasion. "Et fais leur de si doux instants / Qu'ils vivent oublieux de l'heure!" sang the ladies of the St. Cecilia Club. It was an invocation which had already been answered.

Brooklyn Symphony Has Season's Third Concert

MARCH 10 (1943), *NEW YORK HERALD TRIBUNE*

Sir Thomas Beecham conducted the Brooklyn Symphony Orchestra in its third concert of the season last night at the Brooklyn Academy of Music. The ensemble, thanks to extremely painstaking direction, achieved a surprisingly grateful sonorous balance in many passages during the evening, in spite of a good amount of inexpert playing in the woodwinds and brasses.

The program opened with the C Major ("Linz") Symphony of Mozart (K. 425). Sir Thomas kept a pleasing, almost mechanically steady beat which gave energy to the performance. The string section worked handsomely.

Oscar Levant's *Caprice,* for which profuse apologies were made in the program notes, was a short piece in a style which is often unfortunately accepted in the United States as "contemporary." This began by sounding almost like Scriabin. Soon, however, it hit its stride: a familiar mixture of facetiousness and sentimentality. The slow section put one in mind of Milhaud's *Création du monde* with its subdued bucolic atmosphere expressed with the help of metamorphosed jazz figures. Sir Thomas informally announced from the platform that the program had been misprinted and that the audience would not have the opportunity to discuss Mr. Levant's piece until after an "old-fashioned effort" of Liszt (the *Tasso, Lamento e Trionfo,* Symphonic Poem no. 2). His remarks somehow had the effect of making the audience talk and laugh a good deal during the playing of *Caprice.*

Concert Given by the League Of Composers

MARCH 15 (1943), *NEW YORK HERALD TRIBUNE*

The League of Composers program of works by young American composers yesterday afternoon at the New York Public Library; assisting artists: Leonard Bernstein, composer-pianist; Lukas Foss, composer-pianist; Ralph Hersh, viola; Harrison Potter, piano; Janet Fairbank, soprano; Leonard Merrill, barytone; David Oppenheim, clarinet; Ernst Silberstein, cello; and the WQXR String Quartet; in the following program:

Pastoral for Viola and Piano	Elliott Carter
String Quartet	Vincent Persichetti
Songs for Soprano and Songs for Barytone	Beatrice Laufer
Duet for Cello and Piano	Lukas Foss
Group of Songs	Van Vactor, Wilde, Bacon, Bricker, Cage
Sonata for Clarinet and Piano	Leonard Bernstein

The League of Composers' last concert of the season took place yesterday afternoon in Room 213 of the New York Public Library. As to style, the general impression one had was an emergence from the orthodox dissonant manner of the past decades into a not very clearly defined neoromanticism. No one work nor any complete part of one could possibly be labeled thus, yet there were unmistakable signs of such a trend throughout the concert.

Elliott Carter's Pastoral for Viola and Piano was a curiously impersonal short piece whose wayward melodic line was made up of assorted pentatonic figures and sous-entendus. The written line was often flowing and grateful, but a not too sensitive performance weighed it down.

The string quartet of Vincent Persichetti, in the Hindemith tradition, was knowingly wrought and sonorously satisfying. The first movement had the same quality of voluptuous and wistful frustration found in the early Hindemith string works: in fact, there was too much rewriting of the master's music for much originality of expression to come through, save in the third movement, which was a little fresher and more personal. The piece was well performed by the WQXR String Quartet.

Four Songs Are Heard

Of the four songs by Beatrice Laufer, no single one offered enough of taste, prosody, or melodic line to enable the hearer to determine the extent of the composer's talent. When the vocal writing was not more instrumental than vocal, it was of a disheartening sentimentality. The selection of texts was unfortunate, since most of the subjects were not of the sort that would naturally suggest song. The last number, *Percussion,* was particularly embarrassing; a humorous song with a difficult, humorless line is simply a joke that falls flat.

Lukas Foss's duo for cello and piano was technically and emotionally mature, yet the impression left was tentative and indecisive. Its lyricism seemed a bit dutiful and not a part of the work's conception. The idiom was hermetically neutral. It was extremely competent music that made no attempt to convince the listener of any necessity for its own existence. This lack of parti pris of any sort made it singularly unaffecting.

Clarinet Sonata Given

The group of songs offered by Miss Fairbank were for the most part pseduo-archaic in style. In the case of Van Vactor, the memories were of the seventeenth and nineteenth centuries combined. *Late, O Miller,* by Bricker, was almost as undistinguished as the songs in English that come at the end of the average song recital. However, it was singable and Miss Fairbank did it justice. John Cage's *Wonderful Widow of Eighteen Springs* actually comes under the heading of Dadaism. It says: "I can write a song without any of the elements of music." Before the piece began, Mr. Cage carefully closed the lid of the piano.

Leonard Bernstein's Sonata for Clarinet and Piano had something which is at a premium in contemporary music: meaty, logical harmony. It was also alive, tough, and integrated. The idiom was a happy combination of elements from both east and west of the Rhine, but only indirectly from that far away. There were stronger hints of what goes on north and south of the Rio Grande, these perhaps more directly via Copland. Through most of this (the andante seemed less real) ran a quite personal element: a tender, sharp, singing quality which would appear to be Mr. Bernstein's most effective means of making himself articulate. The work was expertly performed by David Oppenheim, with the composer at the piano.

Chavchavadze Gives Town Hall Piano Program

MARCH 23 (1943), *NEW YORK HERALD TRIBUNE*

George Chavchavadze, pianist, at Town Hall Monday night, in the following program:

Sonata in G Minor	Schumann
Nine Preludes: E Major, no. 9; C-sharp Minor, no. 10; F-flat Minor, no. 14; A-flat Major, no. 17; G Minor, no. 22; G Major, no. 3: B Minor, no. 6; A Major, no. 7; D Minor, no. 21	Chopin
Sonata no. 2 in B-flat Minor, op. 35	Chopin
Toccata	Khatchatourian
Prelude no. 11, op. 34	Shostakovich
El Amor brujo	Falla

Mr. Chavchavadze's playing was polished and meticulous. It was not a part of his intention to make a show of physical force (although at times—notably in the last Chopin étude and in one encore—he did not hesitate to punch the keys with a certain violence). Rather he chose to exhibit his admirable proficiency in making music lacy, bright, and sweet. And although his program was made up almost completely of straight Romantic music, there was no embarrassing abandon, no false poetry, and no falling into moods. The only poetry was that written into the music; and mood was created, sustained, held at arm's length rather than bathed in. This would be considered by many music lovers to be the indirect rather than the straight approach. It is certainly the objective one, and for that the more moving, because it reflects a more evolved degree of civilization. Unrationalized emotion is an unlovely manifestation, and has little place in art. Mr. Chavchavadze achieved an intelligent and objective lyricism and he expressed it through a carefully fabricated sonorous clarity.

The Schumann G Minor Sonata has great vitality. Here was romanticism at its cleanest and most bracing. The artist gave it a restrained, undramatic reading which emphasized the legend-making element within the music: each note was an important new word in the tale being told. Dead spots are practically nonexistent in this piece; that this is unfortunately not true of some Chopin was presently demonstrated.

The nine Preludes of Chopin were played without any waits at all between numbers, with some resultant amusing tonal juxtapositions. Sonorities were lean, metallic, with right-hand passages occasionally (as in the C-sharp Minor Prelude) light as thistle-down. The Sonata was given with laudable precision, although one would have appreciated a bit more power in the scherzo.

Russia's two representatives on the program did not shine. Khatchatourian's Toccata had all the squareness and unimaginativeness of any academic product. Shostakovich did nothing interesting in the short Prelude. Of more interest was Falla's *El Amor brujo,* played as a closing number, without, one was happy to discover, the "Danse rituelle du feu." Parts of this are brilliant piano music, better than Albéniz or Granados at their best ("Danse de la frayeur," "Danse du jeu d'amour," "Les cloches du matin"). The arrangement of others, while exacting skill and care for their execution, is not wholly grateful material for the instrument. The dance rhythms were always strongly brought out; it made a nice final number.

Uninsky, Pianist, Gives Carnegie Hall Recital

MARCH 30 (1943), *NEW YORK HERALD TRIBUNE*

Alexander Uninsky, pianist, played last night at Carnegie Hall in a program which began with Mozart's Variations, *Come un Agnello,* and Schumann's Novelette in F-sharp Minor (op. 21, no. 8), continued with the Moussorgsky's *Pictures at an Exhibition* and a group of Chopin numbers, and ended with selections by Debussy, Ravel, and Prokofieff.

It would be interesting to have a scientific graph of Mr. Uninsky's playing of certain pieces, to measure the extent of his deviations from the exact indicated tempo. "Bydlo" of the *Exhibition,* for instance, became at moments a clear 5/8, and again almost a 6/8 at one point. Such a document would also show how often the artist played simultaneously struck notes in spread fashion, both between the two hands and between voices played by the same hand.

These idiosyncracies, however, were not the reason why certain passages sounded blurred (as in "Limoges" of the *Exhibition*) or jumbled (as in the Chopin Ballade in G Minor). Here the main trouble was that Mr. Uninsky had decided to sacrifice everything—feeling, balance, and accuracy—for breathtaking speed.

Yet, in contrast to these imperfect renditions, there emerged an excellent performance of the Chopin Etude in C Major, op. 10, in which every note was in proper relation to every other and the outcome was a delightful quality of tone, not too brittle and not too thick. The G-flat Major Etude also was sensitive and precise. The mystery of the arbitrary tempo in the Ballade remains.

After the intermission the audience stood while Mr. Uninsky played Chopin's *Marche funèbre* in memory of Sergei Rachmaninoff.

Talk About Records

APRIL (1943), *MADEMOISELLE*

Last year at this time I was living in a village down in southern Mexico where even the kids don't use Spanish in their conversations; they speak the ancient Indian language, Zapoteco. There was one juke box in town (they call them *traigadieces,* dime-swallowers), and all the records were *boleros, sones,* and *canciones rancheras.* Yet in their infrequent visits to Ixtepec, the nearest town, they had heard North American swing records and had been excited enough by them to learn the names of the instruments. And, which is more astonishing, when they heard the records I had with me, they were able to identify those instruments in both solo and group work, and expressed no hesitation in picking out the passages they preferred. The Ellington recordings generally made the biggest impression, with *Ko-Ko* leading.

Which brings me to the controversial Ellington concert at Carnegie Hall. *Downbeat* and *Metronome,* after taking the critics of the dailies for a ride because of their generally unfavorable reviews of the great affair, went ahead to claim triumphantly that the Duke, in his "tone parallel to the history of the Negro in America" entitled *Black, Brown and Beige,* had finally effected a true fusion of jazz and symphonic music. Maybe. I doubt it, although I think that if any one piece could accomplish that feat, the Duke would be the man who could write it. But I don't believe such a historic phenomenon (of dubious desirability, anyway) is effected by any single piece, or even by any one individual. True merging of art forms is a process rather than an isolated event. Not that conscious pioneering in that field is reprehensible—certainly Ellington has more right than anyone to do it—but *Black, Brown and Beige* was neither representative of his best jazz, nor was it a good symphonic composition. All those wonderful ideas cried out for real integration in terms of each other musically. The literary description of the piece in the program notes was beside the point; no good piece, symphonic or otherwise, needs to be explained in words to be understood. All it needs is to be listened to.

Priorities plus the Petrillo-vs.-record-companies fight have been making slim pickings for the collector. Blue Note* recently issued some excellent recordings, but these, alas, are Blue Note's swan song. Ammons has two fine pieces on one disk ($1.57): *Suitcase Blues,* his own version of Hersal Thomas's old piece of twenty years ago, in which the bass rolls like a trombone and makes a very satisfying left hand; and *Bass Goin' Crazy,* where the bass doesn't really go berserk. It just plays a chromatic scale in the straight-eight boogie rhythm of the rest of the number. Ammons's varied bass, rather than his showy right hand, is what gives life to his playing.

More restrained and subtle, and therefore to me more expressive, is the purist Lewis in his forceful *Rising Tide Blues* ($1.57), in which practically every chorus is emotionally a step above the one before. Notice the strange broadening effect he gets at the end by shifting imperceptibly from the established rhythm of triplets to one of almost equal eighth notes.

Of the two sides of the Muggsy Spanier disk released by Decca ($.37), I prefer Handy's *Hesitating Blues,* by the Ragtimers, to its reverse, *Little David, Play Your Harp,* by the orchestra, which in spite of Muggsy's own solo contribution remains a little pat and on the dead side because of the tune itself, one of those spirituals that have to be taken about three times as slowly as this or lose all harmonic variety. The opening and closing choruses of *Hesitating Blues* have fine teamwork, and Spanier's cornet and Fazzola's clarinet have solo honors.

Commodore gives us Art Hodes playing two beautiful atmospheric barrelhouse pieces ($1.05): his own *Selection from the Gutter,* done with an easy indolence that gives it a completely relaxed quality; and Clarence Williams's old *Organ Grinder Blues,* taken as a rather static straight eight boogie.

On Decca, Art Hodes plays two good numbers with his ensemble ($.53):

* Blue Note recordings are available only at the Commodore Music Shop, 136 East 42 St., New York.

Liberty Inn Drag, whose principal attraction is the lovely dark piano opening chorus, partially repeated at the end. There is lots of rolling with the right, and the bass comes out well with plenty of character. Brad Gowan's trombone solo is a bit stiff and weighs it down in the middle. The other side is the *Georgia Cake Walk,* ghosts of old Rampart Street. Everything on the downbeat and decisive. Here the trombone sounds swell.

Mel Powell has four numbers put out by Commodore. *Blue Skies* is coupled with *When Did You Leave Heaven?* ($1.05); and *The World Is Waiting for the Sunrise* with *Mood at Twilight* ($1.05). *Blue Skies* is taken at a pleasant, easy tempo. Mel's solos are full of harmonic invention. His runs here sometimes make you think for an instant of Tatum's, but they were less florid. Billy Butterfield's trumpet is vibrant in his solo. In *The World Is Waiting for the Sunrise,* Powell takes the first two choruses, the second with chordal accompaniment, then Jackson the next two with virtuoso clarinetting in which the melodic invention keeps up almost to the end of the passage. Fast tempo. *Mood at Twilight* is slow and languorous. Powell loves sixteenth triplets in the high register of the piano and decorates the edges of the piece with them. Butterfield has a nice, direct, and unassuming solo. All the Powell numbers are clean and airy.

Victor offers two sides by Sidney Bechet and his New Orleans Feetwarmers, playing Bechet's own *Blues in the Air* and his version of Ellington's old *The Mooche* ($.50, excluding tax). This latter is arranged so that Bechet's expressive soprano sax, Henry Goodwin's trumpet, and Victor Dickenson's trombone play the melody in 6/4 minor triads in open position against a regular slow tomtom. Dickenson makes a good Nanton for this number, and Goodwin takes Cootie Williams's place in the "jungle" business.

The Jazz Ear

APRIL (1943), *VIEW*

Not being sure of how to begin my column, I dreamed I had begun it with this sentence: "Poets have ears, but the world of sound is unkempt, chaotic, and barbarous." The next step, after waking up, was to find out exactly what my sentence meant. The explanation seemed to come out saying that persons of sensibility have always agreed about the desirability of arranging the world in such a manner that, insofar as is fairly convenient to all, the eye shall be pleased. Architecture, clothing, the utensils of daily living are created with a certain amount of care as to color, proportion, and line. Ophthalmic migraines don't result from a walk, even along Park Avenue or Hollywood Boulevard. Sight is catered to like a big brother in the family of senses. Naturally. Seeing is believing. Think of today (leaving out the detonations of war, which, changing everything at once, changes nothing), and the fancy Longchamps with antigastric Musak, think of the machines which can do everything but be quiet, of apartments with indirect lighting and porous walls and ceilings which allow noise to filter through from all six directions to plague the inhabitant, of radios designed for home use, but which are capable of augmenting the sound of the human voice far beyond any conceivable necessity. One would never wish to be blind, yet not a day passes in the city that one does not tickle one's imagination with the idea that total deafness might be a delight.

There is also the gloomy reflection to be made that the ear-poet has to deal in his public with a sense which has as yet to be developed. There is no doubt that hearing is considered a secondary sense, one which is less directly connected with the intellect than sight is—more visceral and infinitely less differentiated. Auditory esthetics are pretty much unevolved, so that in spite of music's impressive technical ramifications, it remains a low-grade cultural vehicle. And a great effort is constantly being made to keep it that way.

......

The swing busybodies exerted themselves no end to defend the indefensible Ellington *fausse couche* called *Black, Brown and Beige,* played at his Carnegie Hall concert. (What comes next in the scale of colors? Black, brown, beige—oh, yes, white.) *Metronome* quoted my *Herald Tribune* criticism at length without having the good faith to quote it correctly, just in order to make me out really feeble-minded. *Down Beat* ridiculed my claim that unless there is a steady beat against which to pit syncopations there is no jazz; they offered the example of a slow blues as proof that syncopation is unnecessary. If they can show me a blues of any tempo without syncopation I shall be delighted. Even the honorable Elsa Maxwell devoted a day to protecting the maligned Duke from the horde of "reactionary reviewers" who (fortunately for Ellington) failed to dig his "tone parallel to the history of the Negro in America." But the Duke doesn't need any of it. All he needs is to stop "trying to get away from" jazz. *Metronome* brazenly used that expression, condoning such an attempt as a constructive one. You see, symphonic jazz is a "new art form." A sensible review of the concert, by John Hammond, appeared in *The Jazz Record,* the little sheet edited by Art Hodes, which will, I hope, grow in size and circulation. If the enjoyment of jazz could cease being organized, and administered like an orthodox religion, everyone would be a lot happier.

......

There are not many good jazz records this season. Even though Petrillo has won in his struggle with his enemies, the shellac remains as scarce as ever. One might or might not expect priority restrictions to make the record companies think twice before recording something really lousy (and several of the new albums are all of that), but then, one sometimes forgets that records, like films, are an industry.

Victor has an album of Brazilian pieces, grouped under the heading *Carnival in Rio.* In performing style, most of them are of an ingenuousness not heard this side of the Caribbean since the close of World War I. Even these, however, give off pleasant whiffs of Latin-American Sunday-afternoon band concerts in the *plaza central.* There is one good tune out of the six: *Nao Tenho Lagrimas.*

Columbia has an album of Teddy Wilson exemplifying his neat, airy playing in a variety of tempi. While I cannot find any reason to agree with Panassié, who claims in *The Real Jazz* that Wilson is a bad influence on younger pianists, still his almost excessively polite style has a lightness and nervousness that can tire you out without having moved you. I like him best at a fairly easy tempo, as in *Rosetta,* which gives him a chance to get in a little springiness and flexibility. Those taut chariot-race numbers he likes to get into *(I Know That You Know, China Boy)* are nice virtuoso things, and he has always excelled at them, because his rhythm is impeccable, and he has enough melodic inventiveness to keep everything going all the way through, but they are not really satisfying—at least, not to me. I am also against Gershwinesque introductions, and the practice of playing the first chorus out of tempo in a cocktail lounge mood, and then getting into tempo only in time to make a chorus or two before the piece ends.

Wilson does this only once in this album, in *I Can't Get Started,* but a good many other pianists have fallen into the reprehensible habit.

Lionel Hampton plays for Decca with his orchestra in *Flying Home* coupled with *In the Bag.* In the case of the latter, the tune may be at fault; melodies made up of familiar repeated riffs aren't as effective as they once were. Nor is the use of the whole tone scale indicated when you want a climax. The ensemble passages sound like Basie of 1938, which is all right, but why keep it up? *Flying Home* always sounded fine when the Goodman Sextet played it. Here it is undistinguished. Naturally. It was created for the Sextet, and its interest lay in the juxtaposition of the sonorities made by Benny's clarinet, Charlie Christian's guitar, and Hampton's vibraphone. The United States Marine Band playing an arrangement made for it of Poulenc's Trio for Oboe, Bassoon and Piano would retain about as much of the original savor of the music.

It's a little hard to get excited by such period pieces as Eddie Condon's *Fidgety Feet* and *Don't Leave Me, Daddy,* on Commodore. Not because they are period pieces—Art Hodes and his men have two nice ones on Decca: *Georgia Cake Walk* and *Liberty Inn Drag*—but because they somehow sound tired, a little undone, as if going back two decades meant letting go in intensity, both in the execution and in the care which goes into getting sonorous variety.

Victor's *Sleepy Town Train* by Glenn Miller is Hollywood jazz: slick and energetic, but self-revelatory in its inability to refrain from proving its status as a luxury product by blowing its top whenever it gets a good excuse.

The best records right now come from Commodore and the defunct Blue Note, whose three final offerings appeared in mid-winter. Commodore has two discs by Mel Powell, good all around: *Mood at Twilight* with a fast *World Is Waiting for the Sunrise,* and *Blue Skies* with *When Did You Leave Heaven?* The group is smooth and lively, John Jackson blows a lovable clarinet in *Blue Skies,* and Powell does some precise and fancy right-hand keyboard work in *Mood at Twilight.* The pieces are all pretty distinguished.

Commodore also has Art Hodes playing the old Clarence Williams–Ethel Waters *Organ Grinder Blues,* now a straight-eight boogie. On the reverse side is *A Selection from the Gutter,* Hodes's own version of barrelhouse atmosphere. The latter is more varied; besides, nobody plays boogie quite as Meade Lewis. Not even Ammons. It is not a particularly rewarding form anyway, being a series of variations on a theme which never admits of much variety. The element of repetition has to be made dramatic by progression from the less to the more expressive: a cumulative emotional effect. Ammons and Johnson seem to have other ideas about it. Their playing is generally more brilliant at any given moment, but Lewis has the time element solved; the piece begins and goes on. Compare Blue Note's recording of Ammons playing *Bass Goin' Crazy*—in which there is diversity among the variations, but no sequential arrangement which could be called an inevitable one—with Lewis's moving *Rising Tide Blues* (also Blue Note), where one feels that something is actually taking place as the music proceeds. There is even an *allargando* at the close in which the rhythm changes from one of triplets to an almost even eight.

Recital Devoted by Borovsky to Bach Music

APRIL 22 (1943), *NEW YORK HERALD TRIBUNE*

Alexandra Borovsky, pianist, in all-Bach recital at Town Hall last night. The program:

Toccata in C Minor
English Suite in C Minor
Three Inventions: B Minor in Three Voices, A Minor in Two Voices, A Major in Three Voices
Prelude and Fugue in A Minor (vol. 2, *The Well-Tempered Clavichord*)
Fantasy and Fugue in A Minor
"French Overture," or Partita in B Minor
Prelude and Fugue in B-flat Minor. (vol. 1, *The Well-Tempered Clavichord*)
Two Preludes of Chorales for Organ (arranged by Busoni)

For those who like so much to listen to the music of Bach that merely hearing the proper notes struck in succession is a pleasure, Mr. Borovsky's program last night was most welcome. This listener feels more or less that way about the music; interpretation is largely a matter of taste, "the correct" style is a moot question, and as long as actual deformation is not practiced, he is content to sit and listen as directly as possible to the notes, without too much regard for how the performer understands their implications.

Mr. Borovsky played with resilience and liveliness, and with little striving after special sonorous effects. In certain pieces, such as the Fuga of the C Minor Toccata, one was struck with the cool and detached, clockwork-like quality, which came near to being what one listens for in the best swing pianists. There was room for fantasy in his conception, as if the logic of the music might not always be inevitable, and the unexpected might be lying in wait beyond the next phrase.

The playing was almost always light, even where a less inconsequential sound might have been preferable. The bouncing tempo used in faster passages was pleasant, but there was an annoying tendency to hurry it for an instant now and then. Such sudden *accelerandi* one felt were involuntary and unconscious, and due to preoccupation with technique. Apart from these tempo deviations, and a few smeared right-hand figures, there was little to complain of technically.

Mr. Borowski repeated the dullest and least Bachlike number of the evening, the Busoni arrangement of *Nun freut euch liebe Christen*. The playing of this had all the feeling of a Czerny exercise; its frantic tempo belonged to the "Ben-Hur Chariot Race" as much as anything.

Vivian Rivkin and Carl Stern Present Recital

MAY 13 (1943), *NEW YORK HERALD TRIBUNE*

Vivian Rivkin, pianist, performed last night at Town Hall, assisted by Carl Stern, cellist. The concert was presented by the Department of Welfare Local of the State, County, and Municipal Workers of America.

The second half of the program had a musically unfortunate if ideologically interesting slant. It was labeled: "United Nations Music," and proved to be an incongruous assortment of bad and indifferent pieces from Palestine, England, China, Russia, Brazil, Mexico, and the United States. An idea of the unhappy result can be had if one notes that England was represented by a Percy Grainger arrangement and an improvisatory number by Cyril Scott, and that our country had only Guion to offer, and Mexico a quite unknown person named Defosse. Apart from this abortive political intrusion upon the program, the concert was most enjoyable.

Miss Rivkin played in a refreshingly relaxed manner, her renditions being clear and spirited, if not always absolutely accurate technically. Her reading of the Rondo in C Major, op. 51, no. 1, of Beethoven was unmannered, sonorously a bit clattery. She exhibited a peculiar tendency in the chordal sequences of the Andante of the Schubert A Major Sonata, op. 120, to produce with the left hand an immediate acoustical echo of the right hand, rather than a simultaneous sound. This occurred again in the Palestinian Dance.

The most sustained and pleasing number on the program was the Shostakovich Sonata for Cello and Piano, op. 40, played by Miss Rivkin and Mr. Stern. The piece is typical of its composer's work, the whole of a loose, open quality, as if the music were without any esthetic bias.

Fast, wooden, folk-music-inspired movements alternate with long, slow ones. The fast parts seem arbitrary and somewhat shallow, and the slow parts are really just as shallow, but much more atmospheric and thus more effective. The superficiality is in no sense a drawback to enjoying the music.

A definite detriment to the music's quality is its harmonic structure. The succession of disparate tonalities evokes a feeling of grayness, a kind of sordid disarray. Part of this may be due to the academic redundancy manifested in placing the material. The most effective section was the bridge at the close of the first movement. The sparseness and simplicity here was an example of Shostakovich at his best. Miss Rivkin and Mr. Stern played the sonata with sensitivity and care.

Concert Shows Place of Jazz in Folk Music

MAY 19 (1943), *NEW YORK HERALD TRIBUNE*

The Little Red Schoolhouse presented an evening of music last night at Town Hall, with Virgil Thomson as master of ceremonies and Leonard Bernstein billed as commentator and pianist. The period after intermission was to have been devoted to "examples and discussion of modern compositions that illustrate the influence of folk music and jazz on the contemporary composer." Program complications reduced the amount of time utilized on the exposition of that thesis to ten minutes, which Mr. Bernstein wisely used to play his own excellent unabridged arrangement of Aaron Copland's *El Salón México.*

Influence of Jazz

If the art music of the United States ever arrives at the point where it is completely distinguishable from that of any other part of the world, the important factor in effecting the change will have been the existence here of jazz. The influence of that particular kind of folk music, however, was shown only obliquely last night in Mr. Copland's piece, which contains jazz only, one might say, as a result of his composing habits, a fact which Mr. Bernstein noted in his brief verbal introduction when he remarked that the presence of jazz there was unconscious.

The overwhelmingly long first part of the program contained a varied assortment of old and new art music, played both on the piano and the harmonica, some swing singing, some swing pianistics, some native American ballad-sing, dance numbers, and even some original voodoo songs with Haitian drum accompaniments, sung and played by the composer, Sergeant Osborn Smith, of the National Guard. These improvisations were an interesting example of mimicry heavily impregnated with tradition and atavism. The words were merely invented syllables, yet bore an unmistakable resemblance in sound to what one hears in West African song. Rhythms were uncomplicated, however, and lacked the subtlety of the more evolved percussive accompaniments of that part of the world. The vocal line was based almost exclusively on the pentatonic scale.

American Ballads

Of Richard Dyer-Bennett's American ballads, accompanied by the singer on the guitar, the most touching was *John Henry*. Jane Dudley, mime, performed two dances, one of which, done to a recorded accompaniment of harmonica, voice, and washtub, was often arresting. John Sebastian played some airs by Bach on the harmonica. The instrument was a bit feeble for the vigorous piano playing that went with it, but Mr. Sebastian performed with accuracy and no effect-making. Pearl Bailey sang some popular numbers, with Eddie Hayward at the piano.

It was a bit difficult to see the intention behind the placing of such disparate entertainment in one evening's program, particularly as the summing-up which was to tie the loose ends together was not forthcoming. One would like to see another such program planned and actually carried out, where the influence of jazz on American art music would be clearly demonstrated.

Vilalta, Pianist, Gives Recital at Carnegie Hall

MAY 20 (1943), *NEW YORK HERALD TRIBUNE*

Alejandro Vilalta, pianist, in a recital of Spanish music given in homage to the Spanish composer Enrique Granados, last night at Carnegie Hall. The program:

Aria in E Minor	Rafael Angies
Rondo in A-sharp	Felipe Rodriques
Sonata in A Minor	Antonio Soler
Danes Lenis	Enrique Granados
Allegre de concert	Enrique Granados
Evocacion, El Puerto	Isaac Albéniz
El Patio del farolillo	Victor Granados
Goyescas (Intermezzo, Les Requiebros, La Maja y el Ruiseñor, El Pelele)	Enrique Granados
Andalusa (La Vida breve)	Manuel de Falla

Since Pedrell, practically all Spanish art music has been intended to evoke the sound of the guitar or the gaits, or the vocalizing of the flamenco singer. Unfortunately the technique most common to the process of effecting this evocation is that of the French impressionists. This is not so in the case of Enrique Granados, who managed to make a music unmistakably if somewhat faintly Spanish without the help of his Gallic neighbors. It was in homage to his countryman, the completely romantic Spanish composer, that Alejandro Vilalta gave his recital in Carnegie Hall last night.

Of the Granados pieces, the most enjoyable was the nostalgic Allegro de Concert. This would make a perfect bit of background music for García Lorca's "Dona Rosita la Rollera," with its audience of lace-decorated cushions and potted palms, and the constant faint suggestion of the harsh Andalusian street outside. Here Mr. Vilalta's delicate, restrained playing, and his ability to create soft, clear sounds was it its best. The interpretation seemed perfunctory. Never did it suggest any depth of feeling.

The Albéniz numbers sounded the way Albéniz always sounds: weak and charming, complex and formulated. Mr. Vilalta did some subtle sonority juggling in *El Puerto*.

El Patio del farolillo, by Victor Granados, son of Enrique, was a lamentably characterless potpourri from a ballet of that title. One after the other there appeared literal paraphrases of dances from Falla's *El Amor brujo* and *El Sombrero de tres picos,* not to mention a sequence which amounted practically to a note-for-note quotation of Ravel's *La Vallée des cloches*. The result was cocktail-hour music.

The program began with three eighteenth-century Spanish pieces, of which the Sonata in A Minor by Antonio Soler was the strongest. The fluidity and charm recalled Scarlatti, whose pupil Soler was. There was even something of what Falla admires so much in Scarlatti, and which he calls "inner rhythm."

One may as well admit that the Germanic influence in Granados is scarcely more useful in bringing out the desired local flavor than the later French, and that modern Spanish art music is simply not representative of its country. (The exception is Falla's Harpsichord Concerto.) The pieces from *Goyescas,* which Mr. Vilalta played with pleasant smoothness and elegance, remind one, in their insistence upon decorative detail, of nothing so much as a Churrigueresque façade. Goya and Spain are something quite different from the tiny refinements and delightful languor of the music which made up last night's concert.

Mozart Played by Robert and Gaby Casadesus

MAY 27 (1943), *NEW YORK HERALD TRIBUNE*

Robert and Gaby Casadesus appeared last night at Carnegie Hall in a program of music for one and two pianos, presented for the benefit of the Russian War Relief. Unfortunately, there was such a great amount of time devoted to the raising of money that one was unable to hear any of the second group of two-piano compositions, which included Mr. Casadesus's own *Danse Russe,* Chabrier's *Deuxième Valse romantique* and *Gracia,* by Infante. It was impossible to regret this fact too much, however, basing one's reaction upon the sole piece of two-piano material one heard: the Sonata in D Major (K. 448) of Mozart.

The ever-recurring question apropos of two-piano music would seem to be, even when the maximum in sonorous quality is attained, is this achievement equal in musical interest to the inevitable sacrifice in expressive subtlety exacted by the medium? The performance last night was excellent, yet there was a sameness of tone that tired the ear. The slight sensation of a constant echo gave the sound a faintly inhuman cast; it was mechanical Mozart, particularly in the first and last movements. One is inclined, for instance, to prefer the purposeful mechanical quality in certain modern works for the same medium, where the two negatives, so to speak, cancel each other and bring everything back into the realm of the human.

The central section of the program was taken up by Mr. Casadesus playing Chopin and Debussy. There are probably few pianists more musically articulate. The playing was impeccable, the message always came through clear and complete. The most remarkable readings were those of the Chopin Ballade, op. 23, the Berceuse, op. 57, and the two Debussy Preludes: *La Cathédrale engloutie* and *Feux d'artifice*. The sonorous possibilities of his instrument were fully exploited by the artist in an endless variety of timbres.

On Film Music

JUNE 20 (1943), *NEW YORK HERALD TRIBUNE*

The films are generally considered a most propitious agent for conveying fantasy. The truth is that nothing really looks fantastic on the screen except factual photographs of real events. Everything else gives one the feeling that work was stopped before the ultimate imaginings were reached. The evocation of the wonderful in this medium is especially difficult simply because the possibilities are practically limitless.

One easy way to suggest the fantastic in a film is to use the right music. Since irrationality can be an attribute only of the visual and literary arts, one cannot, properly speaking, use "fantastic" music to set off a fantastic sequence. However, music can be found whose quality will correspond to an intensification of the salient emotional element in a given sequence. This is likely only to accentuate the basic emotion. A more striking procedure is to use music which either points in the opposite direction to that indicated by the visual track or which remains entirely aloof from its emotional implications.

Then, even though the film travels a negligible distance into the realm of irrationality, a new gauge of reality is supplied by the presence of music; and, measured by this, that distance may seem somewhat greater.

Julian Carrillo, venerated by some of his Mexican colleagues as a pioneer in music involving a variety of fractional tones, has written, along with Jorge Perez, the score for the Mexican-produced *La Virgen morena,* the well-known story of how the Blessed Virgin appeared to the Indian Juan Diego and asked for a shrine in her name at Tepeyac. The only effective sounds in the film are those Sr. Carrillo uses for the actual appearance of the Virgin: an ensemble of sliding siren-like notes played ostensibly on zithers—the composer counts among his inventions a harp-zither with ninety-seven tones to the octave—sounds that help stress the unearthly nature of the divine apparition. Unfortunately, just before the first visitation, a scene is shown in which the plotting Aztecs agree to use the howl of the coyote as a war signal; this proves somewhat confusing for a moment or so, until the figure of the Virgin becomes clear enough to remove one's doubt as to what the sound is meant to represent.

Richter's expressionistic *Sie Sehen und Hören,* about a country fair, recently shown at the Museum of Modern Art in an evening of "avant-garde" films, had a far better than average score, by Walter Gronostay. There was reciting of rhythmical verse, sometimes with repetitions of a monotonous spoken phrase for effect, done to an accompaniment of an orchestra whose instruments (one recalls piccolo, banjo, and xylophone particularly) approximated the sonorities made by rustic bands and merry-go-rounds. The mixture of sound effects, these somewhat abstracted bits of music, and occasional spoken words was impressive.

On the same program were two old shorts by Alexeleff and Fischinger, which, although technically inferior, clearly foreshadowed parts of *Fantasia.* Fischinger's wholly abstract visual accompaniment to a Brahms Hungarian dance is naturally more successful than the partly abstract, partly representational opening of the Disney film.

From time to time ever since 1931, Jean Cocteau's *Le Sang d'un poète* has been shown in Paris and around town here. In spite of the spectator's diminishing ability to accept the personal obsessions as valid symbols for any but the maker, the film can still be seen with interest. For, technically inept as what appears on the screen may seem today, the soundtrack, with the probable exception of M. Cocteau's "poetic" commentary, which serves as vocal titles, remains as fresh as the day it was recorded. The score by Georges Auric continues to be a model of intelligent, sensitive, and imaginative film music writing.

Here music is meant not to suggest an atmosphere of irrationality for an isolated sequence in a realistic or factually possible context, but on the contrary to make everything more real, to help render the consistently fantastic argument more acceptable.

There is often a blend of sound effect and music, but since the effects lay slight claim to being auditory counterparts of what transpires on the screen, they must be considered as a part of the music proper. An exception is the end of the card game, where the hero's perturbation is expressed in sound by the use of an actual recording of a human heartbeat. (This technical device was later employed in connection with Louis Gruenberg's excellent score for *The Fight for Life*.)

The impossibly prolonged horn notes, the ratchets, x-ray machine sounds, and motor noises are used to destroy the spectator's sense of time; naturally a steady sound with unchanging pitch and no suggestion of metrical involvement is well qualified to do this. The melodies, reminiscent of French street tunes, have lines which never lead quite where one would expect them to, yet there is enough of the needed familiarity in their feeling to give the listener the false sense of security which aids him in accepting the more irrational elements of the argument, or the dream in general.

The music's texture has the happy faculty of never sounding symphonic, since scoring was done with an ear to the most complete sonorous variety possible. While there are very few actual solo passages, many sections take on the color of one particular prevailing instrument. Judged by what one reasonably imagines Hollywood ears to be—since Hollywood assumes the same prerogative with regard to the ears of the entire country—the score would sound thin and watery, and doubtless would have to be built up with symphonic fat before it would be usable.

Stadium Filled for a Gershwin Concert Again

JULY 7 (1943), *NEW YORK HERALD TRIBUNE*

Gershwin program, played by Philharmonic-Symphony Orchestra, conducted by Alexander Smallens, with Jesús Maria Sanromá, pianist, and

Todd Duncan, barytone, as soloists, with Harriet Jackson, Alma Hubbard, Etta Moten and the Eva Jesaye Choir, at the Lewisohn Stadium last night. Program as follows:

Overture, *Strike Up the Band*
An American in Paris
Piano Concerto in F
A Cuban Overture
Excerpts from *Porgy and Bess*
Rhapsody in Blue

New Yorkers turned out more than 20,000 strong last night to hear the music of their favorite American composer, George Gershwin, in the annual concert devoted to his works at the Lewisohn Stadium.

There seems to be no doubt that some of Gershwin's music is destined to find as secure a place in the esteem of future American music lovers as the songs of Stephen Foster. The question is: Which part of it? Probably the vocal repertory. Last night one became eminently conscious of the fact that he was primarily a songwriter. The instrumental works came off with eclat—particularly where the piano was used as solo instrument (partly because Gershwin was most expressive in writing for his own instrument, and partly because Mr. Sanromá played with admirable feeling and efficiency)—but it was only when the strains of *Summertime* came forth that one felt the presence of the true Gershwin. This, the *Buzzard Song, My Man's Gone Now, I Got Plenty o' Nuttin'*, and *Bess, You Is My Woman Now* were the most touching music of the evening, because here the conception was fully realized in direct fashion and without labored decoration.

It is a pity that Gershwin was not content to be, as Aaron Copland once wrote, the best composer of light music this country has produced. His melodic invention is spontaneous and original; his tunes manifest a healthy gaiety in terms essentially American. It is always with a certain sadness that one views his accosting of the larger forms. The inevitable occurs: the expressive method grows more complex but the vocabulary, remaining the same, appears vulgar in contrast. The aspiring thoughts cannot find the proper material to clothe themselves in. Instead, there is an often painful straining after eloquence which proves largely destructive to the music.

The concert began with Mr. Smallens leading a perfunctory performance of the overture *Strike Up the Band.* It was bright and noisy, and practically a period piece. In *An American in Paris* one was given a clear view of the composer's weaknesses. The piece rambles, clearly devoid of form, alternating boisterous passages with nostalgic ones, but giving nowhere a feeling of continuity or development. The orchestration is uneven and last night it sounded worse because the instruments in the orchestra were not in tune (solo trumpet consistently played sharp, for instance). In suite form, the lack of cohesion perhaps would not be so apparent.

With the playing of his concerto, however, the composer would probably have been highly satisfied. A better solo performance could hardly be imagined than Mr. Sanromá's clear, lyrical, and rhythmical reading. Mr. Smallens kept the balance and timing admirably precise. This piece is Gershwin's most mature work; it marks the apogee of his attempts at symphonic writing.

The vocal soloists sang the excerpts from *Porgy and Bess* beautifully. The choir was kept somewhat in the background, but its swelling and subsiding added much to the general sonority. The audience was especially enthusiastic about Mr. Duncan and Miss Moten in their duet, *Bess, You Is My Woman Now.*

Frank Sinatra Is the Soloist at Lewisohn Stadium Concert

AUGUST 4 (1943), *NEW YORK HERALD TRIBUNE*

A program of film and popular music played by the Philharmonic-Symphony Orchestra. Max Steiner conducting, with Frank Sinatra, popular tenor, as soloist at the Lewisohn Stadium last night. The program follows:

The Informer	Steiner
The Bluebird	Newman
For Whom the Bell Tolls	Young
Songs by Mr. Sinatra	
Gone with the Wind	Steiner
Petite Valse and *Petite Marche*	Steiner
Now, Voyager?	Steiner

Concertgoers present at the Lewisohn Stadium last night were treated to an amazing phenomenon, more revealing sociologically than from a musical viewpoint. One facet of American culture showed itself in all its effete nakedness when Max Steiner led the Philharmonic-Symphony in the performance of film music of his own and other fellow Hollywood composers. As soloist, the popular singing idol of the day, Frank Sinatra, appeared and sang two groups of harmless Tin Pan Alley tunes to the accompaniment of the orchestra and a chorus of hysterical feminine voices screaming in the audience.

Movie music without the movie is not very satisfactory, particularly when it consists of long sequences of unrelated symphonic sounds without unifying ideas to make them even musical figures, not to speak of phrases or melodies. The Hollywood style is a senseless collage of the orchestral effects practiced by the principal composers of the past fifty years or so. In last night's samples one recognized undigested bits of pieces by Ravel, Moussorgsky, Falla, Tchaikovsky, and others, but the likeness generally stopped with the orchestra sonority. Beyond that there seemed to be no desire to use the actual musical ideas of those works.

Screams from Audience

The film scores bore more or less the same resemblance to music that Hollywood films do to life, or as that regimented sentimental fixation which passes for love in this present civilization bears to the real thing. Which brings us to Mr. Sinatra. The hysteria which accompanies his presence in public is in no way part of an artistic manifestation. It is a slightly disturbing spectacle to witness the almost synchronized screams that come from the audience as he closes his eyes or moves his body slightly sideways, because the spontaneous reaction corresponds to no common understanding relating to tradition or technique of performance, nor yet to the meaning of the sung text.

Mr. Sinatra's admirers assured me that last night he was not at his best. Certainly he seemed unsure of the "symphonic" accompaniments that Mr. Steiner was conducting for him, and the microphone was obviously not completely to his taste. His voice was pleasant, and generally under complete control. His diction was excellent and his personality projection satisfactory. In thanking the audience for its enthusiasm he referred to the members of the Philharmonic as "the boys in the band." It was surprising to note that in spite of the almost ferocious fanaticism of the younger feminine spectators, the audience was in reality extremely small. Only about seven thousand persons attended.

Cooper Leads Russian Music at the Stadium

AUGUST 6 (1943), *NEW YORK HERALD TRIBUNE*

The Philharmonic-Symphony Orchestra, in an all-Russian program conducted by Emil Cooper, with Alexander Brailowsky, pianist, as soloist, last night at the Lewisohn Stadium, in the following program:

Symphony in F minor, no. 4, op. 36	Tchaikovsky
Pictures at an Exhibition	Moussorgsky-Ravel
Concerto for Piano and Orchestra in C Minor, no. 2	Rachmaninoff

Emil Cooper, the Russian whose firm hand helped make the New Opera Company's *Fair at Sorochinsk* a pleasurable event last season, made his first appearance at the Lewisohn Stadium last night conducting a program of romantic Russian works.

The orchestra seemed to be in better condition than it has for some time. Sonority was splendid; not the least reason for this was Mr. Cooper's sureness of interpretation and his vigorous conscientiousness in extracting the utmost sound from every note of the scores he read. The playing of the Tchaikovsky Fourth was literal but magnificently unacademic. It had the clarity of the landscape seen on a cold autumn day: each detail was discernable in all its minuteness. Yet there was no straining for effect in the procedure. Naturally this insistence upon utter lucidity cannot give a piece more than is in the music. If a detail is less interesting than another, its highlighting will deaden the impact of that other. This came to pass now and then during the course of the concert. The final movement of the Tchaikovsky seemed a bit slow; one felt that the time had come to let go a bit and allow more freedom to the rhythmical impetus set up by the music.

In the Moussorgsky *Pictures at an Exhibition,* the impression of literalness in interpretation was even stronger. It was almost as if Mr. Cooper were giving an object lesson in the making of sonorities. The piece stood such treatment less well than the preceding one; the effect became a trifle labored eventually. One felt that the real pains had all been taken with the Tchaikovsky number.

Of Mr. Brailowsky's playing of the Rachmaninoff Second Piano Concerto, one can only say that he used a hard, biting touch and that he was accurate. The amplification was such that the tone quality was generally unreal and on the mechanical side. This was especially noticeable in the second movement, where the melody is unfolded in octaves. The piece itself is couched in an unamusing, degenerate style whose sole point seems to be that of keeping the texture every moment at the highest possible degree of richness. Unfortunately the richness palls almost immediately, as greasiness does in cooking, and the listener is left with nothing to follow but melodies whose courses are seriously interfered with by the composer's deficient harmonic sense.

An audience of about nine thousand persons attended.

All-Soviet Works Heard in Carnegie Hall Concert

OCTOBER 25 (1943), *NEW YORK HERALD TRIBUNE*

The American-Russian Institute presented a program of all-Soviet instrumental and vocal solo music last night at Carnegie Hall.

Perhaps the most striking feature about such a concert is the strong impression one has that no recent non-Russian music has penetrated within the borders of the vast union of republics. It would seem that everything comes right out of the end of the nineteenth century. German romanticism, French Impressionism, academic arrangements of Russian folk music, these are present, but there is no sign of Stravinsky, Hindemith, Schoenberg. It is as if everyone had been asleep all these decades.

On last night's program the one item of interest was Shostakovich's Second Piano Sonata, op. 64, which was given its first American concert performance by Vera Brodsky. Here the principal influence appears to be Prokofieff, so that this could be considered a partial exception to the rule, the absorption of recent extra-Russian elements being one step removed. The piano sonata has the looseness and relaxation of Prokofieff, as well as the insistence upon sequential figures which the latter uses for balance. However, the younger man has not Prokofieff's harmonic clarity nor yet his melodic inventiveness. A good deal of the sonata is unpianistic in style and sounds ungrateful as a result. The passacaglia as a final movement seems the most dramatic, but it is too long, and some of the variations are factitious.

Alexander Kipnis sang three songs of Shostakovich, also for the first time in America, the most impressive of which was a Russian setting of Shakespeare's Sonnet No. 66. The curious vocal line and perverse harmonic accompaniment gave one the strange feeling that one was listening to music by an Oriental composer writing in the style of Occidental music. The material was familiar but its use was exotic.

Doris Doree, soprano, and Donald Dame, tenor, sang popular Soviet tunes of the day and Emmanuel Vardi, musician first class, U. S. N., played a suite by Chemberdahki and other shorter works. Donald Ogden Stewart addressed the audience before the second half of the program.

Josef Lhevinne in Carnegie Hall Piano Concert

NOVEMBER 8 (1943), *NEW YORK HERALD TRIBUNE*

Josef Lhevinne, pianist, at Carnegie Hall last night, in the following program:

Chaconne	Bach-Busoni
Nocturne in G Major	Chopin
Five Etudes	Chopin
Op. 10, no. 12	
Op. 10, no. 11	
Op. 25, no. 6	
Op. 25, no. 8	
Op. 10, no. 4	
Sonata in B Minor	Chopin
Cloches à travers les feuilles	Debussy
Masques	Debussy
The Linden Tree	Schubert-Liszt
Hark, Hark, the Lark	Schubert-Liszt
Feux follets	Liszt
La Campanella	Liszt

It is a pleasant thing to have in existence a standard of excellent piano playing, a gauge by which one can measure and judge the various personal stylistic and temperamental vagaries which make for controversy, a standard without which these interesting deviations become meaningless. Josef Lhevinne's performance last night at Carnegie Hall was an example of just such a standard, and his warmly responsive audience seemed fully conscious of the fact.

The program in itself, apart from the five Chopin Etudes, was musically not particularly interesting. The difference between a work by Bach and a Busoni arrangement of a work by Bach seems to this reviewer as great as the difference between the respective cathedrals of Chartres and Saint Patrick's in this city.

Each has its virtues, but they are not by any means the same virtues, and one is entitled to prefer the older structure. Mr. Lhevinne gave as much cohesion as can be given to the rather amorphous *Masques,* and his performance of *Cloches à travers les feuilles* had charm, but these two works are not Debussy's most ravishing by any means. As to the Liszt group, one can only remark that such pieces, during whose performance the spectator's principal excitement lies in witnessing the fingers' safe traversal of chromatic runs, lengthy trills, *bisbigliandi,* and octave passages, can scarcely be expected to evoke the complete interest of every listener.

Delighted smiles on the faces of the audience evinced its complete approval of Mr. Lhevinne's playing of the last two of these Liszt numbers. Certainly his *Campanella* was about the smoothest version one could ever expect to hear. Absolute technical mastery such as that is by no means common. Pure virtuosity, however, always remains just that, whether the performer be Mr. Lhevinne, Larry Adler, or La Nina de los Peines.

Mr. Lhevinne's Chopin had a wonderful way of mixing simultaneous suavity and violence, retaining at the same time, of course, complete balance of volume and tempo. The first and third in his list of Etudes were particularly delicious in quality. The B Minor Sonata became rousing in its sonorities toward the close of the last movement, but the movements all have a way of sounding alike, and the piece can never be so moving as the shorter works.

Marisa Regules Is Heard in Recital at Town Hall

NOVEMBER 13 (1943), *NEW YORK HERALD TRIBUNE*

Marisa Regules, young Argentine pianist, appeared for her third recital at Town Hall last night in a program which numbered several works of a

Hispanic flavor. These included two short pieces by young composers of Argentina, Garcia Morillo and Alberto Ginastera, as well as the traditional offerings from Falla, Granados, and Albéniz.

Played by a pianist with the curiously unreflective approach of Miss Regules, this latter music is more successful than works such as the C Minor Variations of Beethoven or Schumann's Sonata in F-sharp Minor, which came earlier in the program. Miss Regules brings to a piece a clean style and an incisive, strong touch, enviable digital accuracy, and a pleasant tone when she wishes it.

There is such a thing, however, as having a fourth-dimensional grasp of a piece of music, whereby one sees the entire piece from the point of view of time, at one flash. To catch this desirable vista, the performing artist must maintain himself somewhere above the actual working surface. Miss Regules seemed to be right behind every note, busily pushing the piece along before her. The result in sound was a certain trance-like automatism. All the notes of every piece were there, but somehow the piece itself failed to materialize.

There is no denying that few enough musicians possess this kind of insight to a marked degree, but even a little of it can flavor a conception miraculously. It is mentioned here only because Miss Regules's performance seemed to lack it utterly, which is unusual for so talented an artist.

The two Argentine dances, *Danza de los animales al silar del Arca de Noé,* by Morillo, and Ginastera's *Cuyana,* were light compositions, relying for charm on rhythmical *bassi ostinati,* false notes and ingratiating harmonies a la Debussy. *Cuyana* was definitely the more serious of the two, and Miss Regules presented it brightly and with feeling.

Helmann Gives Piano Concert in Town Hall

NOVEMBER 18 (1943), *NEW YORK HERALD TRIBUNE*

Aleksandr Helmann, pianist, presented a program containing several rarely heard works at Town Hall last night. These included the D Major Sonata of Friedrich Wilhelm Rust, contemporary of Mozart, the *Veritables preludes flasques (pour un chien)* by Erik Satie, and Three Funeral Marches by Lord Berners. Parts of the Rust Sonata, notably the second movement, "Wehklage," were couched in an idiom which seemed amazingly far advanced into romanticism for the epoch in which they were conceived.

Of particular interest was Mr. Helmann's choice of Satie for one of the two modern composers represented on his program, inasmuch as this latter-day master's fairly large piano repertory is practically never looked into by performers. Doubtless the prejudice which attaches to Satie's name the inevitable adjective "trivial" has much to do with this, as well as the suspicion that the music does not give them enough to do. One felt last night that Mr. Helmann possibly shared this latter fear, for although the three little canine pieces were the most enjoyable items of the program to this reviewer, the pianist rushed them practically off their feet in apparent terror that they might fail to give a sufficient impression of technical difficulty.

Indeed, this desire to dazzle with technique seemed Mr. Helmann's principal preoccupation throughout his program. With the firm intention of sounding brilliant at all costs, he committed major injustices against much of the music. In his playing of four Chopin Etudes, and in particular the op. 10, no. 4 in C-sharp minor, the artist sacrificed harmonic and rhythmical implications for sonorous effect, which, when attained, had a certain decorative if (in the long run) wilted quality.

Another case in point was to be found in the performance of parts of the Brahms Variations on a Theme by Paganini, where his blatant accuracy in the upper registers of the piano seemed a manifestation of a desire for statistical exactitude rather than a concomitant of any deeper wish to express the sentiments of the music. The tone was narrow, and even when loud, the playing was never strong because it lacked the elements of proportion which make strength possible. Mr. Helmann accomplished the dubious miracle of making the Steinway sound like a Gaveau.

Film Scores by Copland and Tansman

NOVEMBER 21 (1943), *NEW YORK HERALD TRIBUNE*

Aaron Copland has written a convincing score for Lillian Hellman's *North Star*—convincing, that is, in that it sounds very much like the score for a Soviet film. This is not to say that the musical content is not superior to that of practically any Russian movie one can call to mind; however, it is dramatically no more effective than the better importations. The Russian system has been accepted with its assumptions; first: that invisible voices can be used legitimately for the same purpose as an orchestra and, second: that any group of visible Russians can spontaneously and without passing outside the borders of credibility burst into a professional exhibition of part-singing.

It is conceivable that we might be brought to regard the chorus in the movies as we do the orchestra: as an accompanimental medium which evokes no images in our minds to clash with those which are passing before our eyes. I doubt it, however, as the voice has a much more direct connection with the human being, and inevitably conjures up, if not a definite image at least the sensation of the imminence of invisible persons, whereas the use of instruments for accompanimental purposes is a tradition which it would not appear easy or even desirable to violate.

The second assumption is important only in that it has no right to be made in a realistic picture. The pat harmonizing indulged in by the avenging guerrilla fighters is of a piece with the brand-new village sets; it simply fails to convince. One realizes of course that the composer often has little to say about the placing of music. A song is wanted for a certain sequence and he has to write it. The regrets are for the fact that so distinguished a composer as Copland has been forced to compromise to such an extent with elements obviously distasteful to him.

Copland has in fact made all the concessions to Hollywood save that of writing bad music. There are interminable village dances and songs to accompaniment of accordion, there is blood-and-thunder music at the end, and there are three detachable production-number songs, with lyrics by Ira Gershwin. Of these last, two are memorable: *The Younger Generation* and *My Village*. The former particularly, with its quality of Russian popular music flavored with Coplandesque details, has some of the charm, if not to so intensely personal a degree, as the songs of *The Second Hurricane*. Indeed, the final credits music calls again to mind this same work. The score is far more sonorously pretentious than those Copland wrote for *Our Town* and *Of Mice and Men*—not pretentious in the derogatory sense—there is simply none of the chamber-music hall in it. It is straight orthodox symphonic music presented in the Hollywood tradition; and one of its chief virtues is that it manages to use the symphonic idiom really effectively, a thing which is not often accomplished in the films.

......

Universal's present venture into irrationality, called *Flesh and Fantasy,* is a short and timid one to be sure, and it scarcely called for the sort of poetic imagination needed for a *Nosferatu* or a *Caligari,* but even this lumbering, half-hearted apology for the persistence of superstition could have been made more lyrical and convincing by good music. Alexander Tansman's score is very much down-to-earth, and on the whole pretty insensitive. When the soundtrack is expressive, it is likely to be the sound effects getting across rather than the music. Naturally such a film, postulated on the idea of the reality of that dark world just beyond our reach, offers the composer a terrain rich with suggestive possibilities; opportunities for creating atmosphere and evoking mood would conceivably be numerous (although in this case the frightful dialogue often destroys beforehand the possibility of making any such evocation musically).

Tansman's music here has a strange way of being unmelodic and yet not neutral enough. One is conscious of its stationary quality because one hears the music: a fault, since obviously as soon the music is salient enough to be heard, it has got to seem to be saying something or going somewhere. And what one hears is likely to be a bit old-hat: diminished triads in the woodwinds descending chromatically, string tremolos for announcement of murderous intentions on the part of Mr. Edward G. Robinson, ascending sixths for Mr. Boyer being hoisted to his trapeze, some rather inept jazz (pronounced "yatz") for a bar scene on an ocean liner, some vaudevillesque strains to go with Mr. Boyer's simulation of a drunk. None of these sequences adds to the unreal quality which is needed and was obviously desired by the makers of the film. The composer is to be commended for avoiding "screwy" music, such as Ernst Toch provided for the Bob Hope mystery pictures. Moreover, there are a few good corners, such as the circus music and the dream sequence on the boat, which is effective for its rhythmical insistence, if not noteworthy for its melodic, harmonic, or sonorous content. The best bit of auditory expressiveness, however, is accomplished without the aid of music, in the scene where the distant puffing of an approaching locomotive accompanies the reading of Mr. Robinson's palm by a chiromancer, increasing in sound until it vies at the proper moment in intensity with the uttering of the crucial word: "Murder!" The familiar device of taking the voice which represents the inner promptings of the soul and resonating it through the echo chamber is used on various occasions, and it sounds pleasantly reminiscent of a railway station.

Kapell Plays Concerto with the Bostonians

NOVEMBER 22 (1943), *NEW YORK HERALD TRIBUNE*

The Boston Symphony Orchestra, conducted by Serge Koussevitsky, with William Kapell, pianist, as soloist in an all-Russian program Saturday afternoon at Carnegie Hall. The program:

"Classical" Symphony, op. 25	Prokofieff
Piano Concerto	Khatchatourian
Symphony no. 5, op. 47	Shostakovich

The vogue for all-Russian concerts is still in full swing; it has been going on for quite a while and will doubtless continue. There would seem to be no reason to object to it, particularly since during this war we are fortunate enough to be allowed to hear our German friends as well. Saturday afternoon Dr. Koussevitsky presented us with his second all-Russian program of the week, and the orchestra as usual sounded like the perfect instrument that it is.

First the orchestra tossed off the Prokofieff "Classical" Symphony. No sparks flew, but present were the inimitable nonchalance, verve, and finesse with which the Boston gentlemen always approach the work, and which make it a recurrent delight.

Then came the Khatchatourian Concerto, which carries on, in a way, the tradition of Rimsky-Korsakoff. Mr. Kapell advanced boldly into its Near Eastern labyrinths. The composer made the solo pathway relatively clear at the start, and the piano writing was grateful and functional, without much wasted motion. In the first movement this effectiveness was often present in the surrounding orchestration. One section of the development showed a gleaming cloth-of-gold texture which was not equaled in originality, alas, elsewhere in the work.

On arriving at the second movement, one shortly realized that Mr.

Khatchatourian had already said in the first movement what there was to be said. Themes here were childishly repetitive, the Oriental element was stressed in harmonies of rosewater and musk. (Near Eastern melodic turns are always offensive when combined with the harmonic traditions of the West. Only in Spain, with the taking over of guitar harmonies, has it been possible to preserve some sort of integrity in this matter.) The third movement was energetic and playful, and in spots was reminiscent of the last movement of the Gershwin Concerto in F, if not so successful rhythmically as that work.

There was just about enough vitality and inventiveness in the concerto for a piece the length of the first movement. The rest was an unwelcome bonus. Mr. Kapell, however, with incisive energy and a great sense of direction, rode shining through the frivolous-sounding cadenzas, skirting the morasses of blatant instrumentation, to the triumphant end.

Coming on the heels of the Khatchatourian piece, the Shostakovich Fifth Symphony made a startling impression of seriousness. The dramatic impact present in the opening of the first movement and in the whole third movement make it particularly regrettable that the rest of the frame should rely on such flimsy harmonic stays and struts, and that the emotional evocation should be constantly dissipated rather than becoming cumulative.

Only the Boston Symphony could have created the wonderful sense of hollow magnitude which emerged yesterday from the largo, with its cobwebs of string sounds and its diaphanous close. Dr. Koussevitzky made the tempo remarkably slow, and precisely because of that managed to sustain the mood of this peculiarly elongated movement to its last breath. This is excellent Shostakovich, and it is typical of him to follow it with an unwanted, callow finale. Like our own Saroyan in literature, Shostakovich has the careless and destructive habit of treating old sentimentalities and platitudes and tender personal discoveries with equal solicitude.

Andrés Segovia Gives Recital at Town Hall

NOVEMBER 25 (1943), *NEW YORK HERALD TRIBUNE*

Andrés Segovia, guitarist, in a recital last night at Town Hall in the following program:

Three Small Pieces	Purcell
Preambule, Sarabande, and Gavota A	Scarlatti
Sonata	D. Scarlatti
Theme Varie	Sor
Sonata	Castelnuovo-Tedesco
Two Etudes	Villa-Lobos
Madroños	Torroba
Fandanruillo	Turina
Mallorca, Torre Bermeja, Sevilla	Albéniz

Of all the popular music of the Western World, that of Spain is most heavy with the strange quality which, for want of a more accurate word, we can call magic. The Spanish themselves have a splendid word for it: "duende." The poet García Lorca quotes a Spanish musician as saying: "It is not in the throat; it comes up inside you from the earth through the soles of your feet." And another says: "Everything with black sounds in it has magic." The most poignant and expressive instrument in Spain is the guitar. Indeed, to this reviewer it is the most directly human of the stringed instruments. Only the strings and the fingers are needed to conjure up a magic particularly potent in its immediate evocation of antiquity. The guitar and its cousins are the commonest accompanimental instruments for voice both in Europe and in the Americas: only in Spain has the subtle contrapuntal "punteado" technique flowered into perfection. And Segovia is the undisputed master of that technique.

Given all this, it would seem only natural that last night's performance at Town Hall should have had its share of magic. Again and again, the artist's fingers accomplished the apparently impossible during their tremulous flights across the strings and frets. There were hushed moments of complete beauty when the melody moved out and hung above the chanterelle like a hummingbird poised over a flower. The crowded house was vociferous in its approval.

Yet there was no magic, because the program precluded it. The pieces written expressly for the guitar were for the most part distinctly inferior music, and the great music was played in arrangements which, miraculous as they were from the point of view of ingenuity, necessarily made its performance a question primarily of manipulation rather than of poetic expression.

In the pieces by the two Scarlattis, one was too conscious of the difference in sonority between the two kinds of strings. When the same voice had to jump from one string to another, it gave the impression of the pieces having been pulled slightly out of shape to fit the new medium. Of the three composers whose works formed the central part of the program, subtitled: "Works written for the guitar for Mr. Segovia," the most successful was Torroba's *Madroños*. Here the composer had used theme treatments and devices familiar to popular guitarists. It had less of the disappointing softness of texture and roundness of edges than the better known Turina and Albéniz works which followed. As to the Castelnuovo-Tedesco Sonata, its harmonic variety was too plentiful to make charm on the instrument, and its musical interest per se was very low.

Mr. Segovia is a great artist and a fantastically gifted craftsman; if there were none of the black sounds of magic to be heard last night in his performance, it was because his musical material was not simple enough to convey the kind of eloquence his instrument commands.

Lucia di Lammermoor Is Given at Metropolitan with Lily Pons

NOVEMBER 26 (1943), *NEW YORK HERALD TRIBUNE*

Lucia di Lammermoor, opera in three acts, by Gaetano Donizetti, after Sir Walter Scott, revived at the Metropolitan Opera House last night. The cast follows.

Lucia	Lily Pons
Alisa	Thelma Votipka
Edgardo	Jan Peerce
Lord Enrico Ashton	Leonard Warren
Raimondo	Nicola Mossona
Arturo	Alessio De Paolia
Normanno	John Dudley
Conductor	Cesare Sodero
Stage Director	Lothar Wallerstein
Chorus Master	Giacomo Spadoni
Ballet Master	Laurent Novikoff

The season's first performance of Donizetti's ever-popular *Lucia di Lammermoor* was given last night to a crowded and cheering audience at the

Metropolitan Opera House. Once again Lily Pons sang the role of the woefully betrayed Scottish lass whose melodious mental decline has been the delight of operagoers for so many decades. Miss Pons appeared last night to be in excellent voice. The quality was pure as a little silver bell, and the intonation was admirable. Her mad scene was both musically and dramatically convincing, within the strict limitations imposed by the creator of the opera.

She had, unfortunately, not enough physical force to compete in dynamics with Jan Peerce in the first act's duet, "Soltano il nostro foco . . ." But in this scene Mr. Peerce, although he stole the song, enjoyed a Pyrrhic victory. His vocal performance had the unbecoming quality of an extravagant attempt at expressivity without being really expressive at all, since his notes were tonally ambiguous. With more room to move about in during his indignant role in the second act, he was more successful. Time did not permit this reviewer to witness his achievements in "Fra poco a me ricovero . . ." in the last act.

The Sextet came off well, despite the reticent participation of Alessio De Paolia, whose unpleasant tic of twitching his head with every stressed note was more noticeable than his voice. In general, the recitative was accorded careless intonation and too much vibrato, which is almost as annoying a fault as the singing of arias off pitch. The sets were as sumptuous as the interior of a provincial masonic temple, and places in the stage direction could certainly be improved, particularly in the scenes with chorus.

Philharmonic Gives Another Russia Tribute

NOVEMBER 29 (1943), *NEW YORK HERALD TRIBUNE*

Artur Rodzinski led the Philharmonic-Symphony Orchestra yesterday afternoon at Carnegie Hall in another all-Russian program, in which Erica Morini was solo violinist, playing the Glazounoff A Minor Concerto. Judging from this piece and the Glière monstrosity (the Third Symphony) which preceded it, one would say that conductors are getting down toward the bottom of the Russian list, and would do well to start on another one, if they must have nationalistically categorized programs.

Perhaps one of the chief charms in a truly academic work of music is the clarity with which the epoch of its creation stands out after the fading process has set in. It is like the year painted in vermilion under the signature in the corner of a dark and drab still life. Having preoccupied himself above all with the superficialities and styles of the period, Glazounoff unconsciously dated his work as perfectly as a painter would who included in a canvas figures wearing clothes of the epoch. By now there is not much beyond such temporal idiosyncrasies to look for in the concerto of his which Erica Morini played so superlatively yesterday afternoon. There was a sad disparity between the clean attack, the fine control, the unassuming virtuosity displayed by Miss Morini and the indifferent music her splendid playing was predestined to make. The third section was one of the most brilliant performances on the violin that has been heard by this reviewer.

Orchestral sonorities were served all afternoon in an underdone condition. Dr. Rodzinski helped ameliorate the flavor in the Rimsky-Korsakoff *Capriccio Espagnol* at the end of the concert, but it was a bit late. One hazards the guess that the orchestra was too much overcome by its recent confronting of pure horror (and horror which went on unrelieved for forty-seven minutes, the length of time it took to get through the Glière Symphony) to have much appetite left for any sort of music.

Menuhin Plays Bartók Sonata in Concert Here

NOVEMBER 29 (1943), *NEW YORK HERALD TRIBUNE*

Yehudi Menuhin, violinist, last night at Carnegie Hall, Adolph Beiter assisting at the piano, in the following program:

Sonata in A Major	Mozart
Sonata no. 3 in C Major (for violin alone)	Bach
First Sonata	Bartók
Vallée	Debussy
Yemaya (first performance)	Reyes
A Lenda do cabocio (first performance)	Villa-Lobos
Cantiga de niñar (first performance)	Guarnieri
Molly on the Shore	Grainger

A different analogy for use in clarifying the nature of music can be found for every occasion. One might say that a piece of music is a length of surface covered with innumerable little hooks whose business it is to get as far into the consciousness as possible and provoke a response. Sensitivity to music implies more than being actively conscious of sound: it means vulnerability of the affective faculties. The penetration can be effected directly via the ear and the approval of the viscera, or via the ear and the intellect, which last simply means active listening, or keeping the appreciative mechanism always in gear.

To those who contest the legitimacy of this last method, one can reply that taste determined by intellectual convictions is at least as much a part of passion as irrational preferences are. Both methods are valid because both get the music inside where it has to go. It must get inside because it must fill some physical need in the organism, and this applies equally to the composer, the performer, and the audience. Wherever there is a slip-up, there is imperfect musical communication.

It was seldom last night that one felt that the music on the distinguished program which Mr. Menuhin had chosen called forth any response within his own being. One waited in vain through a skimming over the surface of Mozart and a technically admirable performance of Bach to hear even a few measures which meant something important to the artist. There was no suggestion of joy, misery, pleasure, or pain: nothing but an apparent determination to play well. And no one will deny that Mr. Menuhin can play uncommonly well.

When the despairing second movement of Bartók's Sonata came along, one finally felt that a connection had been made and the performance was moving. This, combined with expert violinistics, made it very fine indeed. Mr. Menuhin remained in his element through most of the fragmentary last movement. At last he seemed to be enjoying himself, and at last one could relax and be glad that he was playing. At the end of the piece, composer and performer came forth three times onto the stage crowded with seated spectators in response to the public's appreciation.

After the Bartók came a group of short pieces no one of which was remarkable. Three were first performances: *Yemaya,* by Angel Reyes, which turned out to be a cake-walk couched in whole-tone harmonies: *A Lenda do cabocio,* by Villa-Lobos, a nostalgic number with considerable charm; and another Brazilian work by Guarnieri, *Cantiga de niñar,* a berceuse dedicated to the artist.

Mr. Menuhin played them all with his customary sureness of attack, perfect intonation, and cold and silky tone. Strangely enough, apart from his not being an especially moving violinist, he is not even an easy one to listen to. Part of this may be due to the fact that he seems not to have a very pronounced rhythmical sense. His rhythm does not go without saying; it has to be followed and sometimes stressed in the imagination of the listener. And this very probably has something to do with his tendency to play with the music like a juggler or to play at it like someone manipulates chessmen on a board rather than simply to play it, which would after all be easier and more effective.

Mahler C Minor Symphony Led by Rodzinski

DECEMBER 3 (1943), *NEW YORK HERALD TRIBUNE*

Philharmonic-Symphony Orchestra, conducted by Artur Rodzinski; Astrid Varnay, soprano; Enid Szantho, contralto; and the Westminster Choir. Dr. John Finley Williamson, director, in the following program:

Three Jewish Poems — Bloch
(Conducted by Leonard Bernstein)
Symphony in C Minor, no. 2 — Mahler

Dr. Rodzinski's program last night at Carnegie Hall, announced beforehand as being "dedicated to the suffering of the oppressed," was not exactly a heartening affair, even when those dead, personified by the entire Westminster Chorus, rose to their feet and began to sing (in English) Klopstock's "Resurrection" Ode, used by Gustav Mahler as text for the final part of the fifth movement of his leviathan-like Second Symphony. For this reviewer, the piece is pathetic, but not in the moving sense of the word, because the degree of its insistence on dramatic effect isolates it from the realm of truly important music, and thus deprives it of the right to be judged as such. If the composer had been content to let his work be simply a piece of music, it might have been either a good one or a bad one, but it would at least have stood on its own purely musical merits; however, since he insisted upon making it a shocker, complete with chorus, organ, ten horns, augmented percussion, and offstage flourishes, there is no way open for us to consider it from the point of view so feverishly indicated by its creator: from the point of view of dramatic impact. Today, as a thrill-producing device, it is as outmoded as a stereoscope.

One is sorry that Mahler was fated to live and work in an age when Disney and Fantasound had not made their appearance, not because he would necessarily have been interested in films as a medium of artistic expression (although he might easily have been, and why not?), but because the infinitely superior ability of that medium to express his particular kind of literary-philosophical grandiloquence would have induced him to exercise his talents in fields of expression more appropriate to the art of music.

As it turned out, Mahler's architectural abilities eclipsed his creative sense of proportion, with the result that his music is not situated on a main thoroughfare of musical thought but on a byway. Neither the thematic material of the Second Symphony nor the harmonic treatment of the material is forceful (read: original) enough to assign it to that wide avenue. What is present is a strong personal inflection capable of imbuing his expressive faculty with a high degree of eloquence. But that eloquence is employed almost exclusively to give tongue to a megalomaniacal passion for the grandiose. One has a suspicion that, given the proper circumstances, he might have qualified as a favorite with certain groups in the Third Reich, whose doctrine of glorification of the irrational conditions all esthetic manifestations of that country.

Last night's performance of this enormous hulk of music was impressive in its dynamics. The Misses Szantho and Varnay sang their relatively short bits commendably, although clarity of diction was not stressed either by them or by the chorus.

Leonard Bernstein, whose accidental debut as conductor of the orchestra was made last month in the absence of Bruno Walter, made a formal bow last night, leading the players in the Three Jewish Poems by Bloch. It was an unfortunate occurrence that Mr. Bernstein was given this purely atmospheric work. The orchestra sounded notably limpid in the first section, the best of the three, and less so in the others. Still, Mr. Bernstein saved the piece from falling into the sentimental well which it so dangerously skirted.

Bach Selections Are Conducted by Stokowski

DECEMBER 13 (1943), *NEW YORK HERALD TRIBUNE*

Leopold Stokowski, conducting the N. B. C. Symphony Orchestra in Studio 8-H, Radio City. The program:

Brandenburg Concerto no. 2, in F major	Bach
Chorale-Prelude, "Christ Lay in the Bonds of Death"	Bach
Toccata and Fugue in D Minor	Bach
Prayer—1943	William Schuman

Leopold Stokowski led the N. B. C. Symphony Orchestra yesterday afternoon at Studio 8-H, Radio City, in one of the series of concerts offered by General Motors Symphony of the Air. The program consisted of two of Mr. Stokowski's arrangements for orchestra of Bach organ pieces, the Chorale-Prelude, "Christ Lay in the Bonds of Death," and the familiar D Minor Toccata and Fugue: the Second Brandenburg Concerto in F Major for solo flute, oboe, trumpet, violin, and orchestra, and William Schuman's *Prayer—1943*.

What one imagines to have been the original orchestral texture of this particular Brandenburg Concerto was best exemplified in Mr. Stokowski's sedate reading of the superb second movement, whose sonorities more nearly approached a simplicity apposite to the work than those of the first movement. Here the strings were inclined to outweigh the solo instruments, perhaps because the conductor placed undue stress on the antiphonal element in the writing.

There is no way of comparing Mr. Stokowski's excellent and completely contemporary-minded transcriptions of Bach to Bach's own orchestral works; disparity of performing media precludes it. However, one may suggest one's preference for a linen garment instead of the same garment reproduced in satin and velvet. In any case, sonorities of the two transcriptions offered yesterday were of the usual luxurious variety, with a superlative wind and brass section outdoing itself in making mellifluous sounds. The beat got lost at one point toward the end of the fugue, and it seemed none too steady in the first part of the concerto. However, the sound of this magnificent music was kept almost constantly at a high level of precision and expressive beauty.

The performance of the Schuman *Prayer—1943* was authoritative and earsplitting in its dynamic intensity. There has been a good deal of talk about the inherent healthiness of Schuman's music. It is hard to see why, unless by healthiness is meant the purely physical and obstreperous well-being of the trained athlete. Mr. Schuman's carefully nurtured robustness often seems precarious; one thinks of it as an attitude rather than as a characteristic. From the point of view of sequence of sonorous effect, *Prayer—*

1943 is fragmentary; its climaxes offer no release, but detract from the potential expressiveness of the passages which follow them. This is probably the desired effect, but with all its emotional impact, the work remains intellectually and sensorially unsatisfying.

Trapp Family Singers Give Holiday Concert

DECEMBER 20 (1943), *NEW YORK HERALD TRIBUNE*

The Trapp Family Singers gave the second of two concerts of Christmas music yesterday afternoon. The audience filled Town Hall and half of its stage, the other half being occupied by the several members of the family and a large Christmas tree trimmed with cookies and ribbons. The program was kept strictly informal, and the Baroness Maria von Trapp, acting as spokesman for the group, explained that since she wished the public to go away carrying with it the feeling of Christmas, all encores would be sung before the intermission, leaving the carols for the very end of the program.

Although a good part of the charm exercised by this gifted family over the spectator is purely extramusical, there is no denying that the performances adhere to a high level of good, homely, nonvirtuoso musical ability. The program yesterday was varied, including a cappella group, various combinations of voices, spinet, and recorders, and two delightful Austrian folk dances. One of these, a waltz for octet of recorders, sounded like a careful and very gentle calliope.

The large work of the concert was a Christmas Cantata of the seventeenth century, *I Bid Thee Welcome, Bridegroom Sweet,* by Luebeck, sung with solos by Baroness von Trapp, obbligati on two recorders by two of her daughters and choral work by the others. Dr. Franz Wasner conducted from the spinet, which was beneath the Christmas tree. The freshness of the voices, the effortlessness of the singing and the touching unpretentiousness of the music itself combined to give an impression of purity as simple and bright as an Alpine winter's day. The audience, in a mood to receive just such nostalgic suggestions, responded with great warmth.

Music for *Jane Eyre*

DECEMBER 26 (1943), *NEW YORK HERALD TRIBUNE*

When functional music fulfills its task perfectly, it lays itself open to the charge of being subservient and unoriginal; if it asserts itself, it runs the much greater risk of being accused of trying to steal the show. Perhaps this kind of music needs to offer no more than the negative aspect of originality: it must not sound too familiar. What is desired is the color of newness without its substance. Good film music cannot be more inspired than the film for which it is made without the resulting disparity's causing it to cease to be effective in its function.

Bernard Herrmann's music for Twentieth Century Fox's *Jane Eyre* relies principally for its strength upon orchestral timbre—interplay and juxtaposition of instrumental tone color. It contains some of the most carefully wrought effects to be found in recent film scores, and the effects are musical ones of as high a degree of dramatic appositeness as good sound effects. It is not composers' music, wherein emphasis is placed on themes and development and expression of personality through harmonic originality, although the stuff used in its structure is distinguished, its thematic material is by no means hackneyed, and its harmonies are fresh yet properly unnoticeable. But if there is no particular passage sufficiently compelling to make one wish to listen to it again as to a piece of art music, there are a good many of them which exist very strongly in relation to the film's action. The score is an excellent example of functional composition: it is highly expressive, neutral music which remains at all times a faithful auditory counterpart of the visual drama, and directly motivated by it.

In the pursuance of this course of careful reflection of the film's every mood and incident, the music suffers certain hardships. There is a tendency sometimes to "mickey-mouse" a sequence, to take its action too literally and synchronize it too consistently. The danger here is that the listener may become conscious of the element of imitation in the music, in which case, unless the sequence is a comic one, the music ungraciously detaches itself from the picture and becomes an annoying hindrance to his enjoyment. Nor does the score completely avoid taking on some of the quality of unreal slickness, that well-known varnished and luxurious finish which is the identification-tag of Hollywood films. (It must be noted that *Jane Eyre* fits the Hollywood conception of romanticism very neatly;

its Gothic extravagances and poetic morbidity make it an ideal vehicle for the particular creative abilities of the American filmmakers. The English would probably never have captured the certain disembodied kind of gloominess which permeates the film: their gloom would have been homely and drear.)

Among effective bits in the score are the poignant music for the scene of Jane's first day at school, as she stands in the empty room with the late afternoon sun shining on the floor behind her; the fire scene, convincing in its sounds of blatant hysteria; and the various night shots on the battlements, where groans and screams are circumspectly blended with instrumental noises to produce some memorable effects.

There are one or two spots where silence would have been a definite improvement over music. When Rochester calls "Stop!" to Jane as she plays the piano, and she obeys, the spectator's senses are confused by the immediate entry of loud cello music to replace the sounds of the piano. This lack of perspective in the juxtaposition of realistically motivated music to atmosphere music occurs again when Rochester turns off a music box, and studio music picks up straightway at equal volume. This is the only fault in the score: it is too insistent. Otherwise, Mr. Herrmann shows a fine understanding of the psychological relationships which exist between drama and music, particularly between mood and orchestral timbre, and this is the determining factor in making the score an outstanding one.

1944

In the Theatre

JANUARY–FEBRUARY (1944), *MODERN MUSIC*

The preopening favorable grapevine and subsequent press raves on *Carmen Jones* led me to expect a production combining the glamor of the Met, the vocal and prosodic purity of *Four Saints,* and the acoustical and dramatic punch of a first-rate Broadway musical. This was decidedly not the case the Tuesday evening when I saw the show. Apologists for the piece claim that on the nights when Muriel Smith doesn't appear, the cast is not so cooperative. This may well be true; Miss Smith was taking that evening off, and the show was certainly uninspired.

The principal objection I have to make is that the work is an opera and needs to be performed by voices equipped to sing the music. If the singing is not top-notch, even though everything else is fantastically good, one can scarcely expect a compelling production. And everything else was not fantastically good.

There needed to be a very apparent reason for creating the esthetic disparity which is the inevitable result when a standard work is paraphrased. Incongruities can make perfectly good sense if presented before the public with style, the great justifier. *Carmen Jones* has practically no style of its own, in the true sense of the word: a conscious manner grown out of organic necessity and which is inescapably the work's own. The piece fits all too comfortably into the category of regular Broadway entertainment: it has visual elegance, a properly speedy tempo of action (save for the second scene of the first act, which could be cut if it were not for the scene change going on behind the drop), several good lyrics, and one or two rousing dance sequences. But these things do not give it style, do not help explain why *Carmen,* more than any other piece from the operatic repertory, should have been made over into a work which misses fire in two directions: both as opera and as musical comedy.

The show has a cast which calls for American music and doesn't get it, and conversely it has a score which in spite of the clever verbal transcription into colloquial American still demands voices which can strike and hold its notes. As to the language uttered during the course of the five scenes (this includes song lyrics, dialogue, and recitativo passages), let it be noted that it is not all pure gold. An overall, standard Negro accent was apparently sought, and it was formulated by the use of such familiar and unfortunate devices as the substitution of "d" for the hard "th," and the third person singular verb without regard to subject. This makes both speech and song completely stilted, since the protagonists make it quite obvious that they are not used to employing such variations on their language. No attempt should have been made to create picturesque accents, but since a halfhearted one was made, it would have been better to suggest the difference between Carolina and Chicago, in the first and second acts respectively. It is surprising, since Robert Shaw coached the cast, that neither the choral nor the solo diction should be quite clear. The great exception to this the night I saw the show was Muriel Rahn as Carmen, whose every word, if musically unsatisfactory, was understandable.

All the way on the credit side are the costumes, the admirable rhythmical precision observed by every member of the cast, the pleasant breaks between songs into spoken dialogue over music instead of the tiresome recitativo, and much of Eugene Loring's choreography. A merging of two parallels is amusingly accomplished in the second-act ballet when the dancers come onstage, assuming postures of banderilleros about to place their darts in the bull's neck, and then make way for a mock boxing bout. It is in the moments of looser adherence to the original that the show is most effective, as in the little vaudeville shuffle done by the counterparts of Frasquita, Mercedes, and the smugglers, with the lively *Whizzin' Away* chorus.

Robert Russell Bennett's scoring is neat and absolutely workable, but I'll take Bizet if I may. That, indeed, becomes something of an idée fixe in your mind as you watch the show unfold, and it keeps you from enjoying it in the right way. You make endless comparisons between situations, milieux, characters, dialogue, first lines of songs (which you listen for carefully because you usually can't hear the rest) and at the end you are inclined, if you have resisted seduction by the bright colors, to sum it all up as a clever tour de force, but not one which makes good opera or really good Broadway either.

Martinu Work Is Played Here by Bostonians

JANUARY (1944), *NEW YORK HERALD TRIBUNE*

Boston Symphony Orchestra, Serge Koussevitzky, conductor, with Mischa Elman, violinist, as soloist, last night at Carnegie Hall. The program follows:

Concerto Grosso for String Orchestra in A Minor, no. 12	Handel
Concerto for Violin and Orchestra	Martinu
Symphony no. 7 in A Major, op. 92	Beethoven

Again last night at Carnegie Hall, that admirable organization, the Boston Symphony Orchestra, manifested to New Yorkers the power of perfect discipline. The finest performances of the evening belonged to the beginning and the end of the concert—to Handel and Beethoven. In the Concerto Grosso one heard the familiar massive, pure tone quality which comes only from the true precision of these players' string attack. The music which emerged was completely heartfelt and beautiful.

The new Concerto for Violin and Orchestra by Bohuslav Martinu, which was given its first New York performance last night by Dr. Koussevitzky, is not the best that the distinguished Czech composer has done for us. It gives, on first hearing, the impression of being a hastily conceived and dispatched opus; moreover, the solo writing is rather less brilliant than the orchestral work, and this is true to such an extent that at times one thinks of the violin as an annoying insect whose sound the orchestra sometimes manages to chase away. Then things happen, for the composer has a way with the orchestra and likes to keep it occupied. Indeed, if one makes a quick inventory of the concerto, one discovers the piece relying almost wholly upon orchestral sonority for its effect. The rhythmical complications seem to be more visual than to exist in the audible fabric of the music, there is very little which is remarkable in the way of melody, and the harmony seems to be carrying out a continuous escape from its own natural consequences. Chordal sequences head straight for sentimental involvement, and then cleverly sneak out through an unexpected exit, leaving the music thwarted for an instant in its sense of destination. It is this harmonic unreliability as much as anything which gives the work its generally fragmentary feeling. And it is the variety of effective instrumentation which by keeping up listening interest gives it whatever illusion of continuity it has.

Throughout the concerto there are passages where the shifting quality of the woodwind accompaniments to the solo instrument make an effect which is quite personal and of considerable interest. At times, Mr. Elman, whose performance lacked the sureness which might possibly have lent direction to the piece, suffered in his intonation in these passages, as if their melting borderline consonances were too much to fight against successfully.

The piece is not a trip to any particular place, but rather a tour through a landscape which does not seem to change basically as one moves about in it. Along the way, in the pastoral-like second movement, there is the spectacle of a cadenza assisted by a triangle ringing like a telephone, and on the homeward stretch Mr. Martinu, in the manner of his countryman Dvorák, offers a bit of American folk music. The sudden ending is like the unexpected arrival back at the starting point of the outing; one is a little dazed, but not in a bad humor.

Condon Leads a Jazz Concert at Town Hall

JANUARY 9 (1944), *NEW YORK HERALD TRIBUNE*

Jazz concert, directed by Eddie Condon, at Town Hall yesterday afternoon, with the following participants:

Pianists	Art Hodes, Don Frye
Drummers	Sidney Catlett, Cozy Cole
Cornetists	Sterling Ross, Max Kaminsky, Billy Butterfield
Trombonists	Lou McGarity, Miff Mole
Clarinetists	Buster Bailey, Pee Wee Russell
Bassist	Bob Casey
Guitarist	Eddie Condon

An audience composed largely of young people and servicemen filled Town Hall yesterday afternoon to listen to another jazz concert directed by Eddie Condon. The winners of the *Down Beat* poll (Mr. Condon for his guitar work, Pee Wee Russell, clarinetist, and Lou McGarity, trombonist) received trophies. The seance got under way with most of the band from Nick's playing a group of numbers which included a much appreciated *Easter Parade,* with strong applause for Sidney Catlett on the drums.

As usual, the actual program differed widely from the printed one, being announced by Mr. Condon in somewhat diffident accents which were not rendered any clearer by the gum he chewed all through the concert. In any case, the second part of the program comprised solo work by Buster Bailey, a clarinetist of the polite modern school, who did a very fine *I Know That You Know* in virtuoso vein; Don Frye, who pianized Ellington's *Flamingo* after a long cocktail-hour introduction; Billy Butterfield, who played *Can't We Be Friends* on his cornet, with excellent tone and shading; and Lou McGarity, whose powerful trombone got inside your ears. Art Hodes offered some, but not too much, of his usual boogie-woogie and barrelhouse material.

The jam session, or "impromptu ensemble," as it was programmed, finished the concert as always, with everyone but Art Hodes taking part at one point or another. An unannounced treat was the appearance of Cozy Cole, currently livening up the first act of *Carmen Jones* as the drummer in Billy Pastor's Café.

What went on yesterday at Town Hall is one kind of jazz; certainly it would be bigoted to say that it is the only good kind. There is also room in the world for the great old New Orleans and Kansas City styles, and even, though Condon fans would cry heresy, for arrangements such as the modern name band gives us, providing those arrangements are done right, which means with complete respect for the tradition of the idiom.

National Orchestra Heard in Carnegie Hall Recital

JANUARY 11 (1944), *NEW YORK HERALD TRIBUNE*

Leon Barzin led the National Orchestral Association last night at Carnegie Hall in a concert which included two first hearings. The assisting artists were Carroll Glenn, violinist, and Staff Sergeant Eugene List, pianist, each of whom appeared in a solo concerto, after which they played together in a double concerto written for them by the American composer Fuleihan.

This work, heard for the first time last night, struck one as a strangely savorless example of contemporary music. There was nothing to object to in it, nor was there much to agree with. Its harmonic idiom was a loose diatonism; its continuity was not so much a matter of flow as of babble. The melodic material was oily and difficult to seize: all the angles were too obtuse. The most that can be said of it is that from time to time it achieved an interestingly pallid orchestra effect.

Both Miss Glenn and Mr. List were heard to better advantage in their solo concertos. Even though Miss Glenn had the misfortune to play the unutterably stodgy Vieuxtemps D Minor Concerto, her strong tone and exact intonation helped mitigate the static effect of the piece. More rewarding was the performance of the Second Piano Concerto of Beethoven (B-flat Major, op. 19) played by Mr. List with proper Mozartean lightness, and with a precision which did one's ears good. Here Mr. Barzin inspired better teamwork between soloist and orchestra than in the Vieuxtemps. The other premiere was a brief, light, academic number by George Lessner, called *A Merry Overture,* with which the concert opened.

Milstein Concert

JANUARY 13 (1944), *NEW YORK HERALD TRIBUNE*

Nathan Milstein, violinist, in a benefit concert given for the Vocational Foundation, Inc., last night at Carnegie Hall, Valeria Paviorzky at the piano. The program follows:

Sonata in C Major (K. 296)	Mozart
Partita in B Minor for violin (for violin alone)	Bach
Concerto in D Major (First Movement)	Paganini
Caprice in A Minor, no. 24 (Variations)	Paganini
Two Excerpts from *Romeo and Juliet*	Prokofieff
Russian Maiden's Song	Stravinsky
"Danse russe"	Stravinsky

When a true virtuoso has the good manners never to remind his audience of the fact that he is one but rather to let the audience savor every instant of the music he is performing, he deserves special credit. Musicianship such as that shown last night by Nathan Milstein in his recital at Carnegie Hall is not always accompanied by the utter sincerity and directness with which he approached his work.

There were no wasted motions in Mr. Milstein's procedure; no energy went to the making of decorative visual effects, nor undue portamento nor excessive vibrato. He is the ideal violinist because, although he has the means to do whatever he pleases, he happens to be satisfied to let the violin sound like what it is—a stringed instrument—and he is not tempted to commit the common but highly embarrassing error of imitating the human voice in distress. This does not mean that his tone is not richly resonant and, at its most characteristic, as penetrating and precise in its activity as a needle. And to continue the simile, the listener's attention was like the thread following exactly and at every instant the path indicated by the bright point of sound.

The Bach B Minor Partita for unaccompanied violin was given a superlative reading. The Doubles, particularly those which followed the Allemande and the Corrente, were masterpieces of interpretation; they went by with the speed of a bomber, but the pitch, dynamics, and bowing had the finesse of a Swiss chronograph. The Bourrée was fast, too; Mr. Milstein played it hard and with great resonance, yet the force never caused the unseemly quality of tone which often comes out at this place. And the Paganini Caprice, with all its accoutrements of virtuosity, its harmonics, chordal and plucked, sounded simply like a piece of music perfectly played. Even in its octave passages, the intonation was so accurate that one had to listen carefully to distinguish octaves from unisons.

The pieces with piano fared somewhat less well. In the Mozart C Major Sonata, the piano outweighed the solo instrument dynamically, so that approximately the whole lower octave of the violin was hidden. Both Prokofieff numbers were in early German foxtrot tempo; they were more cute than convincing, and again the piano was too strong.

One is tempted to suggest that Mr. Milstein could get away with something that possibly no other violinist could: an entire program of unaccompanied violin music.

Stravinsky Leads the Boston in an All-Stravinsky Program

JANUARY 15 (1944), *NEW YORK HERALD TRIBUNE*

Boston Symphony Orchestra, Igor Stravinsky conducting, in Symphony Hall, Boston. The program:

Symphony in C Major	Stravinsky
Four Norwegian Moods (first performance)	Stravinsky
Circus Polka (first concert performance)	Stravinsky
Suite from *Pulcinella*	Stravinsky
Jeu de cartes	Stravinsky

The Friday afternoon audience at Symphony Hall gave an extremely warm reception to the program of his own works which Igor Stravinsky conducted with the Boston Symphony Orchestra today.

Any all-Stravinsky program is news, and this was not an ordinary Stravinsky program, which is to say that no works of the so-called first period were given. And of those played, all but one were of the most recent output—representatives of the period in Stravinsky's development which has been a most frequent target for critical excoriation. Such abuse has generally been made on the grounds that the well of invention is nearly dry. It would be difficult for a serious musician to entertain such an opinion even momentarily after hearing today's concert.

Symphony in C Played

The Symphony in C, like most of the master's works dating from the last fifteen years, is a pastiche of romantic music, but it is more than romantic music in modern dress. It is twentieth-century music which relies almost completely on the psychological overtones of sonorities and harmonies which came into being in the nineteenth century, and which would mean nothing to an audience not conversant with romantic music. And like the other recent works, it is classical only in the sense that the music is climaxless. This reviewer had heard the composer conduct the work with the Orquesta Sinfónica in Mexico, and the two performances were almost equally good. The orchestra today seemed tense and somewhat unsure, and sonorous balance came undone in the third movement. This was unfortunate, inasmuch as the work is practically a problem in instrumental proportions, which, if they are not exact, give it a halting aspect. Yet, at any point in any movement, what is going on is more interesting than in a work of any other contemporary composer.

The *Four Norwegian Moods* proved to be four short numbers written to coincide comfortably with popular taste. The subtitles are "Intrada," "Song," "Wedding Dance," and "Cortege," and the subject matter, in spite of the composer's assurances that all themes are right out of Norway, ranges from themes which might be Irish to others which might be Levantine. The first sounds like a fanfare for a procession in a motion picture, the second like a tone poem, perhaps about snow, the third like a beer garden, and the last rather like Stravinsky, with threats of becoming *Petrouchka* now and then. Incidentally, the word "mood" here does not denote what one might think, but is used in a generic sense which Webster defines as "distinction of form in a verb to express the manner in which the action of state it denotes is conceived." Which may or may not have something to do with the four little pieces. The audience reaction was extremely favorable. One would expect this work to figure on many symphonic programs next season.

Circus Polka *Is Repeated*

The *Circus Polka* enjoyed the distinction of being the first work to be repeated by the Boston Symphony Orchestra in Boston since 1924, when *The Flight of the Bumble Bee* was replayed for enthusiastic listeners. This piece is about elephants; it evokes their grave and dignified movements perfectly. The circus band is there, with the bass drums and calliope, and it is a brilliant tour de force, ending with a bit of Schubert.

Mr. Stravinsky is the perfect conductor for his own works because he aims directly at clarity of sound in line and balance, and in this music, which can be made to sound clearer than any music written since Mozart, utter clarity is the only way to achieve dramatic effect. There was no underbrush in his orchestral forest today; one felt that one could walk between the groups of sounds. No orchestra ever sounded more diaphanous than his did today in certain passages of *Jeu de cartes*. All these recent scores, when conducted by him, are the epitome of sonorous richness; indeed, one could say that texture has come to be the motivating passion that rhythm once was with him. And it is this reviewer's contention that the music remains as stimulating as ever.

Virgil Thomson Suite Conducted by Stokowski

JANUARY 17 (1944), *NEW YORK HERALD TRIBUNE*

Leopold Stokowski, conducting the N. B. C. Symphony Orchestra in Studio 8-H, Radio City. The program follows:

Romeo and Juliet	Tchaikovsky
The Plow That Broke the Plains	Virgil Thomson
American Rhapsody	Zimbalist

Leopold Stokowski led another General Motors Symphony of the Air yesterday afternoon in N. B. C.'s Studio 8-H, conducting the N. B. C. Symphony Orchestra. The program included three numbers instead of the scheduled four, with Skilton's *Sunrise Song* being deleted for lack of time. After a somewhat congested-sounding performance of Tchaikovsky's *Romeo and Juliet,* the lack of clarity being due perhaps to imperfect pitch in the wind section, Mr. Stokowski plunged into what was listed as the first radio broadcast of Virgil Thomson's Suite from *The Plow That Broke the Plains.* While certain individual instrumentalists were not completely smooth in their playing, the performance did justice to the work; the sonorous balance, a rather important item in a piece like this, where the orchestral conception is somewhat stark, was conscientiously preserved by the conductor. Mr. Stokowski took the Blues section ("Speculation") faster than is usually done, and it seemed a good idea: the line is more coherent, less jumpy at his tempo.

Another piece about the United States, borrowing native popular themes instead of the religious material used by Mr. Thomson, was Efrem Zimbalist's *American Rhapsody,* with which the concert closed. It was a happy juxtaposition, that of these two numbers side by side on the same program, with the Zimbalist opus as a perfect example of what it is better not to do when you want to make music about America. As has generally been the case when instrumental virtuosi turn their hand to composition, an attempt is made here to compensate for the basic vacuity and purposelessness of the music itself by an overabundance of complex orchestral details. But it is like putting a suit of clothes beside a naked man instead of on him—he seems only the more unclothed. The difference between this piece of Mr. Zimbalist's and the products of other recent executants indulging in creation is that the idiom is somewhat different. *American Rhapsody* is like a fairly successful exercise in how to write a score for one of the more sentimental Disney shorts. No attempt is made to digest the American melodies contained therein. They are simply quoted, with fancy modal accompaniments. Aside from these lumps of familiar tunes, the rest is just the traditional modulatory magma of Hollywood, where everyone plays loud and nothing happens at all.

Jazz Concert Is Presented at Metropolitan

JANUARY 19 (1944), *NEW YORK HERALD TRIBUNE*

Jazz concert, given by "Esquire's" All-American Band last night at the Metropolitan Opera House, for the opening of the Fourth War Loan Drive. The participants: Louis Armstrong, Mildred Ralley, Barney Bigard, Al Casey, Sidney Catlett, Roy Eldridge, Lionel Hampton, Coleman Hawkins, Billie Holiday, Red Norvo, Oscar Pettiford, Art Tatum, Jack Teagarden, Teddy Wilson.

One kind of enthusiastic audience is much like another, and if the Metropolitan Opera House last night often sounded more like Madison Square Garden during a title bout, it was simply because a jazz audience has to feel free to express itself not only between numbers but during them. "Esquire's" All-American Band embraced artists representing many styles of jazz playing, and the inevitable result was that the solo work was far superior to the ensemble. However, it is not every night that one gets the chance to hear such a collection of great interpreters of the contemporary American folk idiom, and practically all of them contributed fine solo performances.

The middle of the program was messed up by some gentlemen from WJZ's Blue Network, who, after giving the spectators a lengthy lesson on how to applaud, as if the concert were being presented only for the pleasure of the radio audience, remained very much in evidence acting as cheerleaders for about half an hour. Once they had got out of the way, the concert continued, and on a rather more interesting level.

Al Casey played his own *Buck Jumpin'* on the electric guitar, introducing a passage in which soft chordal effects were interspersed with repeated single notes. Art Tatum's incredibly smooth and florid piano was starred in *Stompin' at the Savoy,* after which Oscar Pettiford did some virtuoso bass playing with impeccable rhythm in his own *For Bass Faces Only.*

No arrangement of *Flying Home* can touch the original version of Benny Goodman's Sextet, which was played at Carnegie Hall four years ago. The piece was used last night as the final number, and it was played around with in various fashions, with Lionel Hampton doing most of the playing around. As a matter of fact, the evening's excitement began only during *Flying Home.* A lady in sequins in the dress circle was suddenly "sent" by Roy Eldridge's spectacular overblowing of his trumpet. Her agonized screams and frantic gestures were the signal for a mass demonstration of approval on the part of the audience. The uproar which ensued lasted through a drum duet between Sidney Catlett and Mr. Hampton, a sort of follow-the-leader game which made a rhythmical canon in stretto; and it went on through a bit of antiphonal vibraharping by Mr. Hampton and Red Norvo, which ended in a final chorus taken by them together on the same instrument.

There is no point in making comparisons of individual styles. The best numbers were those which were not arranged, where a soloist played against the quartet of piano, guitar, bass, and drums. For ensemble work, perhaps the most memorable bit was *Back o' Town Blues,* not alone because of Louis Armstrong's important part in it, but because it was in an idiom which everyone seemed to feel the same way about, and therefore the improvisation had room for expression in it.

Francine Nola Marcus Gives Accordion Recital

JANUARY 24 (1944), *NEW YORK HERALD TRIBUNE*

Francine Nola Marcus, child accordionist, gave a recital yesterday afternoon at Carnegie Chamber Music Hall. Her program was made up largely of arrangements of familiar numbers, and pieces in the American popular idiom by John Gart.

Miss Marcus played with great ease and a good rhythmical sense, and showed finesse in managing the bellows. She is obviously an extremely musical child and dominates her instrument already with the sureness of an adult.

There is not much to be said about the accordion as a solo instrument. Either its sounds please you or they fail to. Since its musical expressiveness is next to nothing, its possibilities stop with virtuosity, which means playing with a maximum of speed and accuracy. This is not achieved every day; complete mastery of the bass keys is no mean feat. One of the most cogent reasons for the tendency among serious musicians to disregard the instrument is its miserable repertory, in which musical interest is very scarce indeed. This, in spite of the arbitrary harmonic character of the bass, is not wholly inevitable. Interesting music can be and has been composed for the accordion. No such material was forthcoming yesterday, however.

Copeland Gives Piano Recital in Carnegie Hall

JANUARY 28 (1944), *NEW YORK HERALD TRIBUNE*

George Copeland, pianist, in a recital at Carnegie Hall last night. The program follows:

Two Sonatas	Scarlatti
Fantasia in C Minor	Mozart
Valse, Nocturne, Ballade no. 3	Chopin
Sonatine	Ravel
Feuilles mortes	Debussy
Poissons d'or	Debussy
Feux d'artifice	Debussy
Seguidilla	Albéniz
Zortrico	Albéniz
Recuerdos	Grovlez

Debussy, the man largely responsible for the transformation of piano writing from its nineteenth-century state to its present one of gong and other percussive imitation, probably never had a more eloquent and impassioned interpreter than George Copeland. Last night at Carnegie Hall Mr. Copeland gave his audience at least three examples of perfect Debussy readings, study of which should be made available and even compulsory for every pianist who plans ever to play a piece by the French master. Perhaps in that way the completely false tradition of preciousness in interpretation which has come to be associated with his music would be destroyed.

The most clarifying performance was the one of *Clair de lune,* given as an encore. It was played rather quickly, with no hesitations, no poetic underlinings, yet with an intuitive sense of the simple inevitability of the line which savored not at all of studied understatement but rather of two ordinary things: complete comprehension of the piece and absolute mastery of the tone-producing means required to play it.

These are the things which make Mr. Copeland a delight to listen to when he plays Debussy: his articulateness in transferring his imaginative powers immediately to his performance and his admirable ability to create and juxtapose a variety of qualities of tone without confusing them. Probably in no other composer's works for piano is a concomitance of these abilities of such cardinal importance as in Debussy's, and to a somewhat lesser degree, in Ravel's. Therefore it is only natural that Mr. Copeland, who has always been an expert in this department of piano music, should tend to exploit the talents which are particularly his, even when he is not playing the music of these two composers. Such a procedure is not without its drawbacks, for other considerations take precedence when the music is by Scarlatti, Mozart, or Chopin, all of whom were represented on last night's program.

Thus it was that the two Scarlatti sonatas were limp, moist, and indistinct rather than hard, dry, and clear, and the Mozart C Minor Fantasia was more sedate than dramatic. Two of the Chopin numbers were delightful in a relaxed, almost casual fashion, but the Ballade in A-flat, no. 3, followed in much the same vein, without the tension one is accustomed to look for there.

The fact that Mr. Copeland played latter-day Spanish music by Albéniz of Spain and Grovlez of France (they might just as well both have been Swiss), although the readings were vigorous and rhythmical, was too calculated a bow in the direction of the audience to be pleasurable. More Debussy would have been in order. One hears that sort of thing too seldom to waste an opportunity of getting more of it.

Ballad Singers

FEBRUARY 7 (1944), *NEW YORK HERALD TRIBUNE*

Last night at City Center the American Ballad Singers, led by Elle Siegmeister, were heard in a program of American songs. Most of the material was of folk origin, sung in arrangement form, although there were two early numbers by Jezeniah Summer and William Billings, as well as three contemporary ballads written by Mr. Siegmeister to celebrate the deeds of three American heroes: the legendary Paul Bunyan, Abraham Lincoln, and Douglas MacArthur.

Mr. Siegmeister delivered rather lengthy program annotations over a public address system before each group of pieces. This did not appear to dampen the enthusiasm of his audience, whose attention was directed principally to the lyrics of the songs.

Fortunately the group's enunciation was on the whole excellent, so that the listener was accorded the full savor of nationalism with which colloquialisms can endow the sung text. However, concert choral arrangements of folk songs are likely to prove embarrassing to the listener. The attempt at mere reproduction of the traditional idiosyncrasies and ineptitudes of untrained folk singers is usually destined to artistic failure when carried out by a trained group such as this. Thus the less insistence that was made upon characterization last night, the more satisfying was the performance.

A notable exception was the collection of street cries, among which there was one immediately recognized and appreciated by the audience—that of the strawberry vendors who pass through the streets of New York.

Many of the songs had what used to be called "social significance" and now come under the head of human interest. There were work songs, religious songs, children's games, ballads, and a cycle taken from the lore of the various national minorities, called "The Melting Pot." For a group of six people, singing for the most part without accompaniment, the American Ballad Singers managed to present a lively program of far more interest than is generally found in a conventional choral concert.

Jorge Bolet Recital

FEBRUARY 8 (1944), *NEW YORK HERALD TRIBUNE*

Jorge Bolet, Cuban pianist, played last night at Carnegie Hall. Like most Latins, he seems to prefer and understand best that kind of piano music whose principal interest lies in its physical sound: music like that of the French impressionists and the latter-day Spanish composers. And like many Latins, he is inclined to consider practically any piece a legitimate place to hang a curtain of shimmering, aqueous sound texture. It sounds well in Ravel. Why shouldn't it in a similar passage in Scarlatti? There are plenty of reasons why it doesn't, but the important thing is that it never can sound well and thus should never be tried.

Mr. Bolet has an admirable technique. He plays with such visual ease and grace that he appears to be lifting the sounds effortlessly from the keys rather than applying pressure to them. He gave a performance of the Schubert "Wanderer" Fantasia in C Major (op. 15) which was a marvel of verve, accuracy, and dramatic imagination. This and *Ondine* of the group of Debussy Preludes were perhaps the two clearest examples of his pianistic powers. Yet, although both were a complete delight, *Ondine* was right, and the Schubert work sounded stylistically a little strange because of the sonorities he gave it.

Mr. Bolet appeared in the uniform of a Cuban lieutenant, and the program was interspersed with rather long waits, as if it were being broadcast to Latin America. The large audience was most appreciative.

Brailowsky Recital

FEBRUARY 9 (1944), *NEW YORK HERALD TRIBUNE*

That acrobatics can in themselves be esthetically satisfying if they are done daringly and with a true sense of style was made evident last night by Alexander Brailowsky at his Carnegie Hall recital. Seldom does one hear the music of Domenico Scarlatti, more Spanish than the Spanish themselves, given a treatment so breathtakingly brilliant on the sonorous side, and with such a complete appreciation of the rhythmical subtleties within its structure.

Mr. Brailowsky's Scarlatti was fine-grained, almost powdery. His Ravel *(Jeux d'eau)* was soft, clear, never vague. His "Mephisto" Waltz of Liszt was bristling with imagination and sounded as though it had been written this morning. One heard all three of these pieces with the kind of clarity with which one sees window displays where the glass is at an angle so that there are no confusing reflected images. Everything was incredibly distinct.

In all these numbers a great many notes have to be hit within a very short space of time, and every one must count. At this Mr. Brailowsky is unexcelled. To the rest of the program he gave rather varying degrees of care. In certain numbers, the last movement of the Beethoven E-flat Major Sonata and the Chopin D-flat Major Nocturne and A-flat Tarantella, he seemed utterly bored. While always efficient, the readings were perfunctory.

Copland Work Is Played Here by Bostonians

FEBRUARY 13 (1944), *NEW YORK HERALD TRIBUNE*

Boston Symphony Orchestra, conducted by Serge Koussevitzky, yesterday afternoon at Carnegie Hall, in the following program:

Symphony no. 3 in E-flat Major, "Eroica"	Beethoven
A Lincoln Portrait (Speaker: Will Geer)	Copland
Francesca da Rimini	Tchaikovsky

Dr. Serge Koussevitzky offered his second Carnegie Hall concert of the week with the Boston Symphony Orchestra yesterday afternoon, terminating it with a beautifully rousing performance of Sousa's *Stars and Stripes Forever,* complete with some fine piccolo playing. One felt that he owed his listeners a work with a little substance to it, in the way of a bonus, after forcing upon them Tchaikovsky's *Francesca da Rimini.* They appreciated his thoughtfulness and responded with a salvo of cheers.

As yesterday was Lincoln's Birthday, Dr. Koussevitzky paid homage to the Civil War president by giving Aaron Copland's *Lincoln Portrait,* for which Will Geer was the speaker. The work has been widely discussed, and it is generally agreed that the second, or picturesque, section, with its poignant evocation of a particular time and place, is the most successful. (It also sounds the most like Mr. Copland's film and ballet music, where he is always adroit in creating definite atmosphere.) The piece has some of each quality that one looks for in a work by Copland: the Mahler-like theatricality near the beginning and at the end, the touching suggestions of melody with their open, sparse but tremendously effective harmonic support, and the taut, electric rhythms, which he is fortunately able to keep going longer than most composers. The action of rhythms like Copland's is cumulative and hypnotic, and so must continue in order to have impact. There is nothing more disappointing than a seductive rhythm which stops too soon; it is like a film sequence of a landscape taken from the front end of a locomotive. One hopes it will go on and on.

The final section, judged by its musical effectiveness, is less pleasing. The performance by the orchestra was excellent in its aiming and balance, with the musical punctuations actually making the spoken prosody clearer rather than confusing it. Nevertheless, no matter how great and how true Lincoln's political utterances may have been, or how apposite they appear today, the symphonic concert scarcely seems the place to restate them, either in spoken or sung form. The public obviously thought otherwise and Mr. Copland was called several times to the stage to acknowledge its applause.

The playing yesterday, while on the deliberate side, was always perfectly integrated sonorously. In the Beethoven Third Symphony, which occupied the first half of the program, the second movement benefited particularly from Dr. Koussevitzky's loving care. The performance of Tchaikovsky's *Francesca da Rimini* was as lucid in its elaboration as an exercise in orchestration, which is the ideal treatment for such a work.

Modern Songs by Americans Are Presented

FEBRUARY 14 (1944), *NEW YORK HERALD TRIBUNE*

> League of Composers, presenting a program of new songs and piano works, yesterday at the New York Public Library. Assisting artists: Ethel Luening, soprano; Janet Fairbank, soprano; Lydia Hoffmann-Behrendt, piano. Songs by Lockwood, Luening, Bauer, Chanler, Nordoff, Goossens, Bacon, Diamond, Wilda, Edmunds, Ames. Piano works by Sessions, Cone, Luening, Tremblay, Phillips.

A program of contemporary American songs and piano works was presented yesterday afternoon at the New York Public Library under the auspices of the League of Composers. The greater part of the concert was devoted to songs, so that one was able to get a fairly comprehensive view of what American composers are producing in the way of art music for solo voice with piano accompaniment.

In general it must be admitted that the works presented yesterday were unvocal, as if the composers would prefer to be writing instrumental music. Often one felt that the basic idea was a purely musical one to which a text had been arbitrarily fitted without sufficient regard for literary overtones.

Strong Accompaniments

This impression was strengthened by the fact that accompaniments seemed to have received more care and thought than vocal lines, so much so that many songs were simply piano pieces with vocal obbligato. In such cases it is only natural and practically inevitable that prosody as well as lyrical expressiveness should suffer. Unless a very special point is being made, there must be some resemblance (and the more the better) between the line's direction and the inflections of speech, and this applies not only to the accenting of syllables within a word and of words within a phrase, but to the treatment of the line from beginning to end with regard to its extramusical meaning.

This extramusical meaning is notably absent from contemporary song. The composers write a song as they would write a piece of instrumental music, using the text more as an excuse than as the impulse which must animate every corner of the work's frame if it is to live—that is, if the result is to be an expression which must inescapably have been couched in intoned words.

Yesterday's texts were for the most part by eminent poets; Whitman, Blake, Dickinson, and Cummings each figured as the lyricist of more than one song. Of these, Whitman is the only one whose choice could be questioned seriously. American composers inspired by Whitman's ideas have reacted by rushing to pay him the honor of setting his words to music. Unfortunately, it always turns out to be a poor sort of homage because his words, aside from not being so worthy of attention as his ideas, are moreover far from singable.

Thus yesterday we heard lines such as "I myself do not expose them" sung in a serious song. In general the level of musical taste in these modern songs was far above that of the choice and treatment of words. The discrepancy reached indicates a discouraging degree of literary insensitivity in the modern composer.

Songs by Bacon

There were a group of pleasant, melodious songs by Ernst Bacon, an extremely delicate one by Theodore Chanler called *Memory,* and a short one in the manner of the French Impressionists, most singable, entitled *The Dust of Snow,* by William Ames.

On the piano solo side of the program, Miss Hoffmann-Behrendt played some dark, moody, fragmentary pieces by Edward T. Cone; some slightly more lyrical ones by Roger Sessions, of which the second was pleasantly reminiscent of the Fauré-like first movement of his Piano Sonata; a series of preludes by Otto Luening, two of which, quizzical and amusing, displayed a family resemblance to Stravinsky's *Sérénade en la*; and six Divertimenti by Burrill Phillips. The program varied considerably from the printed one because Maria Maximovitch, who had been scheduled to appear, was indisposed and was replaced by Janet Fairbank and Ethel Luening, both sopranos.

The Philadelphians

FEBRUARY 16 (1944), *NEW YORK HERALD TRIBUNE*

Bruno Walter led the Philadelphia Orchestra last night at Carnegie Hall in a program which included the Mozart G Minor Symphony (no. 40, K. 550), Strauss's tone-poem *Tod und Verklaerung,* and the Brahms Second Symphony. To hear the magnificent sonorities produced by this ensemble after listening to our own Philharmonic-Symphony is like putting a new needle into a gramophone after the ear has long been accustomed to the indistinctnesses produced by a worn needle. It was this quality of overwhelming immediacy which characterized last night's performances and infused each work with a quality of aliveness which one does not always realize one has been missing until one discovers anew that it exists.

Mr. Walter modified the tempi in the first movement of the Mozart, taking the second theme more slowly than might have been expected; the movement thus lost the beauty which strictness can impart to it. The third movement was particularly fine, with the superlative string section sounding out to full advantage.

The lightning-like clarity of the orchestra's playing showed the Strauss tone poem in all its fascinating hideousness. The work, with its phrases which are completely estranged from the natural accents of human utterance, needs a perfect performance like last night's to be at all successful in its frantic attempt to play terrier to the emotions' rat.

The violins reached a maximum of pleading convincingness in the final passages. The piece is a wonderful product of that stage in the degenerescence of romantic music before the maggots of modernism had brought a new kind of life to the general mass of decomposition.

N.B.C. Symphony

FEBRUARY 21 (1944), *NEW YORK HERALD TRIBUNE*

Leopold Stokowski led the N. B. C. Orchestra yesterday afternoon for the General Motors Symphony of the Air, at Studio 8-H, Radio City. The all-Russian program began with a brilliant performance of Rimsky-Korsakoff's chef d'oeuvre of orchestration, *Capriccio espagñol.* The concert suite from Stravinsky's *Petrouchka* came next, with its arbitrary ending. It was given a glittering performance; the "Semaine grasse" music was taken extremely fast. This is an error. The sonorities here are sufficient to hold interest.

The program closed with the world premiere of Amfiteatroff's *De Profundis Clamavi,* whose erudite title in no way succeeded in disguising the music's quality of purpose. Harmonically and melodramatically, the work was reminiscent of Mrs. Carrie Jacobs Bond; the instrumentation sounded vaguely like Respighi. The result was in high Hollywood style, and the film which ought to have been shown with the music would presumably have been a knockout.

The piece begins with forebodings of doom. There is a long love scene in the tower of the haunted manor, interrupted by a bolt of lightning which hits the tower, announcing the arrival of the Nazis, whose marching is heard approaching. The ship is overtaken by a storm, founders with groans, sinks, and the Nazis appear again, greatly reinforced and squealing with rage. The girl is left weeping at her lover's grave (for quite a long time), after which she has a vision which assures her it has not all been in vain. She prepares to ascend to Heaven, the Nazis rush in gnashing their tusks, but she is too quick for them, and triumphantly she soars aloft. The entire first violin section had to play this fifteen-minute saga standing up, although there seemed to be no clear quotation of the *Star-Spangled Banner* in the score.

Povla Frijsh Gives Last of Three Song Recitals

FEBRUARY 23 (1944), *NEW YORK HERALD TRIBUNE*

Povla Frijsh gave the third of her three song recitals of the season yesterday afternoon to a public which filled Town Hall. This public (as well as the composers whose songs she often tinges with magic) is fortunate in still having someone like Miss Frijsh, who never fails to evoke poignant memories of a civilization which has just finished existing, and which is for that reason all the more touching. For it is in the calling up of nostalgia that she particularly excels; such songs as *Infidélité* of Hahn, Trenet's charming *Les enfants s'ennuient le dimanche,* Poulenc's *Voyage à Paris,* and the brilliant *Chanson fuer Hochwohlgeborene,* sung in German, were accorded performances which one can only characterize as perfect.

Several American songs received first hearings. These included Chávez's *North Carolina Blues,* which had a most ungrateful vocal line; Wilder's *Summer the Lovely,* Barger's *Monks and Raisins,* and *Song of an Old Woman* by Bowles.

Philharmonic

FEBRUARY 25 (1944), *NEW YORK HERALD TRIBUNE*

Philharmonic-Symphony Orchestra, Artur Rodzinski conducting at Carnegie Hall last night, in the following program:

Symphony no. 40 in G Minor	Mozart
Also Sprach Zarathustra	Richard Strauss
Symphony in E Minor, no. 4	Brahms

While Strauss's glorification of the Uebermensch was in the act of being played last night, one found oneself wondering why, unless he wished to make as obvious a contrast as possible between the sublime and the ridiculous in music, Dr. Rodzinski had chosen to expose the ugly form and character of *Also Sprach Zarathustra* to the Carnegie Hall public directly after the miraculous G Minor Symphony of Mozart. Throughout the course of its convulsions, one thinks of the behavior of some venomous insect or reptile which refuses to stop moving even after it has been hacked into pieces. When the last harmonica-like chord had been uttered and the piece had come to its end, one understood why the time necessary to a sonorously integrated performance such as last night's had been spent on the work—the public likes this kind of music!

Thus there is no more to say on the subject, save to express one's ingenuous wonder that this same public should not demand, in a work where the composer screams "wolf!" so very many times, that he produce such an animal somewhere between the beginning and the end of the piece.

The Mozart Symphony in G Minor (not the "Haffner," which was listed on the programs) was given a straight, healthy, and fairly unsubtle performance, with even tempi and a certain amount of acidity in the higher strings. In both this and the Brahms Fourth the sonorous surface, especially at the orchestrational joints, needed a bit more sandpapering.

Heifetz in Recital

MARCH 2 (1944), *NEW YORK HERALD TRIBUNE*

Jascha Heifetz played last night at Carnegie Hall on a platform crowded with members of the armed forces, male and female.

For some reason which it was not possible to determine, in the first half of his program, comprising the classical works, his tone was small to the point of being occasionally inaudible. The piano was partially open. During the latter portion of the evening, one would have said he was using a different instrument, which may indeed have been the case. At the playing of the first phrase of the Bruch Concerto, it was immediately obvious that a change had been effected: the tone was full and rich and the performance had little in common sonorously with what had gone on before. To help matters, the piano's lid had been lowered, so that a balance was found more easily.

There is a remarkable quality in Mr. Heifetz's treatment of practically all lengthy or slow legato passages. These mark his most expressive playing, but one feels that the artist means them to be expressive of unhappiness, as if intensity of feeling could be interpreted on the violin only by means of sobs and wails. This conception is not peculiar to Mr. Heifetz, but it is a bit surprising to find it in a man who can give such a fine reading of a work like the Bach Sonata, whose fugue and final movement were played with a rare combination of fire and technical smoothness. Perhaps the reluctance with which one accepts his quasi-lachrymose style of rendering the more emotional sections of the works he plays is a part of one's distaste for the idea of a great artist's playing down, even a little, to the public.

Folksong Recital Given by Richard Dyer-Bennet

MARCH 5 (1944), *NEW YORK HERALD TRIBUNE*

Richard Dyer-Bennet, folksinger, or "Twentieth-Century Minstrel," as he is billed, made his concert debut last night at Town Hall, and the house was full. Mr. Dyer-Bennet, who is accustomed to performing in the intimacy of a small nightclub, sings softly and accompanies himself lightly and with finesse on the guitar, which meant that a good part of his audience last night had to listen with concentration. Fortunately his diction is of the very best, so that it was a rare occasion when a word got lost, even though it was barely whispered.

His program was drawn from Anglo-Saxon and Celtic musical folklore of both sides of the Atlantic, and most of the numbers were either love songs of various kinds or ballads. The voice is soft, high, and husky, without the unpleasant signs of partial cultivation which might easily be present in such a case. When he sings a song straight through simply and without too many art-effects, he is eminently enjoyable. He has, however, a tendency to exaggerate the mood of some of his numbers, particularly the ballads, by slowing down when he comes to a soft passage, and singing loud when he comes to a fast section. This hyperbole in interpretation can become a definite fault, and it did last night in the case of *Lord Rendal* and *Binnorie*.

The expressive conventions of art music as regards dynamics and tempo cannot be observed to the same degree in the case of folk music without weakening the folk music. Mr. Dyer-Bennet should beware of making "concert ballads" out of his splendid repertory. It has been done with spirituals, and with very sad results.

Portia White Debut

MARCH 15 (1944), *NEW YORK HERALD TRIBUNE*

Portia White, contralto, showed the public at her Town Hall debut Monday night that she not only has a magnificent vocal instrument, but that she also has sufficient musicianship and intelligence to do what she wishes with it. Scattered throughout her varied program were passages of superb singing, done in strong, straightforward fashion and with a purity of tonal quality the like of which one encounters all too seldom. She used force in every part of her range, attaining an amazing volume, without sacrificing pitch or tone. Her diction was gratifyingly clear, even though her pronunciation of languages other than English was on the English side, and if the group of songs by latter-day British composers were the most difficult to understand, it was Miss White's fault only in that she chose to sing material which numbered, among its many faults, a most inexpert sort of prosody.

Rarely does one hear a florid line given with such a close approach to perfection as the artist's singing of Purcell's *I Attempt From Love's Sickness to Fly,* and just as infrequently does one find a singer who can sing a long song unaccompanied and make every second important and, what is more, come out at the end right on pitch. Miss White did it with *I Wonder as I Wander,* one of John Jacob Miles's discoveries in Kentucky. One must voice one's objection to a repeatedly shown tendency to slide up to the opening note of a phrase, rather than hitting it directly, and this is a definite fault, because it robs Miss White's work of some of its precision.

Horowitz Concert

MARCH 16 (1944), *NEW YORK HERALD TRIBUNE*

There is something to be said for potboilers in music. At the mercy of a consummate artist they do more by their very transformation to convince us of his skill than a dozen pieces we consider beautiful in themselves.

Vladimir Horowitz could probably make Gottschalk's *Dying Poet* touching if he chose; last night at Carnegie Hall he made Liszt's Sixth Hungarian Rhapsody a straightforward, lilting, and tremendously exciting work, and that, considering the music, is an act of white magic.

In this piece, which closed the program, and in the third movement of the Sonata no. 7 of Prokofieff, the first New York performance of which he gave last night, Mr. Horowitz accomplished memorable piano playing, thrilling in its relentlessness, exactitude, and power. His delicacies and charms in other works, notably the Scarlatti and Chopin pieces, are not lost on the ear, neither are they things a few other pianists cannot produce; but the vertiginous tension he can create, in a purely visceral sense, by an absolutely smooth, scrupulous observance of tempo in rapid, rhythmical, forte passages is unequalled by anyone.

Of the Prokofieff Sonata, written in three movements, the last two were easier to enjoy on first hearing than the somewhat erratic first, with its recurrent martial air interrupted by contrasting sections of nostalgic calm, and its Hindemithian middle section.

Indeed, one might say that the composer has shamelessly enrolled himself with the eclectics of the day in this work. There are echoes of Shostakovich in the wandering close of the first movement; echoes, and strong ones, of the German Romanticism of a century ago, as well as of Moussorgsky in the melancholy second movement; and more echoes, this time of Stravinsky, in the reiterated bass figure of the third movement. This last is the big number, with its unpredictability in repetition and its thunderous end.

Thanks to an electrifying performance, it became almost unbearable just a few seconds before it stopped, so that the emotional effect was that of a headlong precipitation into the silence that followed, which, one takes it, was what the composer wanted. Certainly it represented the acme of physical excitement during the evening.

Recorded Popular Music

MARCH 19 (1944), *NEW YORK HERALD TRIBUNE*

"Popular" here is used in a strict sense and can be construed as embracing all shades of non–art music, from the purely folk product to the purely commercial. Naturally it is not the passage of money between persons in payment for a piece which makes it commercial, but rather the impression the music gives of having been conceived with the idea of salability as the chief consideration. Involved here is the importance of distinguishing a popular idiom before it becomes self-conscious from the same idiom after the discovery of its exploitational possibilities. There is an element of truth in the former which is absent in the latter, and since truth is stranger than fiction (strangeness, like originality, being never so marketable as usualisms and repetition with minor variation), commercial music turns out to be as homogeneous as possible, and consequently not very interesting.

With regard to jazz (and swing), in view of the violent denunciations which are forthcoming from many directions whenever anyone opens his mouth to speak on the subject (a manifestation as encouraging in its healthiness as it is discouraging in its lack of objectivity), it would be well for this listener to declare his nonimplication in any tendency or school. He is not interested in bringing back the dead days of Storyville, nor in keeping jazz free from contaminating influences, nor yet in seeing it "raised" to any particular degree of sophistication. He judges it exactly as he does any other music—a Mozart sonata, a Chilean *triste,* a *java* in the Rue de Lappa: first, is the relationship between the means employed and the end achieved such as to arouse admiration? And second, does the music function as something which is fun to listen to?

It is, of course, a platitude to say that the piece is not made by the tune but by the quality of the arrangement (in swing), and the quality of the ensemble improvisation (in jazz), and certainly by the personnel of the performing organization in both cases. This means that it is not too important what music a band records. Whether this is one cause for, or one result of, a general dearth of good tunes is not very important either. Occasionally, there is a well-tuned melodic line by a not-so-well-known songwriter. One of these is *When They Ask About You,* by Sam Stept, recorded by Sonny Dunham on Hit, and fortunate in its vocalist. Another, more static, less convincing, and not nearly so fortunate in its singer, is *I'll Be Around,* by Alec Wilder, also by Dunham on Hit. Wilder's pieces for his octet with harpsichord are more amusing and personal.

Commodore has two records, both by the gang at Nick's, of which one is a twelve-inch and is labeled *Panama* and *That's a Plenty,* played by

"Wild Bill" Davison and his Commodores. The other is *Ugly Chile* and *That Da-Da Strain,* and the group is billed as George Brunis and His Jazz Band. The ensemble is made up in both cases of George Brunis, trombone; Davison, trumpet; Pee Wee Russell, clarinet; Eddie Condon, guitar; Gene Schroeder, piano; Bob Casey, bass; and George Wettling, drums. My favorite of these is *Panama,* which has a fine tune that never palls. These numbers, like all true jazz, have the fascination and beauty of handmade objects which the perfection of machine-made goods (and careful arrangements) can seldom attain.

Seldom is used advisedly, since the greatest exception to the above statement is the work of Duke Ellington, whose magnificent arrangements are certainly of the most careful sort and yet leave the music absolutely fresh and unlabored. Ellington lovers had better begin worrying, for the recent release of his *Main Stem* and *Johnny Come Lately* marks the end of his records made before the ban in 1942, and no more will be forthcoming until differences are settled. *Main Stem* is a show-piece, with sections of superb orchestrational invention which far surpass anything being done these days. *Johnny Come Lately,* by the other arranging genius of the organization, Billy Strayhorn, is harmonically more exciting and boasts some wonderful cornet playing by Rex Stewart.

Now I Know, a pretentious tune, can be had sung by Pearl Bailey in a purple arrangement played by Cootie Williams on Hit (a far cry from the lost days when Cootie lent his name and talent to Ellington for the "Rug-Cutters" on Vocalion), or by Dinah Shore on Victor, accompanied by a rhythmless mixed chorus which sounds like a group of elderly kindergarten teachers soothing their charges with close harmony.

Decca gives out with Ella Fitzgerald singing *When My Sugar Walks Down the Street,* the same old piece I had a record of in grade school and improved now by a slower tempo and Ella's expressive little voice. If you must have that stirring marching song *Mairzy Doats* in your discoteca, I suggest the classical version by the Merry Macs on Decca, in place of the unorthodox one by the King Sisters on Bluebird. It is also less painful to put up with Jerry Wald's relatively harmless playing of *Poinciana* on Decca than it is to attempt to un-Ravel David Rose's daffy and cloying paraphrase of the same piece on Victor. This and *Holiday for Strings* loom high on the list of sickly tendencies of the last year.

Victor offers an album of reissued Swing Classics garnered from the output of the last seven years, including Goodman's *Stompin' at the Savoy,* Shaw's *Begin the Beguine,* and Miller's *Tuxedo Junction.* The differences among the musical sounds made by these excellent bands are in general superficial, since they all agree upon the target.

French Recital

MARCH 21 (1944), *NEW YORK HERALD TRIBUNE*

There is not a very great probability that French culture, which to many people is all but synonymous with Western culture itself, is in danger of immediate disappearance. In spite of the fears which are constantly being voiced on this point, the influence France has exerted upon music alone in recent times guarantees a continuance of her tradition.

Two American composers who can be counted on to further that tradition, one of tasteful precision in considering the proportion of form to matter, are Virgil Thomson and Theodore Chanler. Both Mr. Thomson and Mr. Chanler conducted choral works of their own last night at the concert given at the French Institute in honor of the people of France. Mr. Chanler's piece, heard for the first time here, was a simple but somber setting of a sixteenth-century poem by Bertaut, written completely in unison, a device which enhanced the directness of its prosodic effect. Mr. Thomson's *Scenes from the Holy Infancy,* moving in its childlike clarity, was a magnificent example of effective English prosody. No less admirable was the diction he elicited from the Emanu-El Choir.

Sir Thomas Beecham opened the concert, conducting the choir in two sixteenth-century French works, and Lazare Saminsky, the regular director of the choir, led its members in a vigorous first performance of his own *France, Glory to New Hosts,* after a text by Victor Hugo. Mildred Dilling played three rococo numbers by Duphly, Rameau, and Couperin on that French instrument, the harp. The result was somewhat unexpected, but amusing. Felix Salmond performed the Sonata for Cello and Piano of Debussy, and Dr. Saminsky again conducted his choir in two first New York performances of latter-day French works by Honegger and Caplet. The concert, whose proceeds are for the destitute children of France, was one of three which are being given in honor of the people of France, Britain, and the Soviet Union, respectively.

Philharmonic

MARCH 24 (1944), *NEW YORK HERALD TRIBUNE*

Once in a while (the phrase is purposely vague), the Philharmonic-Symphony Orchestra gives a program which is completely dead, the meaning of whose material seems to be effectively out of touch with present-day musical thought. Last night's concert at Carnegie Hall was such a one. Even Milhaud's *Cortège funèbre*, heard for the first time and dedicated to the Allied soldiers lost in the present war, failed to establish emotional or philosophical contact. The piece in its idiom would seem to be a flashback to the period when the composer had just visited Brazil; it is more like a maxixe than anything else. Perhaps at a different tempo from the one taken by Dr. Rodzinski, it might have seemed more to the programmatic point. There is a dissonant and perturbed climax, a steady marching beat, and a soft snare-drum sequence at the end. Otherwise, the instrumental syncopations present from the beginning suggest something quite other than a funeral procession.

The Franck Symphony made up in lugubriousness for the lack of it in the Milhaud opus, after which in reverse order from that announced in the program came two more romantic works: the Kodaly *Dances from Galanta* and the Rachmaninoff Second Piano Concerto in C Minor, the solo part of which was played by the young American pianist William Kapell.

Mr. Kapell's performance was visually elegant and auditorially satisfactory but noncommittal, in the sense that it was impossible to know whether or not the artist was enjoying his part in the music-making. Personally this reviewer hoped he was not, and that he was simply fulfilling a contractual obligation which left him free to think of pleasanter things while he worked.

Miss Rosen Presents Recital on the Theremin

MARCH 27 (1944), *NEW YORK HERALD TRIBUNE*

Lucie Bigelow Rosen, thereminist, presented a concert of music played on that instrument Sunday night at Town Hall. The program included works by Bach, Beethoven, and Debussy, as well as two pieces written for the theremin by John Haussermann and Mortimer Browning.

The sound of the instrument is, of course, unfamiliar to ears accustomed to the exact intervals of Western music. Perhaps for that reason it would be advisable in writing for the theremin to avoid any attempt to use a tempered scale. Certainly its sound, when accompanied by the piano, is not what would generally be called pleasing.

Sunday night it was made apparent that exact pitch, except in the case of notes of long time value, is not an easy feat to accomplish. Used as sound effect in the orchestra, the instrument could obviously be impressive. Also a kind of sound-music can be made with it, as Varèse demonstrated several years ago with his *Equatorial.* It is, however, not the ideal thing to use for playing *Clair de lune* and the Meditation from *Thaïs,* which were attempted Sunday night.

Miss Rosen played several encores and gave a brief talk on the therapeutic uses of the theremin. Frank Chatterton accompanied at the piano.

Bernstein's First

MARCH 30 (1944), *NEW YORK HERALD TRIBUNE*

Leonard Bernstein, the twenty-five-year-old conductor, scored a double-barreled success last night at Carnegie Hall leading the Philharmonic-Symphony Orchestra in a program which included the New York premiere of his own First Symphony. This work, which he calls *Jeremiah,* outranks every other symphonic product by any American composer of what is called the younger generation (meaning people up to forty).

Not that it is of equal excellence from beginning to end. The flighty second movement cuts into its sustained atmosphere of mystery and beauty, and also shares some of the brutality of harmonic and sonorous treatment typical of the contemporary American school. (By harmonic brutality I mean the summary handling of the psychological effect which the sounding of any tonality inevitably establishes.) But those interested will search far and wide before they will come upon another young American work so sophisticated and at the same time so straightforward and exciting. The work is in no sense inventive; it profits rather from the pioneering experimentation of others, using with complete ease an idiom which one is accustomed to hearing used only haltingly.

The work does not sound American. It is hard to assign a geographical tendency to it, and this is not said because of its text in Hebrew. If anything, it rather resembles what comes out of Russia today, except that, barring Prokofieff, no one there writes with the same show of awareness of worldwide contemporary musical thought. Shostakovich's music is like a talented poor relation who hasn't been around very much; Bernstein's piece bespeaks perfect schooling.

The performance was startling in its near approach to sonorous perfection. Miss Jennie Tourel sang the vocal part in its third movement (from the Book of Lamentations), with a power and emotion which did much to make that section the most moving of the three, although it is at the same time the most original and least impersonal. For in spite of the echoes of Stravinsky, both straight from the source and via Copland, there is a definite personal tenderness expressed in the simplest and most direct of terms, and this is the work's own quality.

Mr. Bernstein gave an intense and poetic reading of the Overture-Fantasy, *Romeo and Juliet* of Tchaikovsky, which brought great applause from his public, although his delicate and tempo-precise treatment of the "Italian" Symphony of Mendelssohn was more pleasing to this reviewer. Copland's *Salón México,* with its rhythmical warfare, produced a certain amount of firing out of turn, but the battle was finally won.

As a conductor Mr. Bernstein is enjoyable to watch, with his passionate entreaties and gestured innuendoes to the men. One would like to see a close-up of his successive expressions. Indeed, it is not unlikely that we shall see just this in the not too far removed future.

Fats Waller Salute

APRIL 4 (1944), *NEW YORK HERALD TRIBUNE*

The American Youth for Democracy not only promised a great show, as is always the case with large jazz get-togethers, but actually produced one in its Salute to Fats Waller Sunday night at Carnegie Hall. The affair was so much more successful than "Esquire's" shindig at the Metropolitan a while back that it wasn't even funny. In an impressive succession of stars who performed one after another it is impossible even to list all of them, but it is enough to note that an evening's entertainment which included Bill Robinson, Duke Ellington, Count Basie and his orchestra, Jimmy Savo, Teddy Wilson and his band, Paul Draper, Earl Hines, James P.

Johnson, Billie Holiday, Zero Mostel, the Berry Brothers, Josh White, and Mary Lou Williams could scarcely contain a dull moment.

Of course the three tunes most often interpreted were *Ain't Misbehavin', Honeysuckle Rose,* and *I'm Gonna Sit Right Down and Write Myself a Letter.* Count Basie and his men played a powerful arrangement of the first, and Bojangles dedicated two choruses of the same piece to Fats's memory. Paul Draper did one of his graceful and fancy-free improvisations on the second, accompanied by a group which included Art Hodes and Mezz Mezzrow, and James Rushing was one of the several who chose the last.

It was fitting that James P. Johnson, of whom Waller was a disciple, should have appeared, and that the other great dean of jazz pianists, Earl Hines, should have played his boogie version of the *Saint Louis Blues,* whose creator, W. C. Handy, in the audience, was introduced and asked how he liked Hines's interpretation. "It always sounds good," Mr. Handy shouted.

The concert ended at midnight with a jam session on two Gershwin tunes: *Lady Be Good* and *I've Got Rhythm.* Will Geer was spokesman for the second half of the concert. A tribute to Waller by Andy Rasaf, his collaborator, was read at intermission time. But the real tribute was the magnificent music, the breath-taking dancing (the Berry Brothers, as well as Mr. Draper, actually brought down the house), and the spirit of cooperation shown by all the artists who appeared to honor the memory of a colleague they respected.

Collegiate Chorale

APRIL 6 (1944), *NEW YORK HERALD TRIBUNE*

The final event of the season's series of Town Hall Endowment Concerts was given last night when the Collegiate Chorale, directed by Robert Shaw, presented a concert of American choral music to a delighted audience at Town Hall. The program opened with three songs by the New England composer of Revolutionary days, William Billings. Included were first performances of works by contemporary men; these were *He Only Comes and Goes Away,* by Charles Warner; Credo, a textless piece by Morris Gedzelman, a member of the chorus; and *The Mystic Trumpeter* by Norman Dello Joio.

This last work, obviously sincere and musicianly, found itself hampered by its text, a thing which is only too likely to happen when a composer chooses to set a poem by Walt Whitman. *The Mystic Trumpeter,* as Whitman wrote it, is didactic and complete in itself, and thus automatically repulses any invitation to be set to music. Here the trumpeter was busy playing a French horn, and passages of the text were whispered over a line held by solo voice. Choral writing was proficient, the effect was hard and healthy, and if the long piece failed to make its musical point it was because the text, with the insistence of a campaigning politician, foiled the music at every turn with its own imperious ideological point.

Mr. Shaw mixed these serious works with what he unabashedly called "commercial" arrangements of standard and popular songs, Negro spirituals, sea-chants, and Southern white "folk-hymns."

In the case of these last, he warned the audience that the songs, taken from *Southern Harmony* and the *Original Sacred Harp,* are really sung "without expression" and in strict tempo, but that the Chorale would not sing them that way, which indeed proved to be the case. What one wondered was why liberties had been taken which obviously robbed the material of its own peculiar character.

The program closed with William Schuman's secular cantata, *A Free Song,* also on a text of Whitman. Several encores were given.

Goffin's *Jazz*

APRIL 9 (1944), *NEW YORK HERALD TRIBUNE*

To the list of books on so-called "hot jazz" can now be added Robert Goffin's *Jazz,* subtitled: "From the Congo to the Metropolitan," and published by Doubleday-Doran. M. Goffin is a Belgian lawyer and writer who claims a preoccupation with American dance music extending back to the days before people here were taking the matter seriously. One of the first things to occur to him two decades ago was the idea that jazz is an essentially democratic phenomenon, inasmuch as it encourages in its performance the fraternizing of Negroes and whites. This is an important conclusion, but M. Goffin makes little of it, because he is out to exhaust his subject.

The book is difficult to categorize. It is not likely to please many readers; those who already are acquainted with the facts will probably prefer a book like Down Beat's *Yearbook of Swing* or even Panassié's *The Real Jazz*, where bands, personnel, and singers are listed alphabetically. And those who are approaching the subject with only an open mind and good will can scarcely be seduced by the writing, even though the best stylistic strawberries are placed at the top of the basket in the form of an atmospheric introduction which sets the scene pleasantly for the drama that ought to, but does not, follow.

New Orleans in the middle and late nineteenth century is evoked by means of frequent and lengthy quotations from the works of several seekers after the picturesque. The African elements in jazz are suggested (never defined), the influence of French folk tunes upon its melodic line is stressed, and from there on the attention is devoted to personalities who have figured in the production of jazz in the brief period during which it has been possible to record it. However, since M. Goffin is only too ready to admit that it is not the individual who is of prime importance in the making of jazz, but rather the group, the consideration given these many separate people would seem to be exaggerated in a work whose title suggests a comprehensive coverage of the material in question.

Perhaps it is being fractious to ask that a book be something other than what it is. Yet it does not seem unreasonable to expect it to have a definite purpose. If one is going to write a book on folk music, one can describe it, which involves a musicological analysis; one can theorize about it, which is to say that one takes an intellectual inventory of its psychological, social, ethnographical, and other implications; or one can make an encyclopedia of its personnel, literature, and terminology. These approaches assume a highly specialized technical knowledge on the part of the investigator, commentator, or compiler. Lacking this knowledge, the writer may attack the subject from the "What the Melodies of the Deep South Mean to Me" angle, but in this case, where the writer moves, so to speak, at the technical level of the laity, unless he has a truly irresistible personality and style, he will probably not impress the members of that group with the descriptions of reactions which they can experience firsthand.

The writing is loaded with lists and quotations. The lists are not always accurate or complete, and could scarcely be used as reference material because there is no particular logic in the order of their presentation, and the book has no index. The quotations are engaging enough—the best writing in the book is perhaps to be found in them—but they happen to be examples of other people's styles, and not of M. Goffin's.

Perhaps the author, who is obviously a true lover of jazz, felt that by using a subjective approach to an art the appreciation of which he justifiably insists is primarily a visceral matter, he could communicate his enthusiasm to others. Such a desire would be laudable, if futile, inasmuch as the music is a far more persuasive envoy for its own cause than any words about it could ever be. But the reader's impression is more likely to be that the author is somewhat too possessive about jazz, that he is above all interested in proving his pioneerhood in recognizing the idiom as an art form. Granting him some degree of seniority in the brotherhood of jazz lovers, one must still admit that definition is a more interesting function than praise.

If he had given evidence of even a minimum of analytical curiosity regarding the musical side of jazz, one could disregard the strain of presumptuousness which taints his pages. It would then be easier to overlook his denigrating attitude toward American taste and esthetic attainment. ("American art lacked self-confidence." "Need I add that jazz has not made any important contribution to serious American music." "When . . . jazz has been universalized by the movies, the most advanced of the American critics will be able to tackle the subject and study it at length. In the meantime there have been nothing more than well-meaning amateurs.") One could smile at the ever-handy quotations from an earlier tome of his called "Aux Frontières du jazz," in which he makes it clear that he considers his personal reactions of momentous importance; one could smile at his stubborn attempt to put jazz into the same dish with surrealism—he suggests that the success of jazz was facilitated by "the discoveries of Freud," and quotes Baudelaire, Lautréamont, and Cocteau to bolster, one fears, the "cultural" element in his pontifical demeanor—and above all one could smile at his amusing cultural chauvinism (M. Goffin is a Belgian) and art lovers will be interested to discover that the Parisian school of painters consists of a progression from James Ensor to Jean Delvaux (both are Belgians).

All these author's foibles could, as I say, be indulgently dismissed if they were offset by something other than personal reminiscences couched in dubious hyperbole (of the Lido-Venice band, heard by him in Brussels, he says: "These were the most immortal moments I have ever spent"). And if, together with the welter of documentation and expression of opinions, practically all of which are esthetically valid, incidentally, M. Goffin gave evidence of being himself something more than a "well-meaning amateur" (in the French sense of the word), one could forgive the aggressive tone of the book, for it would be something quite different from what it is. A good book on jazz, starting at the point where Winthrop Sergeant left off in his *Jazz, Hot and Hybrid,* would be most welcome.

One more thing: the author, along with a good many other jazz-worshipers, shows a fallacious tendency to consider jazz a unique phenomenon in music. ("Jazz really brought something incredibly new into the world. Until it appeared, a piece of music continued to be played according to the same unchanging conception; Beethoven's Fifth Symphony, for example, will remain identical to the last syllable of recorded time.") The error here consists in the apparent assumption that jazz has no relation to its counterpart in other sections of the world, where cross-breeding of musical traditions exists (e.g., Japan, South America, Mexico, West and North Africa). This confusion of categories gives rise to a hypothesis too patently false to require refutation. As a book of information, *Jazz* is disorganized; as a book of entertainment, it is ponderous. It might more accurately have been called "Memoirs of a Jazz Record Collector."

Istomin, Pianist, Makes His Concert Debut Here

APRIL 19 (1944), *NEW YORK HERALD TRIBUNE*

Eugene Istomin, eighteen-year-old American pianist who already has appeared as soloist with the Philharmonic and the Philadelphia Orchestra, made his New York concert debut last night at Town Hall. From the opening of the program, one was conscious of being in the presence of a first-rate musical talent. One may not have agreed every time with Mr. Istomin's very personal interpretations, but precisely because these were the result of a young artist's intense feelings about music and not a synthesis of other people's ideas, they compelled the listener's admiration. Seldom does one hear Chopin played with such complete evidence of the pianist's having understood its kind of poetry, and seldom does that poetry find an instrument so naturally adapted to its expression as Mr. Istomin's sensitive fingers.

Much of the intuitive grace in the playing last night was traceable to the pianist's great preoccupation, perhaps unconscious, with sonority. If his rhythmical sense sometimes lapsed because of a youthful overabundance of enthusiasm and energy, and if the clarity of a passage was occasionally sacrificed by the use of the pedal to the making of a more impressive effect, his already fully mature tone more than made up for these minor flaws.

One admired the sonorous solidity of the Mozart Fantasie and Fugue in C Major, the emphasis without heaviness of the repeated bass chords in the first movement of Beethoven's "Waldstein" Sonata, but one never felt circumspectness behind the playing. The music was simply coming out as it was being felt. Where this method is safe, nothing can beat it. And it proved quite safe last night, because Mr. Istomin is an artist.

Donald Dame Offers Recital at Town Hall

APRIL 25 (1944), *NEW YORK HERALD TRIBUNE*

Donald Dame, the young tenor recently acquired by the Metropolitan Opera, gave an interesting recital Monday night at Town Hall. A thorough and intelligent musician, Mr. Dame carefully chose a program of popular appeal, varied and unfamiliar; moreover it was designed to show his lyrical gifts to best advantage. Eschewing the temporary wartime custom of starting concerts with *The Star-Spangled Banner,* the artist began instead with Beethoven's *God Is My Song,* and proceeded directly into a series of folk songs from Ireland, England, Italy, Mexico, France, and the Hebrides.

Following these, Mr. Dame gave the first performance here of a modern English work: Ralph Vaughan-Williams's Four Hymns, accompanied by piano and viola. Of these, the first and last, on the exuberant side, seemed less convincing than the two middle songs, with their subdued sweetness and agreeable modal turns. *Come Love, Come Lord* especially gave the artist an opportunity to exhibit his admirable mezzo-voce, as had *L'Angelus* in the preceding group.

Four Grieg songs, done in Norwegian, necessitated the using of text sheets; this struck a slightly false note in a program of such direct audience-appeal. Eminently successful was Mr. Dame's presentation of Private First Class Emanuel Rosenberg's *Complete Misanthropist* in the group of contemporary American songs which received their first performances at the end of the program. Here the simple nightclub-song treatment of a set of amusing lyrics and the singer's perfect diction brought off the comic tour de force and delighted the audience the first time and when it was repeated. Mr. Dame introduced Paul Bowles's *Night Without Sleep* by remarking that it was a song which could be understood only by those who had suffered from insomnia. Apparently a good percentage of the Town Hall audience had, and were not worried about it, as the song provoked considerable laughter. The Gene Bone and Howard Fenton setting of *Finnegans Wake* was sung with high spirits and plenty of characterization.

Performances throughout the evening were marked by a high degree of musical sensitivity and dramatic imagination. Also Mr. Dame happens to have an exceedingly fine voice, which he can make triumphantly free of any trace of vibrato. His phrasing is perfect, and he sings without using portamento. It must be noted, however, that Monday night the voice was sometimes tight when the vowel was an emphasized short "i" or "e." Otherwise the concert was vocally a delight. Stuart Ross assisted at the piano, and Hugo Fiorito provided the viola accompaniments.

Records, Mostly Afro-American

APRIL 30 (1944), *NEW YORK HERALD TRIBUNE*

It's not so much a question of what has been recorded or even reissued lately as it is of what you can get. Many items are exhausted almost as soon as they appear; thus it behooves the collector to buy quickly after release of the record. This is particularly true of the few lonesome selections of good jazz which still get born now and then. There's little enough of this, but as long as Blue Note continues to record, it won't be true that jazz is dead and gone. Whatever Blue Note puts out is bound to be good. Recently they have put on the market six very fine twelve-inch records, of which four (eight sides) are piano solos by James P. Johnson, Waller's onetime mentor. With Fats gone, Johnson carries on that particular tradition pretty much by himself. These pieces are rich in feeling and brilliantly played: there are examples of rags, stomps, blues, and boogie. Johnson is at his best in the stomps. His playing is a bit less exact and rhythmically emphatic than Waller's, but listen to *Carolina Balmoral,* with its shining treble figures against the powerful bass. The tempo breezes along practically at that of the *Caprice Flag,* which is a little confused once in a while but has some wonderful passages near the end. His blues are excellent, but the piano is not the ideal instrument for the form. One misses the sustained vocal or instrumental line: the trills don't really hold it all the way up. Each succeeding trill is automatically weaker in its effect. Johnson's boogie playing is satisfying. *J. P. Boogie* contains figures not usually associated with the idiom, and this accomplishes for it some welcome freshening up. In addition, halfway through he modulates down a fifth and never returns to the original key. This also helps, by breaking into the tonality of the one-four-five-one tyranny.

The other four sides are devoted to Edmond Hall's Blue Note Jazz Men, which group includes Hall's clarinet, Sidney de Paris with his trumpet, and Vic Dickenson on the trombone, with the rhythm section comprising Johnson at the piano, Arthur Shirley on the guitar, Israel Crosby on bass, and Sidney Catlett as drummer. This music is the sort of thing you can't get for love or money these days, with a wonderful purity of sound and poetry of invention which makes mere swing seem like music by and for robots. Of the two slow numbers, *Blues at Blue Note* has the more brilliant solo work and is the dirtier, Hall's clarinet embarks on a fruitful voyage of discovery, Dickenson's cadential trombone solo is strong on personality. (Cf. Paramount Record 12816: Ike Rodgers's *It Hurts So Good.*) The other easy-going one, *Night Shift Blues* is a fraction slower, and the ensemble work is admirable. There is also the old march, *High Society,* exuberant and fast.

Hit has a remarkable album called *Spirituals in Verse and Song,* recorded by the Juanita Hall Choir. These are really not spirituals at all, of either the concert or the real variety, but performances of poems by James Weldon Johnson in the manner of church sermons. In spite of an overdose of arranged singing, the records attain an extraordinary degree of realism and beauty. The sine qua non of the Negro religious service is satisfyingly present: those punctuations of agreement shouted and sung by the congregation. There are fine moments in the preaching of Robert Harvey in *The Creation,* but the most moving part is *Listen, Lord,* where Fredye Marshall does a magnificent job. At the outset her sermon is sung on a single note, the tonic, with the ends of phrases hanging unaccented below it. Then, slowly adding to her tonal palette, she begins to use the third, then the fifth, then the flatted seventh, then the octave. Finally, having ineluctably set the tonality for the congregation, she abandons intonation and speaks simply above one repeated chord in the chorus.

Bluebird has two rhythmical religious songs by the Southern Sons: *Lord, Have Mercy* and *I Want Two Wings*. This quintet sounds rather like the Golden Gate Quartet's work and is a little too sophisticated for my taste, which inclines to groups like Mitchell's Christian Singers. Also on Bluebird are two familiar blues singers: Tampa Red (who has always been one of the musically less interesting of the male exponents of the form), singing *Baby, You're Gonna Miss Me When I'm Gone,* and Jazz Gillum, who used to sing straighter and better a few years back than he does now in *Deep Water Blues,* which nevertheless has its points.

The addition of the milk bottle to the percussion sections of the Boston and Philadelphia Symphonies to meet the demands of certain scores by contemporary composers has apparently escaped the notice of Mr. Petrilla; otherwise he would not have permitted the inclusion of an entire case of these musical instruments in the otherwise vocal accompaniment of the King Sisters' *Milkman, Keep Those Bottles Quiet* on Bluebird.

Lena Horne sounds like Helen Morgan doing *My Bill* in *Good-for-Nothing Joe,* with Charlie Barnet on Bluebird. Cole Porter's *Mexican Hayride* success, *I Love You,* is on Hit by Madriguera and on Victor by Perry Como. *San Fernando Valley* turns up on Hit with Liz Tilton's squawking livening up Jan Garber's version on Hit, and the King Sisters being not nearly so agreeable in their own on Bluebird. Decca has two show albums: *Winged Victory* with four sides, and *Carmen Jones,* with twelve, all twelve-inch disks.

Besides being far too short-lived as to playing possibilities, the present records enjoy a most delicate health, which makes it impossible for many of them to survive the physical stress put on them by the record-changer. They just break in half, dying young and innocent, before the tenth playing grays their grooves.

In the Theatre

MAY–JUNE (1944), *MODERN MUSIC*

Another old operetta on the list of the New Opera Company's offerings is *Helen Goes to Troy.* By not even intimating that either the vehicle or the production is anything but the toughest kind of field corn, this one manages not to be offensive. That is if one can accustom one's eyes to the hideousness of the visual spectacle, which is, after all, probably no more unbeautiful than any table of prize lampshades and vases at a Luna Park shooting gallery.

Humor in wartime, like many other things, has a tendency to revert to its less subtle manifestations. The only moment of the concerted romp which seemed amusing in a distraught way was Massine's *Procreation Dance,* where the studied gaga quality was heightened by emphasis on Truex and Novotna, neither of whom danced a step and simply swayed clumsily back and forth like two people busy at charades.

For me, Novotna was the whole show. At last she was done up to look like Dietrich, and at last her pure, small voice didn't have to reach a block across the Met. She seemed perfectly at home in her kewpie-doll trappings, in her burnished gold bathtub, in her bed built for three with flesh georgette sheets. Her diction, already careful, was made more pointed with the aid of her very movable eyes, and her spoken dialogue was distinguished both in its accent and in its faintly succulent modulations.

The score has of course little in common with the original. It contains no fewer than sixteen numbers from Offenbach operettas other than *La Belle Hélène*, whose music the adapter, Erich Wolfgang Korngold, considered "wilted" for Broadway audiences. As in *Rosalinda,* the music has been slicked up, weighted with contemporary clichés, and made generally acceptable to movie-radio taste standards.

Mr. Korngold's men in the pit blared out his vulgarized version of the music, a fitting frame for this Beverly Hills vaudeville show. The one pleasant thing about the production is that its brashness is homogeneous. No one moment is more enjoyable than any other. There is no let-down because there is no build-up; you are thus spared the constant shocks occasioned in a show like *Carmen Jones,* which really gets off the ground now and then.

......

Not having seen the original unabridged Guild production of *Porgy and Bess,* I can't compare its respective shortcomings and virtues with those of the recent revival of Cheryl Crawford's pocket edition at the City Center. But it seems exaggeratedly sanguine of critics to acclaim this work as the long-awaited American opera. The construction is too casual for serious opera, and the material and its treatment too Broadway to let it be a true folk opera. Say rather that it is a super-musical-comedy with several excellent songs and a good deal of less distinguished recitative. Whether Gershwin did better in his straight commercial work is a moot question, to be debated between those who like their Tin Pan Alley unconscious or circumspect.

......

You can hear suggestions of several Cole Porter tunes in *Mexican Hayride,* but they are from other days. *The Good-Will Movement* is reminiscent of *Let's Do It*; *Sing to Me, Guitar* sounds here and there vaguely like *Begin the Beguine*; and even *I Love You*, roared over the nowadays inevitable P.A. system by an acid baritone, makes you think the first three times you hear it that *Night and Day* might come out at any moment. Eventually, of course, *I Love You* establishes itself as a real song. It's a fair show, the costumes naturally come from Argentina and the Andes as well as from Tehuantepec, the sets are more or less Fourteenth Street display windows, and the acting, on the brighter side, is like a sophisticated adaptation of what actually goes on in a higher-priced *carpa* along Santa Maria la Redonda in Mexico's capital. I liked Bobby Clark as an Indian lady in the Taxco *zocalo,* and as a *mariachi* flutist playing Paderewski's *Minuet* in Xochimilco. Also the reassuring lyrics to the macabre hymn, *Count Your Blessings*. I did not like Porter's treatment of *Guadalajara* in *Carlotta* or of *Cielito lindo* in the last scene; he used to be a very clever man who could have done pleasant things to some Mexican rhythms.

Band Symphony

JUNE 29 (1944), *NEW YORK HERALD TRIBUNE*

A concert of music composed directly for band was given last night on the Mall in Central Park by the Goldman Band, Edwin Franko Goldman conducting. The event of the evening was the premiere of the Symphony in B-flat for Concert Band by Robert L. Sanders, who is the Dean of the School of Music at the University of Indiana. Before introducing Mr. Sanders, who conducted his own work, Dr. Goldman recounted briefly to the public his struggle to raise the level of band music during the twenty-seven years he has been giving the Central Park concerts. He announced the Sanders Symphony as a serious work, which indeed it turned out to be, without, however, being particularly impressive.

The piece's failure to impose itself to any marked degree upon the listener's consciousness was not due in any manner to uninteresting or incompetent instrumentation, for the workmanship was more than adequate. The harmony was sometimes compelling in detail, even if the correlation between consonance and dissonance appeared to be arbitrary and forced; the counterpoint was occasionally engrossing, but the themes and their vicissitudes were unable to command sufficient attention. The three movements seemed discursive and fragmentary in spite of (or, if you like, precisely because of) the obvious effort expended to make them sequential and interesting. Yet how right Dr. Goldman is to persist in his search for good band music! A few years ago a work of the high musical caliber of the Sanders Symphony would have been inconceivable, nor would a park audience have countenanced its playing, much less offered it an enthusiastic reception such as last night's.

The program also contained works by Samuel Barber, Ralph Vaughan Williams, and Jaromir Weinberger.

Recorded Popular Music

JULY 2 (1944), *NEW YORK HERALD TRIBUNE*

Latin America comes up to us in a maze of translation and transcription. Columbia has an album called *Mexico,* by Xavier Cugat. It arrived in May, the night before I was to leave for that country. I played the records and was in no way reminded of anything I had known there in other years. Still, there had been rumors of great changes below the border in recent months. Perhaps even the music? . . . I was quickly reassured upon arriving in Guadalajara: it had only been Señor Cugat's imagination. An old tune we used to hear in every cantina down there a few years back, called *Amor, amor, amor*, has been recorded on Columbia by Señor Cugat, who categorizes it as a bolero, and on Victor by Wayne King, who thinks the word "beguine" looks nice after it. I suppose Mr. King is thinking of Cole Porter. Certainly he's not thinking of Martinique. Another old melody, Agustin Lara's *Solamente una vez,* has become *You Belong to My Heart,* and Musicraft issues it.

A very pleasant surprise was Columbia's album *Blues by Basie,* not a collection of reissues, and with eight excellent recordings of blues, most of them familiar. The sly, tentative little figures which endeared Count Basie's piano playing to jazz lovers nearly a decade ago, and which have little by little been obscured by the systematic augmentation of his band, are here the motivating force of the music, just as they used to be. Some pieces boast trumpet and sax, others only a rhythm section, but in both cases the style is beyond reproach, without concessions to commercialism. One of the best rhythmically is *Cafe Society Blues,* where the tempo is perfect and everyone seems very happy in it. I also admire the sustained calm of *Way Back Blues,* the nonchalant exactitude of *Farewell Blues,* and the fantasy of the piano playing in *How Long Blues.*

If you want one, Commodore has perhaps the most amusing version of *Begin the Beguine* that has been recorded. It is a twelve-incher by Eddie Heywood, who plays solo piano until the final cadence. The other side is a lush (but not shamefully so) arrangement by Heywood of *I Cover the Waterfront.* Commodore has several period pieces: *Oh, Katharina!* and *Basin Street Blues,* directed by Eddie Condon with the old gang, also "Wild Bill" Davison making a lifelike resuscitation of the *Original Dixieland One-Step* and *Clarinet Marmalade.* For a tremendous dose of Rampart Street, get the Climax set (made by Blue Note) of ten old Crescent City numbers by George Lewis and his New Orleans Stompers, including two sacred songs played hot: *Just a Closer Walk With Thee* and *Just a Little While to Stay Here.* The rest of the group shows such familiar faces as *Milenberg Joys, Careless Love, Fidgety Feet,* as well as Buddy Bolden's *Don't Go 'Way, Nobody.* The band is pretty basic, but full of life.

Edmond Hall's Quintet

My favorite of the new jazz records this time is Blue Note's twelve-inch *Blue Interval,* a splendid invention played by Edmond Hall's Quintet, which consists of clarinet, piano, vibraphone, guitar, and bass. Names of performing artists are not on the label, but it is not difficult to spot Teddy Wilson's smooth piano style. Red Norvo is the vibraphonist and Hall himself is, of course, on the clarinet. Everything in *Blue Interval* works out just right, and it would be hard to imagine a piece in that idiom with greater charm. This and three other pieces by the quintet (*Seein' Red,*

Smooth Sailing, and *Rompin' in '44*) supply the need which has existed for that special kind of sophisticated "chamber" jazz since the Goodman Sextet records stopped appearing.

Assorted Swing

There seems to be at least one thing by almost everybody this month. All the old favorite bands pop up with an offering; the only catch is that many of them don't sound the way they used to. I suppose it is essentially fear of being considered old-fashioned which has made them all cover their original styles with slick new arrangements for extra instruments and impossible vocal groups that result in their all sounding equally fancy and uninteresting. Both Glenn Miller on Victor and Harry James on Columbia have *On a Little Street in Singapore*. As a tune it's just more fodder for the corn-fed juke boxes. James has, of course, his own trumpet and Sinatra for the vocal chorus, both items helping make for the desired languor. Better, however, is James's circumspect but effective *Memphis Blues,* coupled with *Sleepy Time Gal* on Columbia.

On Okeh, Cab Calloway appears in *Let's Go, Joe,* an old riff-tune played and sung with what doubtless means to be heat. The other side is called *A Smooth One* and seems endless in its lack of imagination. This month's prizes for arrangements go to *Someone,* written and played by Duke Ellington for Victor (at times reminiscent of his *In a Sentimental Mood*), and to *Darktown Strutters' Ball* by Benny Goodman for Columbia, although both men have, of course, done far better in the past. The reverse of the Duke's piece is a bit of tripe à la Whiteman, 1924, called *My Little Brown Book,* by the usually gifted Billy Strayhorn, and Benny's other side is *After You've Gone,* which, along with *Strutters' Ball* is a fine old tune rendered in a fashion which is sonorously tops in the field of synthetic inspiration. Columbia also has *Flatbush Flanagan,* written and played by Harry James. Erskine Hawkins's *Bear Mash Blues* on Bluebird is more fun.

If you admire Coleman Hawkins's prowess on the tenor sax, there is Bluebird's *Body and Soul,* which he embroiders from beginning to end in a strangely static sort of design, which to me is uninteresting from every point of view save the technical. This is backed by Earl Hines in a completely Hollywoodian choral version of *It Had to Be You.*

The arrangement of *Things Ain't What They Used to Be,* played by

Cootie Williams on Hit, has some good harmonic invention in it. The tune is traditional, and if Basie's old *Sent for You Yesterday* springs to mind before any other of a dozen versions, it is because Cootie's lively vocalist, Eddie Vinson, sounds rather like James Rushing in that ancient recording. On the other side, in *Red Blues,* Mr. V. sounds like Joe Turner, except that his voice breaks into a hysterical falsetto at unexpected moments. Johnny Temple did this amazingly several years ago. I remember particularly a piece called *Big Leg Woman.*

Victor has an album of reissues, a companion volume to their *Up Swing,* called *Smoke Rings.* It is a collection of dreamy "away" numbers, among which are Ellington's excellent *I Got It Bad,* Goodman's eight-year-old *These Foolish Things,* Artie Shaw's version of his father-in-law's great song, *All the Things You Are,* and Larry Clinton's metamorphosed Debussy opus, *My Reverie.*

Ellington Albums

There is much wonderful material in both volumes 1 and 2 of Brunswick's two *Ellingtonia* albums, which, rather than tracing the Duke's development through the period of from 1927 to 1940, as does the Victor Ellington album, consist solely of early masterpieces, with the most recent of the sixteen sides dating from January, 1931. Volume 1 contains such classics as *Mood Indigo, East Saint Louis Toodle-oo,* and *The Mooche,* which three are in the Victor book. Of the first two named, I prefer the Victor versions, but Brunswick's *Mooche* is definitely superior. You also get *Rockin' in Rhythm* and *Black and Tan Fantasy.* Volume 2 offers the brilliant *Creole Rhapsody,* with some sensational pianistics by the Duke, and the simple, touching *Awful Sad.* Brunswick performs a very real service in making these recordings available to the public. Personally, I hope they go on indefinitely with the series, and I hope that among the pieces to reappear I shall find *Lazy Rhapsody, Black Beauty,* the original *Solitude, Sweet Dreams of Love, Rude Interlude, In a Sentimental Mood, I Let a Song Go Out of My Heart,* and *Dallas Doings.* A set of the same sort of music under the labeling of "Cootie Williams and His Rug-Cutters" would be most welcome, too, including *Downtown Uproar, Delta Mood, Echoes of Harlem,* and *Have a Heart,* all Ellington tunes, if I remember correctly. It's an important part of America's musical lore.

Stadium Concert

JULY 14 (1944), *NEW YORK HERALD TRIBUNE*

Philharmonic-Symphony Orchestra, Leonard Bernstein conducting, at the Lewisohn Stadium last night. Nathan Milstein, violin soloist. The program follows:

"American Festival" Overture	William Schuman
Concerto for Violin and Orchestra in E Minor, op. 64	Mendelssohn
Symphony in E Minor, no. 1, op. 38	Sibelius

The spectacular young conductor Leonard Bernstein made his debut at Lewisohn Stadium last night before an audience of 10,500 enthusiastic persons. It is unfortunate that the exigencies of present-day concert tradition are such that a young man whose particular genius it is to make living interpretations of living music must go through the same old motions of playing the same old pieces exactly as if he were one of the more aged conductors innocent of the ways of new music.

Still, the career formula demands sacrifices, and the audience was certainly not displeased last night. Moreover, as part of a normal program, there was one contemporary work, the "American Festival" Overture of William Schuman. This vigorous and ugly piece received a rather frantic reading which may not have done justice to certain details in the writing, but which definitely made its effect from moment to moment, and cumulatively as well.

Mr. Milstein, as soloist in the Mendelssohn Violin Concerto, was perfection itself. There is probably no other violinist who can reach and sustain his degree of technical perfection and emotional convincingness. His faultless tone production and immaculate pitch go without saying; moreover there is a certain wonderful control at work whenever he is playing, which makes being a spectator particularly engrossing and rewarding. He combines the passion and precision of the complete artist.

Last night's combination of Mr. Mendelssohn, Mr. Bernstein, Mr. Milstein, and the orchestra was a happy occasion, the music coming out with airy grace and a fitting sense of effortlessness.

"Army and Navy Night" at Lewisohn Stadium

JULY 31 (1944), *NEW YORK HERALD TRIBUNE*

It was "Army and Navy Night" at the Lewisohn Stadium on Saturday; the conductor, three soloists, one composer, and a large part of the audience wore uniforms. The program was bright-sounding and pleasantly varied. Warrant Officer Thor Johnson, who made his Stadium debut in this concert, dedicated to the men in the Allied armed forces, got a lively response from the men in the orchestra, particularly in the three Slavonic Dances of Dvorak which opened the program and in the Tchaikovsky "1812 Overture."

Of New Horizons, by Ulysses Kay, Musician 2d Class, U. S. N., was given its first performance. The horizons concerned are presumably poetic and not musical ones. The piece is episodic, opening with a declamatory and somewhat Coplandesque phrase whose feeling has little to do with the subsequent material. Sonorous texturc is well handled, harmonies are diffuse, and melodies are not of the directly communicative variety. (On first hearing, they seem more like "theoretical" melodies than real ones.)

Seamen 1st Class Arthur Whittemore and Jack Lowe, duo-pianists, presented a group of numbers largely of Latin flavor, of which the best was also the simplest: Morton Gould's *Guaracha.* There was also an insufficiently rhythmical version of *Begin the Beguine,* and a very slick *Boléro.* Messrs. Whittemore and Lowe are very smooth performers, but one wishes they were a little less in love with the sort of ingenuous chichi which comes out of things like keyboard-length glissandi. They gave three encores, all of which showed the same perfect teamwork.

Sergeant Eugene List was soloist with the orchestra playing Gershwin's *Rhapsody in Blue.* Aside from a few separations at the end, things went along pretty well between ensemble and piano, although in the solo sequences one sometimes felt one was listening to a Hungarian instead of a Tin Pan Alley rhapsody. This reviewer is inclined to Oscar Levant's more strict interpretation. The audience loved every minute of it, however, and was given two encores, the First and Third Gershwin Preludes, and would have had more if Sergeant List had only been willing.

Records: Folk, Jazz, And Commercial

AUGUST 13 (1944), *NEW YORK HERALD TRIBUNE*

I have privately been wondering for some time why Columbia did not reissue a series of Goodman Sextet pressings in an album. Now they have—eight good examples of this admirably eloquent and precise musical art. Several of the group's best recordings are here: *Flying Home,* where the fine guitarist Charles Christian and Benny practically create a new instrument between them in the first chorus, playing their respective instruments in unison. Two representatives of the velvet-smooth slow style are *Rose Room* and *Poor Butterfly,* and *Boy Meets Goy* is here under the title *Grand Slam*. Instead of *As Long As I Live,* where the pitch of Benny's clarinet is just sharp enough to make the atmosphere slightly acid (it always made me uncomfortable, at any rate), I wish they had used *Six Appeal.*

In these days of general cultural regression, Musicraft gets into the swing of things by issuing two groups of records which ought to prove mighty popular in the corner taverns. One pile consists of eight luscious waltzes, such numbers as *Kiss in the Dark, Missouri Waltz, Beautiful Ohio, Let Me Call You Sweetheart,* played by Paul Lavalle and his String Orchestra. The other set is something which was apparently designed to keep up prestige without sacrificing sales: a series of hillbilly songs which are categorized as "Folk." Some of these ditties are stylistically fairly convincing, although at times one is tempted to question the geographical pedigree of the singers' accents. Then there are others with novachord accompaniment, and still others with electric guitar used in the howling, or "Hawaiian," manner. Singers include Red River Dave and Esmereldy. But what right have they to list these patently commercial disks as "Folk"?

Is it the attitude of a musical tourist to resent the changes which take place in folk music, depriving it of the picturesque local color it has retained during the period of its isolation, and to decry the newly hybridized and urbanized product which results from contact with other manifestations of musical culture? Does it seem so selfish and irresponsible of the listener to deplore the fact that a folk art does not remain reasonably pure, even after the culture it represents has been reached by the ever-expanding stain of twentieth-century kitsch? One can get pretty indignant about such little things and, I think, with justification.

For a good American folk piece, turn to *The Wave on the Sea,* sung, and accompanied on the auto-harp and guitars, by the properly forlorn-sounding Carter Family. This, along with most of the best items of Americana of the present time (exclusive of jazz), is issued by Bluebird. This label also gives us two square dances with intoned calls by Shorty McCoy: *Buffalo Gals* and *Cindy*; as well as two typically sad blues by Lonnie Johnson: *Lonesome Road* (nothing to do with "Look down, etc.") and *Baby, Remember Me*; and the more obstreperous Sonny Boy Williamson, who in *Love Me, Baby* waxes enthusiastic during its harmonica interlude. On the other side, *Decoration Day Blues, No. 2,* he disposes beautifully of some tough problems in prosody.

Victor has an album called *Fats Waller,* a timely tribute to the talent of the splendid pianist. Thomas Waller was really at his most brilliantly inventive when he was playing alone at the keyboard. For that reason I can't help wishing that the "memorial album" had comprised piano solo material, and even an old organ number or two like *Messin' Around with the Blues* or *The Rusty Pail.* There are only two solos in the collection: *Ain't Misbehavin'* and *Honey-suckle Rose,* which is played, according to the label, in the respective styles of Bach, Beethoven, Brahms, and Waller. The recording is the only one of the eight sides which is not a reissue, but it is not likely to move the Waller faithful to new expressions of praise. As a bandleader and vocalist, Waller was most successful in comic fantasy, and several pieces in that vein are present: *Your Feet's Too Big, Hold Tight, I Can't Give You Anything but Love,* and *The Joint Is Jumpin'*. There is also the excellent old *Minor Drag,* made before Fats's "Buddies" became his "Rhythm."

Other items on Victor's list are two albums of eight swing reissues each. One is devoted to the music of Tommy Dorsey and the other to that of Glenn Miller. If I had to choose between them, I'd take the Miller set. The arrangements are more original, ensemble playing is smoother, and there's not so much vocal nonsense. Included among the Miller numbers chosen by Victor to be rejuvenated are *In the Mood, Star Dust,* and *Tuxedo Junction.*

On Columbia there is Harry James doing solo work in a not-so-awful-as-you-might-think arrangement of that inevitable old *Estrellita,* whose partner is *My Beloved Is Rugged (Since He's in the Army)*. Another grammatical anomaly in titles is *If I Knew Then What I Know Now,* played on Victor by Sammy Kaye. To get back to Columbia, Gene Krupa (with drums) plays *Bolero at the Savoy*. *Side by Side* is coupled with this, and Anita O'Day, the vocal soloist, tries to sound like Ivy Anderson in both numbers. Also for Columbia, Claude Thornhill pushes out a languorous symphonic version of Dick Rodgers's *There's a Small Hotel,* backed by *Moonlight Bay,* a bit less in the discreetly lowered-lights tradition. They also have an album of songs of World War I, sung by Buddy Clark. An addition to the Brunswick Collectors Series is a volume of Bing Crosby's early successes, including *Out of Nowhere, I Surrender Dear,* and *Good Night, Sweetheart.* While we're on the subject, Victor has reissued Sinatra's *Night and Day.* I'm afraid I prefer Frank to Bing; he is less emotional, and less of a virtuoso, but he is also less corny.

Disque International sends an album of Enny de Vries singing French café songs. Two are by Charles Trenet: *Boum* and *Ménilmontant,* which has the best tune of the six pieces. Miss de Vries sings pleasantly in the "boîte intime" fashion: arch, tearfully wistful, little voice quivers that seem to express the right mixture of helplessness and defiance. However, her diction is not always completely clear.

The best new jazz record is Blue Note's *Victory Stride*, by James P. Johnson, played by James P. Johnson's Blue Note Jazz Men, to wit: Sidney de Paris, trumpet; Vic Dickenson, trombone; Ben Webster, tenor sax; Arthur Shirley, guitar; John Simmons, bass; Sidney Catlett, drums; and Johnson, of course, at the piano. The texture is consistently a bit dark for want of a clarinet, and the tune is certainly not inspiredly new, but the solo passages are fine, and the piece has integrity of style and atmosphere. The reverse side is *Blue Mizz,* by the same setup. It is hotter, much slower, and its effect is less distinguished.

Alec Templeton Is Heard with Philharmonic

AUGUST 14 (1944), *NEW YORK HERALD TRIBUNE*

Alec Templeton appeared Saturday night at the Lewisohn Stadium in what one might call a twofold capacity. First, he was solo pianist with the Philharmonic-Symphony Orchestra under Alexander Smallens in Mozart's B-flat Major Concerto (K. 595). Then he entertained his audience with a series of "improvised" paraphrases of well-known hit-song and serious themes, done in the contemporary popular idiom. Mr. Templeton's performance of the Mozart work was gratifyingly clean in execution and unaffected in style. It may be that he lacks sufficient sureness and strength of hand to attain perfection in the playing of certain of the runs, but these minor shortcomings did not detract too much from the pleasure one derived from hearing the lovely work. As to pianistic tone achieved, again one can only say that because of the amplification it was impossible to have more than a very imprecise idea of the kind of sound Mr. Templeton was making.

As to his improvisatory tricks, which are to music about what after-dinner repartee is to literature, it suffices to say the public went for them in a big way. Handel's F Major Concerto Grosso became "Handel With Care," and the listener was treated to one more example of how easily the Alberti bass can become a left-hand boogie-woogie figure. Five notes of the chromatic scale were chosen at random by various members of the audience and shouted at the performer, who then ostensibly improvised a short piece based on the given letters. Other extemporized stylistic highjinks were offered, with the audience always clamoring for more. Mr. Templeton then sang an imitation of Jimmy Durante doing *Give a Man a Horse He Can Ride,* and Cab Calloway in a scat version of *Largo al Factotum.* Applause went on and boos greeted the removing of the piano from the center of the stage.

It was too bad that Aaron Copland's *Billy the Kid Suite* was saved for the end of the program. After the mood of pure amusement created by Mr. Templeton's pranks, the audience found it difficult to get back to music, so that there was a constant and disturbing exodus of impatient listeners during the entire playing of this affecting score. The performance was rhythmically on the loose side, with the opening theme and the nickelodeon-like saloon music showing to best advantage. The cutting did not have entirely satisfactory results.

Mr. Smallens also gave the first performance in this city of Burrill Phillips's *Courthouse Square,* an academically-minded piece in the Grofé tradition, more sophisticated in the choice of its musical material, perhaps, than the works of Grofé, but not in its final effect. About 10,500 persons attended the concert.

Shostakovich 8th Played by Philharmonic

OCTOBER 13 (1994), *NEW YORK HERALD TRIBUNE*

Philharmonic-Symphony Orchestra, Artur Rodzinski conductor, at Carnegie Hall last night. The program:

Symphony in B Minor, no. 2	Borodin
Symphony No. 8, op. 65	Shostakovich

The Philharmonic-Symphony Orchestra played last night under Artur Rodzinski in Carnegie Hall, and the program consisted of Borodin's Second Symphony and Shostakovich's Eighth, introduced to the New York public last April by Mr. Rodzinski. Having missed the initial performance of this recent work of the Soviet composer, I cannot compare performances, but the consensus of opinion seemed to be that last night's reading, with faster tempos, was far superior to last spring's. Certainly if for no other reason than that the piece becomes the orchestra, the Philharmonic would be justified in playing the Eighth regularly. It is the sort of music Mr. Rodzinski and his men can do to perfection, and it obviously had received careful preparation, to judge from the ringing sonorities achieved last night, sonorities whose maximum effect must be reached, in fact, to put the piece across at all.

A good deal has been said about Shostakovich's propensity for stringing things out, as well as about his unique scoring habits. A normal quota of these traits is in the Eighth. There is no question that to be able to keep a piece going as long as possible is the main problem of form, but only insofar as the music really does keep going. In the fantastically horizontal writing of the first movement, for instance, the emphasis shifts too often from matter to manner, from idea to mood. It is hard to know exactly how to listen to it: one can be active only so far, and then it forces one into passive participation by its inevitable turn to subjectivity. In this sense it wavers between the nineteenth and the twentieth centuries. Again, there is none of the twentieth century's knack of establishing tension immediately. The idiom is so relaxed that it takes time to work up impetus. The result naturally tends to be cumbersome. But for those who like sheer weight, the time element undoubtedly aids in building it up. And these same listeners are likely to approve of the extension of the Wagnerian technique and of the episodic overall effect of the writing.

The fourth movement, as an unabashedly Romantic Largo, is the most compelling section on first hearing because there is no ambiguity in its intent. The mood of somber desolation is poignantly effective. The fast third movement is brilliant, raucous, amusing.

The important thing to notice is that Shostakovich is a highly individual composer and one who is prolific. Good passages succeed bad ones, invention comes suddenly on the heels of tired repetition, delectable bits of sound follow masses of harassing noise, and if the result is never animated with subtlety or charm, it is often powerful.

Recorded Popular Music

OCTOBER 15 (1944), *NEW YORK HERALD TRIBUNE*

Asch Records has issued a fine volume by the already legendary Huddie Ledbetter, known as "Leadbelly." The songs he sings provide excellent material for the argument against the theory of a quasi-spontaneous and anonymous growth of musical folk tradition. His versions of work songs, spirituals, blues, prison songs, and shouts are often pretty much of his own fashioning, yet many of them are likely to sound more valid, more "right" than other versions. This would incline one to believe that the element of personal artistry is of enormous importance in the genesis of any folk music, and that individual style can enjoy complete freedom without violating the limits of the music's tradition. Indeed, it is more than likely that an entire tradition can be made up of efforts to retain and emulate the combined memories of a few such individual styles.

However this may be, Leadbelly's voice and guitar have given us many splendid examples of American music in a period when (unlike the days when the older bard Lemon Jefferson recorded for Paramount) faithful auditory documents can be made for future use. And obviously every recording is important, inasmuch as the tradition is undergoing a violent metamorphosis (which will probably be tantamount to its extinction) as a result of contact, via radio and films, with present-day popular culture.

While none of the songs in the Asch album is of great musical interest, the collaboration of another distinguished Negro artist, the harmonica player Sonny Terry, makes some of the numbers doubly engrossing. The teamwork is at its best in *John Henry,* where the strange dichotomy of tonality, always present in such harmonica accompaniments, is especially audible and exciting.

This bitonal element (which, incidentally, can also be found in square dances, with their calls and use of open strings) comes about because again and again the key chosen for the piece is a fourth below the fixed one of the harmonica. It evidently is more important to the harmonica players to be able to include the flatted seventh of the scale in their harmony than to be able to play a tonic triad, a thing thereby made manifestly impossible, since the harmonica's tonic triad falls on the fourth note of the piece's scale. Thus occurs a series of dissonances which can only be considered as consciously perpetrated, desired effects. When there comes to be a widespread manner of playing such "wrong" notes (and the practice is not confined to Sonny Terry), we have a tradition. Considering that harmonic variety is the only weak point in our American folk music, it is worthwhile to look into any example one can find today of truly indigenous harmony. Preoccupation with harmony on the part of some of the best latter-day jazz makers attests to a desire to enlarge the basic I-IV-V structure of jazz. It is unfortunate that their additions to the harmonic consciousness of our music have been primarily devices lifted from European, especially French, art music, when many more apposite and effective harmonic extensions could be made directly from our own "primitive" material.

The Muse of the Midway, responsible for inspiring such phenomena as the Three Stooges and, in popular songs, such exotic ballads as *Lena Was the Queen of Palesteena, I Wish That I Was Born in Borneo, I've Got a Bimbo down on a Bamboo Isle,* and *So Long, Oo Long, How Long Ya Gonna Be Gone?* has come forth from long hiding and dictated a song called *Babylon,* which is sung by the Barry Sisters for Hit Records.

Elman Is Heard in Concert at Carnegie Hall

OCTOBER 21 (1944), *NEW YORK HERALD TRIBUNE*

Mischa Elman, violinist, played last night at Carnegie Hall to a large and enthusiastic audience.

The enthusiasm was notably evinced, and rightly so, after his faultless performance of the Richard Strauss Sonata. This work couched in honeyed accents is the perfect vehicle for Mr. Elman, his tone quality having attained such incredible perfection and smoothness that one is convinced he is incapable of producing anything else.

Listening to him drawing the rich, round strains from his instrument, one is inclined to forget the variety of strange noises which the passing of the bow across the strings can evoke when the violinist is less well equipped, or less obsessed by the importance of creating "beautiful" sound.

Naturally, the making of music for the purpose of inducing a state of euphoria is by no means an uncommon thing, but the practice defeats its own purpose when the effect is attained at too great a sacrifice of other musical values.

Such immunity from any possibility of making a harsh sound as Mr. Elman has achieved is likely to involve the neglecting of other equally important considerations.

Last night, above all one missed the element of variety in feeling, the sense of adventure that must be present for the intellectual enjoyment of such a program.

The Mozart D Major Concerto was as unsuited to Mr. Elman's playing as the Strauss Sonata was apposite to it. Nor did the Waspish Rapsodia Iberica of Nin do much to alleviate the continuous sedative mood.

If the therapeutic value of lovely sound can be considered a legitimate substitute for the spiritual stimulus of music (and perhaps it can during times like these), one can salute Mr. Elman as a public benefactor.

He offered five encores.

Leopold Mittman assisted at the piano.

Artur Rubinstein Heard in an All-Chopin Recital

OCTOBER 30 (1944), *NEW YORK HERALD TRIBUNE*

The piano playing that took place last night in Carnegie Hall at Artur Rubinstein's all-Chopin concert was of the sort that inevitably calls forth endless metaphors in an attempt to describe its matchless texture. When such a degree of mastery has been attained, the listener can sit back and remain royally oblivious to things like technique and tone quality. Like the components of the air, those elements are so completely present and in such correct proportion in Mr. Rubinstein's playing that one looks through them at the more subtle things which go to make up a great performance.

The lack of external formal attributes in Chopin makes the problem of keeping up interest in interpretation a personal and subjective affair. It is a question of the proper treatment of blending and juxtaposition of succeeding emotional elements. The architecture can be given or taken away by such a small thing as the underemphasizing of a strategic chord in his wonderfully complex harmonic structure.

Mr. Rubinstein played all the works with surpassing sensitivity. His treatment of such difficult music as the third movement of the B Minor Sonata, where the single melody has almost the declamatory quality of a vocal line, was wholly admirable. The entire sonata, with its lacy Scherzo and its passionate and robust final movement, was a masterpiece of piano playing. (One must except the runs in the right hand at the close of the last movement, which lacked precision.) Again, the cantilena in the B Minor Scherzo was given with a rare understanding of how to make a simple melody infinitely meaningful and touching.

Prolonged applause greeted Mr. Rubinstein's interpretation of the G Minor Ballade (op. 23), and of the program's final selection, the A-flat Polonaise (op. 53). This last work, while given an incredibly fine reading, might have been even better if it had been accorded some slight fire. One felt that the artist was just a little tired.

City Symphony Has Totenberg as Its Soloist

NOVEMBER 30 (1944), *NEW YORK HERALD TRIBUNE*

New York Symphony, Leopold Stokowski, conductor, at the City Center last night in the following program:

Overture in D Minor	Handel
Symphony no. 1	Brahms
Concerto for Violin and Orchestra (Roman Totenberg, solo violinist)	S. Barber
Prelude and Love-Death from *Tristan and Isolde*	Wagner

The New York City Symphony under Leopold Stokowski had another opportunity last night in its concert at the City Center to show that it is on its way to becoming a really integrated ensemble. As usual, the sound was finer in tutti and legato passages than in the solution of ticklish balance problems or managing the give and take of short phrases. It may be the acoustics of the Grand Guignol set in which the men play, but the ensemble makes an imminent sound like that of an enlarged chamber orchestra, which in a way precludes the more distant and blended tension which one has come to associate with the symphony. This is not to be construed as disparagement.

The evening's main dish was the playing by Roman Totenberg of Samuel Barber's Concerto for Violin and Orchestra, a work somewhat enigmatic in its unexpected combination of philosophic reflection and dry whimsy. The first two movements, which seem to stand in the shadow of Brahms, Mr. Totenberg played with intensity of feeling, switching in the tarantella-like third part to tough virtuosity. But that is the way the piece is. The bright last movement is full of amusing *trouvailles* of instrumentation, and is thoroughly enjoyable. It was too bad for this piece, as well as for the Brahms, that the horns were not better, but perhaps even they will improve shortly.

Mr. Stokowski obliged his public with an encore, which he prefaced with a few remarks on the religion of the Mayans in Guatemala. The stifled little arrangement of what purported to be a ceremonial procession in the Sierra of that Central American republic sounded more like Cadman than like what this reviewer has heard in Guatemala. The real thing reminds one much more of a sort of super-early Stravinsky, and is, needless to say, a good deal more exciting. But it was a thoughtful gesture and the audience was delighted.

Philadelphia Orchestra Plays Shostakovich Fifth

NOVEMBER 9 (1944), *NEW YORK HERALD TRIBUNE*

Philadelphia Orchestra, Eugene Ormandy conducting, with William Kapell as piano soloist, Tuesday night at Carnegie Hall. The program follows:

Symphony no. 21 (in one movement)	Miaskovsky
Rhapsody on a Theme of Paganini, op. 43	Rachmaninoff
Symphony no. 5, op. 47	Shostakovich

An election night audience, crowding Carnegie Hall Tuesday night, sat in absolute silence, without even the customary salvos of coughs, listening to Eugene Ormandy lead the Philadelphia Orchestra across the vast regions of Shostakovich's Fifth Symphony. For pure delight in sound there has been little like it recently. If a piece is really as good as its best possible performance, then this work is very good indeed, after all, for Tuesday night's reading surrounded it with an unexpectedly wide horizon of sonorous variety. One had almost forgotten that the symphony orchestra was capable of so many kinds of juxtaposition of dynamics and timbre.

William Kappell, the brilliant young pianist, was the evening's catch and he received an ovation after his excellent performance of a mediocre piece, the Rachmaninoff Rhapsody on a Theme by Paganini. He, too, ran the dynamic gamut, although his tone was more successful in soft passages than otherwise. His fine rhythmic sense made for perfect teamwork, and his technical accuracy was beyond necessity for comment.

The Miaskovsky Symphony was a pleasant piece, pitched rather low in intensity of emotion and romantic by way of Rachmaninoff as much as anyone else. It is surprisingly difficult to remember it with any precision after hearing the breathtaking performance of the Shostakovich work.

Piano Recital at Times Hall by Kirkpatrick

NOVEMBER 14 (1944), *NEW YORK HERALD TRIBUNE*

John Kirkpatrick, pianist, Monday night at Times Hall, in the following program:

L'Amphibie, Les Barricades misterieuses, Le Rossignol en amour, Les Vendangeuses, L'Unique, La Reveille-matin	Couperin
Evocations (four chants for piano)	Carl Ruggles
Third Sonata in E (First performance)	R. L. Finney
Motet	de Vitry
Four Pieces	Anonymous (French, about 1300)
Musette en rondeau, Le Rappel des oiseaux, Les Cyclopes	Rameau
Sixth Nocturne, Fourth Valse Caprice	Fauré
Old Folks at Home Variations (First performance)	Stephen Foster
Anadolla, Old Folks Quadrilles	Stephen Foster

John Kirkpatrick is a pianist who can always be expected to present an unusual program in a style of playing notable for its wealth of personal musical ideas. At the same time, he provides the spectacle of a performer who is admirably self-effacing in his devotion to the music and in his desire to place it before the spectator in the clearest possible manner.

Monday night at his Times Hall concert, Mr. Kirkpatrick offered another of his unorthodox programs, this one called "Music of France and the United States." With the exception of two short pieces by Fauré, all the French music was old, the most recent being a group of pieces by Rameau, from whom the field extended backward chronologically through Couperin into the early fourteenth century. The question which immediately arises in the mind of the person seeing such a program in print is whether or not such music, which has no difficulty in sounding complete on the psaltery, spinet, or harpsichord, can be made to sound as well on the modern piano, which lacks so many of the sonorous elements around which the writing developed. The answer would seem to be that it depends on the piece. Certain of the Couperin numbers were satisfying and delightful; others, using ornamentations inapposite to the piano, produced in the listener an acute nostalgia for the sound of an earlier instrument. However, Mr. Kirkpatrick painstakingly and with consummate skill managed to provide each piece with the stylistic frame that set it off to best advantage.

At the antipodes of musical expression and technique were the American selections: Four *Evocations* by Carl Ruggles, and Ross Lee Finney's Third Sonata, in E, which was given its first performance. The brisk first movement was the most pianistic and gave the impression of being the best constructed; it had direction. The other movements were more loosely woven and less individual in style, although the decisive line of the final section made a good impression. In these modern works, Mr. Kirkpatrick's touch was springy, his tone delectable, his fingerwork and phrasing of such a meticulous accuracy as to give one the sense of infallibility. Few pianists of his taste and ability take such pains with material which at first sight would seem so ungrateful and potentially so unrewarding. And of those who would undertake such a program, practically none could carry it to so successful a conclusion.

Recorded Popular Music

NOVEMBER 19 (1944), *NEW YORK HERALD TRIBUNE*

Now that Mr. Petrillo has signed up Victor and Columbia, the buyer can expect many new things from these two companies, which have been slowly feeding him with reissues of former favorites and what "new" two-year-old recordings were left. Ban-time record companies which have been using lesser-known bands will find the going harder; for the most part it will make no difference whether they fold up or not. One hopes, however, that the sudden availability of new name material will not squeeze out such specialists as Blue Note, Commodore, and Asch. So far, no new recordings have arrived since the lifting of the ban.

Victor offers the bright, young two-piano team of Whittemore and Lowe in an album of popular tunes played in a cocktail-hour fashion. The collection is called *Doubling on the Ivories,* and includes such things as *Begin the Beguine* and *Temptation*. The two most engaging numbers, however, are by Alec Wilder and bear titles typical of the composer's whimsy: *Seldom the Sun* and *Neurotic Goldfish*.

Blue Note has two twelve-inch disks by Art Hodes's Blue Note Jazz Men, where such players as Kaminsky and Edmond Hall are heard working together. The tunes are familiar, the style pleasingly pure. Solo work holds up better than ensemble, even though the latter has a minimum of prearrangement.

The group numbers in Asch's Mary Lou Williams album are completely arranged, but inasmuch as instrumental sonorities are used more or less as garnishments for her free piano work, the result is not too much out of focus, although the harmonies in both arrangement and piano are on their way toward what is known as sophistication, and show the sort of circumspection one is used to seeing presented with a higher degree of sonorous organization.

Both Asch and Columbia have made a Burl Ives album; all the songs are different, and, surprisingly enough, one collection is as good as the other. Ives is the most delightfully unaffected of all the bards who go about singing Anglo-American folk tunes. When you hear him sing them you really believe they are a part of him and not something he has discovered and decided to exploit.

Hit has an album of eight sides by Cootie Williams, of which the key piece is a rather better-behaved version of his old *Echoes of Harlem,* recorded for Vocalion by his (Ellingtonian) Rug Cutters in the middle twenties. Good behavior here is a detriment. With regard to this one piece the principal lack, aside from the rich instrumental backing he had then, is the cross-rhythm of drums on alternate beats of what is now plain 6/8 meter. I could also do without the Near Eastern unison singing in the middle. However, this and all the other numbers stand up under repeated playing. If one can't quite rave, it's only because inevitably one compares it all to Ellington.

Among recent contributions to recorded American music is an album by Asch Records called *Blues*. Herein are six twelve-inch numbers. Josh White accompanies himself on the guitar in a characteristic *T. B. Blues,* coupled with another *Careless Love,* recorded two years ago by the same artist for Blue Note. The new version shows quite a different Josh White: the early one has fewer subtleties, is more in the old blues-singing tradition. The Asch waxing reveals refinements of vocalization, due, no doubt, to constant and careful use of the mike.

One misses the freedom of vocal expression, as well as Sidney Bechet's eloquent clarinet interpolations. On the other hand, the Asch recording is far better and gives a faithful impression of the artist as he is today. Woody Guthrie sings a white blues in harmony with Cisco Houston. As might be expected, this is nearer to the Methodist hymnal than to most blues. Jack Dupree sings *Too Evil to Cry* with a fine primitive self-accompaniment on the piano in the style which has influenced Art Hodes. Mary Lou Williams plays behind Nora Lee King's voice in *Until My Baby Comes Home*. By far the finest piece in the album is Sonny Terry's *Lonesome Train,* as thrilling a bit of primitive Americana as has been heard in a long time, for its intensity of expression, purity of style and, in the category, for brilliant technicianship.

Victor has issued a memorial album of the late Bunny Berigan's most popular recordings, all of them made five and six years ago. These include such things as *High Society, Jelly Roll Blues, Black Bottom, Frankie and Johnnie,* and *I Can't Get Started,* which last is one of the best, and has a vocal chorus by the popular trumpeter himself.

Another Bing Crosby album has come, bearing the Columbia stamp. This collection has *I've Got the World on a String, How Deep Is the Ocean? Thanks for the Memory, The Last Round-Up,* and *Some of These Days*, containing a scat chorus which to these ears is nothing short of embarrassing, but doubtless the Crosby fans feel otherwise.

Olga Coelho has recorded two twelve-inch records for Hargall. The songs include four from Brazil, two from Inca sources and two from Spain. Most are adaptations of folk material, but there are two songs by Guarnieri and one by Falla, and it is in these that the performer seems happiest. Her folk songs are too often dressed in kid gloves. There is *Bambalele,* an *embolada* like those Elsie Houston used to sing. To satisfy my curiosity I should like to hear such a song done by a musically illiterate Brazilian Negro artist.

Isa Kremer, Vocal Mime, Heard at Carnegie Hall

NOVEMBER 20 (1944), *NEW YORK HERALD TRIBUNE*

Isa Kremer, Bessarabian vocal mime, was known to audiences here prior to her five-year sojourn in Buenos Aires, from which she recently returned. Her public manifestly has not forgotten her, for a large number of spectators gathered last night at her Carnegie Hall recital, and they were loud in their appreciation.

Miss Kremer's art cannot properly be called singing, nor was she billed on the program as a singer. The effects she makes rely fully as much upon gesture, bodily movement, facial expression, and stylistic vocal mimicry as upon the normal properties of vocal expression in music. When she sang a lullaby, she sat in a chair and rocked an invisible cradle, or held an equally hypothetical infant in her arms and stroked its head; when she sang Russian sailors' songs, she swaggered about in front of the piano with her hands behind her and pretended to have a cap on her head.

The program was marked in its variety of material. Among the heterogeneous items offered were a group of soldiers' songs from Greece, Spain, the Soviet Union, and Argentina; songs in American Negro dialect, in Yiddish, French, and Russian; and another group of old Russian folk songs. Ivan Basilevsky assisted at the piano.

Dorothy Minty Heard in Recital at Town Hall

NOVEMBER 21 (1944), *NEW YORK HERALD TRIBUNE*

Highly pleasurable violin playing was heard last night at Town Hall in the recital of Dorothy Minty, who, inexplicably enough, gives a New York concert only every four years, having been last heard here in 1940, and before that, in 1936. Surely we deserve to hear such an able performer more often than that.

Miss Minty showed all the qualities one can ask for in a violinist, with the exception (probably damning in the eyes of many present-day devotees of the instrument) of that great, wide, rich tone which is the stock-in-trade of the big-name virtuosi. She possesses a gratifyingly sure intonation, a sensitive and powerful bowing arm, a fine sense of rhythm. She also has musical taste and the ability to impose that taste successfully upon her audience, thanks in part to her gracefully imposing personal presence, and in part to the fact that she inspires a conviction in the listener that she is playing exactly what she means to play.

Her reading of the Debussy Sonata was a model of the proper juxtaposition of restraint and abandon essential in a good performance of the work. Especially lovely was the "Intermède," with its strange blending of bizarrerie and nostalgia. The Glazounov Concerto in A Minor received the same carefully considered and beautifully executed kind of treatment, the third movement being carried off with bravura and an incisive rhythmic attack. It's a dull piece, but Miss Minty did admirably by it. She also gave an excellent performance of the Bach Sonata in A Minor for violin alone. Here her prowess in achieving really exact pitch more than made up for an occasionally tenuous quality of tone. The andante revealed a fine continuous sense of flow, a certain amount of which the fugue could have used.

George Reeves provided "active" accompaniments for Miss Minty instead of the usual disinterested sort of background that seems to be present only because it has to be. His playing was creative in its subtle integration with the solo instrument, providing a rich palette of timbres against which the sustained sound of the violin became infinitely more effective.

Koutzen Heard in Violin Recital as Composer and Performer

NOVEMBER 23 (1944), *NEW YORK HERALD TRIBUNE*

Boris Koutzen, violinist and head of the violin departments of both Philadelphia Conservatory of Music and Vassar College, appeared last night in a two-fold capacity at his Town Hall recital: as both executant and composer. Surprisingly enough, his work as composer is more mature and shows more style than his violin playing. His Second String Quartet, in which he played first violin along with Bernard Robbins, Carlton Cooley, and Harvey Shapiro, is a carefully written, somewhat impersonal work in the erudite idiom, but all three of its movements get across to the listener's understanding.

The fabric is excessively contrapuntal; its tight writing shuts out the air. From beginning to end it uses a practically constant tutti, save for a fughetta in the first movement. The pleasantest part on first hearing is probably the melodic second movement, but one suspects that the final allegro, with its contrasting sections and ingratiating harmonic sequences, might well prove to be the most interesting. The work was given an excellent performance; its well-planned sonorities were achieved with intelligence.

As a violinist Mr. Koutzen leaves a bit more to be desired. His understanding of and sympathy for the Beethoven C Minor Sonata (op. 30, no. 2) surpassed his capacity for expressing it in terms sufficiently accurate to carry across his version of its message. One felt he had no right to show temperament unless he was going to play on pitch. After all, if there is a sine qua non of performance, it is precision; after that, if there is room in the executant's bag of talents, comes a show of feeling. Mr. Koutzen seemed satisfied with approximate pitch and a querulous tone, and neither tone nor pitch was ameliorated by his overtly emotional approach.

His best performance came with the playing of the Bach Sonata in A Minor, no. 2, for violin alone. Here there was a stronger attack, better intonation, a larger tone if not a smoother one, and in general a manifestation of more true interest in the music. Vladimir Padwa assisted in the works using piano accompaniment.

Martial Singher Presents Recital at Town Hall

NOVEMBER 27 (1944), *NEW YORK HERALD TRIBUNE*

Martial Singher, barytone, who for a decade sang at the Paris Opera and is now a member of the Metropolitan Opera Association, last night gave his second Town Hall recital since taking up residence in this country. The audience was large, distinguished, and highly appreciative; it seemed loath to let the artist go after the concert was over, staying and insisting upon numerous encores.

The program, consisting solely of French music, from Lully through

Rameau and Grétry on down to Debussy, Ravel, and a contemporary or two, was well balanced and, happy to relate, contained not a single "rollicking" song. When one considers the barytone repertory, one feels this was a minor miracle.

But Mr. Singher would scarcely try to sing that kind of pseudo-hearty material. He is a barytone with a tenor quality; his two great virtues are clarity and charm—clarity of diction, phrasing, and style, and charm in presentation. A song to him means a great deal more than a succession of notes and words to be got through correctly, and while not every song last night was equally successful from the vocal standpoint, certainly there was not one whose character and meaning had not been painstakingly considered by the artist, and its personality as it were enhanced by such scrutiny.

The songs which showed Mr. Singher's voice at its brilliant best were not the most musically interesting on the program. For some reason the artist seemed less sure of the notes in Debussy's *Trois Ballades de François Villon* (he left out almost a measure in *A la Requeste de sa mère,* and his agile accompanist, Paul Ulanowsky, cleverly hid the omission). It was in the *Chanson de labour,* with its melody that reminded one of songs from Asturias, and the *Berceuse,* from Cantaloube's *Songs of Auvergne,* that his work was perfection itself; again in the Hebraic Song and the Italian Song from Ravel's *Quatre chants populaires,* his voice rang out without any suggestion of constraint or insecurity.

This is not meant to imply that Mr. Singher does not possess an impressive and very sensitive pianissimo. It is simply that in many places the full voice was not equal in quality to the voice in passages where he used more restrained dynamics. And, paradoxically enough, in the Canteloube songs (in Auvergnat dialect) and the Ravel songs (in Yiddish and Italian), he realized his full vocal powers, which are very fine indeed.

Shura Dvorine, Pianist, Makes Town Hall Debut

NOVEMBER 28 (1944), *NEW YORK HERALD TRIBUNE*

A brilliant new addition to the growing list of young American piano virtuosi was made last night at the Town Hall debut of twenty-year-old Shura Dvorine. Whatever one may have thought of his very definite stylistic mannerisms, here was a young man whose massive and precise technique one could not help admiring. The playing was imaginative, intelligent, and very often of infinite elegance.

If Mr. Dvorine failed to make complete sense of the latter part of the Beethoven op. 111, this understandable shortcoming was more than compensated for in the magnificent performance he gave the Bach-Busoni Prelude and Fugue in E-flat Minor. Here and in the modern works, one sensed more fully his fine feeling for rhythm and his indefatigable and powerful finger work. This is quite as one would expect; it would be strange if a pianist so obviously sympathetic to twentieth-century music should enjoy playing nineteenth so much as seventeenth and eighteenth century products.

Thus Mr. Dvorine's Chopin was less moving than his Stravinsky or his Copland. The former's clever collage, *Circus Polka,* was played with alternating thunder and neat rhythmical lilt and received the most intense applause of the evening. Nabokov's *Dulcinée,* in which the Scriabin tradition is carried on, was given a sensitive reading, as was the early student-day Copland *Passacaglia.* Above all, the artist impressed with his absolute sureness of technique and style. His tone was mat; it could have stood more contrasting. It will be surprising if one does not hear a good bit about Mr. Dvorine in the near future.

Philharmonic Plays a Tribute to a Musical Ace of the R.A.F.

DECEMBER 1 (1944), *NEW YORK HERALD TRIBUNE*

The all-Britain program given last night at Carnegie Hall by the Philharmonic-Symphony Orchestra under Artur Rodzinski began with the playing of R. A. F. Wing Commander John Wooldridge's composition, *A Solemn Hymn for Victory.*

Dr. Rodzinski previously had promised the English composer to play one work of his for every five enemy planes he shot down. Last night's performance was presumably in payment for the first pentad. The piece began in the guise of a thinly scored and harmonically diffuse little work and developed into an overstuffed, fat one. It lasted a short time and received prolonged applause predicated on the composer's appearance upon the stage and, one supposed, on the unusual circumstances of its performance.

Ralph Vaughan Williams, whose Fifth Symphony in D Major was given its first performance on this side of the Atlantic at last night's concert, had inscribed on the score: "Dedicated without permission to Jan Sibelius." It would not be necessary to know this fact in order to find the work reactionary in intent. It is anti-intellectual music, and as such is not of this century. While it cannot be called program music, it seems constantly to be providing an emotional accompaniment to some undefined flow of extramusical ideas, with the emphasis on the sustaining of the emotion rather than on intramusical motivations. The sound itself does not provide the interest, nor does the sequence of sounds or phrases divulge any particular musical raison d'être.

The first movement says most of what there is to be said: that ancient England was a most charming place; the other movements show in how many ways that charm was exemplified.

One feels that the composer has been emotionally "taken in," in the most literal sense, by his own creation (another reason why the work is not of this day). It is not that one does not admire Mr. Vaughan Williams for his great ability to do just what he wishes: it is simply that one is not terribly much inclined to appreciate his wishing to do it.

The Westminster Choir was in evidence all evening, completely filling that part of the stage not occupied by the orchestra. It was a pleasure to hear its members sing *The Star-Spangled Banner*: a loud vocal rendition of that song is highly acceptable now and then.

Miss Schumann Is Soloist with City Symphony

DECEMBER 5 (1944), *NEW YORK HERALD TRIBUNE*

Leopold Stokowski's all-Russian program last night at City Center proved to be a little more varied than some such musical efforts at inter-Allied solidarity. In fact, Mr. Stokowski's fare is practically always interesting from the point of view of selection. The unfortunate circumstance about the New York City Symphony is the fact that it has to play in a hall whose acoustics are about as antisymphonic as one can conceive. In a sonority whose imminence and immediacy permit of no confounding of one instrument with another, where the component elements of sound refuse to blend, and sforzandi go off with the concussion of a bomb in the bathroom, it is pretty difficult to mold a true symphonic-sounding whole; it is to the great credit of Mr. Stokowski that he avoids racket as often as he does.

Henrietta Schumann, the young pianist who played the solo part in the Kabalevsky Piano Concerto no. 1, made an excellent impression, both visually and musically, with her clean-cut, decisive performance. She showed a high-spirited style and admirable control in ripping off the showy banalities of the piece, which is little more than a workmanlike and academic hash made up of the dry leftovers of Romanticism. The third movement brought out a few examples of rhythmical uncertainty on the parts of both Mr. Stokowski and Miss Schumann, but the final effect was one of buoyancy and good spirits.

The really delightful music of the evening was the little suite taken from Prokofieff's score for the film, *Lieutenant Kije.* Excepting the final movement, which is not successful in tying the other parts together as they require, the group is an ideal example of the best grade of contemporary thought and technique in music.

Tchaikovsky's Sixth Symphony suffered rather more than the recent works from the lack of acoustical cushions, particularly in the first two movements, where the instruments just couldn't merge. The program began with Deems Taylor's *Fanfare for the People of Russia,* and *Ivan the Terrible* of Rimsky-Korsakov.

Philharmonic Is Heard in Tchaikovsky Program

DECEMBER 8 (1944), *NEW YORK HERALD TRIBUNE*

Artur Rodzinski led the Philharmonic-Symphony Orchestra last night at Carnegie Hall in an all-Tchaikovsky program which comprised three works: the "Mozartiana" Suite, the Violin Concerto in D Major, and the Sixth Symphony.

The evening's warmest applause went to Isaac Stern, young American violinist, whose masterful reading of the concerto earned him every second of it. Mr. Stern is a mature instrumentalist and a fine musician.

Seldom does one find such a wide, ingratiating, reliable tone being produced simultaneously with such consistently controlled and admirably accurate pitch. In the first movement, certain of his détaché notes were wiry, but the display of enthusiasm on the part of the audience at the end of this section appeared to fire the artist with the necessary assurance, since from then on his playing was technically impeccable and imbued with a delightful quality of intimacy. The last movement especially was carried off with imagination and verve. It was a pleasure both to watch and to listen to the results in sound of the incisive but delicate bowing he used in the final passages. Prolonged manifestations of appreciation greeted this eminently clean and spirited reading, for which Mr. Rodzinski provided a sensitive orchestra accompaniment.

Lt. Bolet of Cuban Army in Carnegie Hall Recital

DECEMBER 8 (1944), *NEW YORK HERALD TRIBUNE*

First Lieutenant Jorge Bolet of the Cuban Army, now Assistant Military Attaché at the Cuban Embassy in Washington, gave a highly successful piano recital last night at Carnegie Hall. Lieutenant Bolet is a generously gifted pianist; his technical equipment leaves little to be desired. Primarily a colorist in the French tradition, he nevertheless has a basic feeling for the broad line. The quality of his sound is capable of taking on a variety of characteristics, but in general it can be said that he has a wide, soft tone. He is likely to play loud and fast, however, when he can possibly justify such action. Thus in the French Suite in E Major of Bach, the Courante, although meticulously fingered, was taken at such a speed that rhythmical integration was largely lost; so was the Bourée, to a slightly less marked degree, while the Gigue was so heavy and rapid that it sounded more like Czerny.

His playing of the Brahms Variations and Fugue on a Theme of Handel, although a little unimaginative in its interpretation, was technically impeccable. In forte passages the notes came forth like a volley of bullets. Fortunately, Lieutenant Bolet's marksmanship was excellent; all targets were hit. His reading of the Chopin G Minor Ballade was caressing and heroic by turns. It was probably the finest playing of the evening.

The only contemporary work listed was the Dello Joio Sonata no. 2, through whose fibrous fabric the artist slashed with brilliant effect. One would say the piece is taxing to the executant because it is not easy to extract a dramatic effect from it; its esthetic of angularity and intransigeance would seem to hold performer and listener at arm's length.

Lieutenant Bolet can play the piano beautifully, too well, in fact, not to exercise his imagination just a little bit more, not on the subject of sonorous effects but on that of his own personal conception of the music's content.

Nadia Reisenberg Heard in Recital at Town Hall

DECEMBER 12 (1944), *NEW YORK HERALD TRIBUNE*

Nadia Reisenburg, pianist, played last night at Town Hall in recital. Her audience was large and attentive, and as one listened to her expound the Schumann Sonata in F-sharp Minor, one understood at least part of the appeal she obviously has to music lovers. It is not a charming and subtle performance that she offers her listeners, nor an overwhelming technique. But, musically speaking, she is a good show; when she is at her best she keeps the music directly in front of one's attention all the time. The playing is persuasive, sometimes eloquent, because she manages to make the thread of the music's thought an imminent thing. This was especially the case in the second and third movements of the Schumann work.

In the final section what had been eloquence gave way to mere oratory; strenuous passages were likely to find her placing too much emphasis on purely dynamic possibilities. Miss Reisenburg is a capable pianist with a fine, wholesome tone. She is prone to allow a little too much leeway to a natural impetuousness which on occasion, when the work requires more reticence, disturbs the sound of the music. Of the three Chopin pieces she played, the Barcarolle, op. 60; the E-flat Major Nocturne, no. 2, op. 55; and the Tarantella, op. 43, only the last remained uninjured by her undue vigor.

Philharmonic Is Heard Under Szell's Direction

DECEMBER 15 (1944), *NEW YORK HERALD TRIBUNE*

George Szell began his two-week period as conductor of the Philharmonic-Symphony Orchestra last night at Carnegie Hall with a program whose principal work was the Beethoven "Eroica" Symphony. His readings of this work and the others of the concert were factual, studious, well planned.

Nothing particularly striking in the way of sound occurred during the evening, the orchestra making a better show in forte passages than in the more restrained moments. In the Beethoven work there was a certain unaccustomed sweetness of sound, however, which disappeared in Smetana's *Vlatava,* when one became unduly conscious of the discrepancy in pitch between certain of the woodwinds and the string section.

Mr. Szell has a rhythmically precise and decisive beat; and it was this quality in his conducting that gave the simple Smetana piece, with its dearth of musical ideas, whatever interest it presented. Without some of the thunder, it would be most useful in musical therapy. The old Strauss period-piece, *Till Eulenspiegel,* not very "lustig" any more, finished off the program. Sonorous consistency was a bit lumpy, but one could scarcely mind. The work is only more bearable than most Strauss in that it does not take itself seriously, and consequently makes a little less racket.

ARTICLES AND REVIEWS

......

1945

Commercial and Popular Records

JANUARY 14 (1945), *NEW YORK HERALD TRIBUNE*

Black and White Records (named, I presume, from the fact that its music is made by Negroes and whites together) has several items of interest in the chamber-music jazz province. These are played by various boys-about-town, put together in different groupings, among whom are James P. Johnson, Pee Wee Russell, Mezz Mezzrow, Bob Casey, George Wettling, and Willie "the Lion" Smith. Among my favorites is *Everybody Loves My Baby,* where toward the end Mezzrow gets his clarinet going and arrives at a passage reminiscent partly of a *sher* and partly of a dance from Saudi Arabia. The same label makes a twelve-inch "experimental pressing" of *Make Me a Pallet on the Floor* on the new unbreakable material we hope will soon be the rule instead of the exception. The tone is excellent, and surface noise seems no heavier than usual, even after many playings.

Two new and vigorous additions to the six virtuoso numbers by the Art Tatum Trio which Comet Records issued awhile back are Asch's *Topsy* and *Soft Winds,* another old Goodman Sextet piece (Tatum always seems at home in these); like the Comet waxings, this is a twelve-incher. Invention and technique are both on a high level. Asch has a Stuff Smith Trio album where the special personality of the popular hot-fiddler proves still projectable and essentially the same as it was nine years ago. The music is necessarily more subdued, less frantic in character than when he had his little band. Among the better sides are Stuff's own *Look at Me,* where pianist Jimmy Jones, bassist John Levy (erroneously labeled guitarist on all the records), and the unpredictable Mr. Smith go out together for some amusing harmonic adventures which penetrate beyond the old Debussy-Ravel frontier into Szymanowskiland. There is also the Russian-sounding *Desert Sands* and a very nice slow tune by Stuff called *Don't You Think,* which he plays like a slightly crazy gypsy.

Lena Horne sings Ellington's *I Didn't Know About You,* formerly known as *Sentimental Lady,* for Victor. Ellington can turn out just about the most satisfying commercial melodies around when he tries, an unusual faculty for a man who is primarily a harmonic and sonorous innovator. But they have consistent sticking power in the memory, releases and all. His fine new *I'm Beginning to See the Light* is on Victor, interpreted by the Duke himself and his men, with a new girl, Joya Sherrill, as soloist. The reverse is *Don't You Know I Care,* also by Mr. Ellington. *I'm Beginning to See the Light* is on Columbia by Harry James, with Kitty Kallen singing; she sounds much like Miss Sherrill, but she is less engaging in character. This is backed by Vernon Duke's hit tune from *Sadie Thompson, The Love I Long For,* which is given a suave Hollywoodian treatment by Mr. James, with his high but not hot trumpet alternating with the caresses of violins. The same good melody is done on Victor by Vaughan Monroe, with Mr. Monroe giving us a clearer version of the Dietz lyrics than James's vocalist manages to do.

Hit Records has a new Cootie Williams release, *Round Midnight,* a distinguished tune presented in an impressive arrangement, featuring Cootie in a beautiful open trumpet solo against an impressively dark background. The other side is a blues, *Somebody's Got to Go,* with the characterful Eddie Vinson shouting between the too-heavily orchestrated choruses.

I am wondering when we shall have an album of music from *On the Town.* Leonard Bernstein's songs will sound even better on records than they do on the stage.

Rudolf Serkin Is Heard in Carnegie Hall Recital

JANUARY 16 (1945), *NEW YORK HERALD TRIBUNE*

Masterly readings of piano music by nineteenth-century composers were heard by the large audience which came last night to Carnegie Hall to hear the Czech pianist Rudolf Serkin. He is an artist about whose playing one feels that everything is right. His technique is such that it can be taken for granted that there will be no untoward detail in its working. There is no stressing of personality or individual specialties; he is attempting to prove nothing about himself. His touch is virile, not violent; not even in the loudest moments was there a suggestion of uncontrolled force or pounding. At the same time his delicacy never comes near the borderlines of vagueness or sentimentality.

If anything can be offered in the way of suggestion to Mr. Serkin, it is that he consider the possibilities of a more varied program. The greater part of his concert was given over last night to music that made (and was supposed to make) the same kind of sound. The Variations and Fugue on a Theme by Bach, op. 81 of Reger; the four piano pieces, op. 119, of Brahms; and the four Czech dances by Smetana all use more or less the same kind of piano writing. And they were all given equally brilliant performances, which meant that by the time the Smetana suite arrived, the listening faculties were a bit fed up with that particular kind of rich sonority. In any case, to this reviewer, the Reger opus combines several of the less happy features of nineteenth-century style; it seems to him to have too many notes both per square inch and per second; it seems pompous and lengthy, quite out of proportion in size and treatment to its musical, if not to its architectural, ideas. Mr. Serkin gave it, however, a massive physical grandeur which brought forth salvos of applause when it was over.

In such a succession of authoritative readings, it is difficult to single out any one for particular praise; one is likely to be influenced by one's appreciation for the music rather than for the performance. But in the first Intermezzo of the Brahms group, there was a feeling of absolute perfection as each note fell into its proper place in the unfolding of the design.

Philharmonic Concludes Series Under Stravinsky

FEBRUARY 5 (1945), *NEW YORK HERALD TRIBUNE*

The last of a series of four concerts given by the Philharmonic-Symphony Orchestra under the direction of Igor Stravinsky took place yesterday afternoon at Carnegie Hall. The program, with the exception of the new *Scenes de Ballet,* which received its first concert performance Saturday night, was the same as that of the Thursday and Friday concerts.

It is somewhat disappointing to see the greatest living composer standing in front of an audience with a large orchestra at his disposal, and yet able to offer that audience only the lightest sort of music. For the *Scenes de Ballet,* commissioned by Mr. Billy Rose, who uses sections of it in the current *Seven Lively Arts,* is, for all the high quality of the stuff of which it is made and the elegance of its cut, a garment designed strictly for the dance. It is not so profound as the various earlier dance works it suggests.

The fragmentary sense given to the material by the stressing of different kinds of accompanimental figures, as in *Jeu de Cartes,* the constant halts of *Danses Concertantes,* and in general the sequinned sonorities and intertwining of sweet and sour harmonies characteristic of the most recent pieces; these qualities are all present, but no one of them takes over. There is an impressive apotheosis, and the conception is consistently graceful and apposite to the dance—more so, perhaps, than any Stravinsky ballet since *Apollon.* The piece makes no effort, however, to sustain a mood, and this lowers its vitality as concert music. The performance, which was given after a minimum of rehearsal time, was far better than that accorded to the unfortunate Piano Concerto on Thursday night. *Scenes de Ballet* should have been the light piece on the program, yet it was followed by the even more frivolous *Norwegian Moods* and the *Circus Polka.*

Villa-Lobos Directs Own Works in Concert with City Symphony

FEBRUARY 13 (1945), *NEW YORK HERALD TRIBUNE*

Heitor Villa-Lobos, the visiting composer from Brazil, is reported in this week's *New Yorker* as being fond of vanilla ice cream. It is stated that he considers it more or less as useful to the body as music is to the soul. This remark makes more sense than it might seem to when one listens to Villa-Lobos's own music. It is refreshing, it slides down easily, it contains a certain amount of nourishment and, if no effort is made to pretend it is anything more important, no one ought to be disappointed.

Last night at the City Center, the talented Brazilian composer led the New York City Symphony in two of his new works: *Uirapuru,* a tone-poem on Indian folk material, and the Seventh of his *Bachianas Brasileiras.*

In some respects the two works are alike. They both are primarily color music, and the color is laid on violently; it is of the successful unorthodox kind that comes from having the freedom to experiment with sonorities. Both pieces are quite lacking in harmonic and melodic interest, and even in organic rhythmical impetus, the excitement being created via the purely physical channels of instrumentation. With his nineteenth-century predilection for musical picture-making, Villa-Lobos reminds one of a southern Sibelius.

Fortunately, the tropical landscape is engaging. It came out as something fresh and compelling in *Uirapuru*. Often the intent here skirted Varèse's realm of pure noise. But the noise was not objective: it represented, and beautifully, the insect, bird, reptile, and animal sounds of the jungle night.

The *Bachianas Brasileiras* No. 7 is less amorphous, but it is also less inventive. There is no way here to pretend that frogs are croaking and crickets are chirping: one has to sit and listen to what amounts to a symphony in four long movements. The scoring is more expected, save for the inclusion of the marimba, and the material, though much of it comes unashamedly from popular sources, is neither folk music presented straight, nor yet transformed, but folk music beaten willy-nilly in with some Bach-like figures and poured all unmixed into the large bowl of French impressionism. And this makes very little sense, save that it provides an occasion for Mr. Villa-Lobos to write counterpoint. In his conducting, he bounced along with the beat animatedly and managed to keep the sometimes complicated rhythms clear of each other. But, to get back to his music, one feels that here is a composer who should completely forget tradition. The further afield he goes, the more likely he is to bring back discoveries of true charm and value.

During the first part of the evening Leopold Stokowski led the orchestra in an enthusiastically received performance of Beethoven's "Pastoral" Symphony. This was preceded by Henry Cowell's *Fanfare for the Forces of Our Latin-American Allies* and a transcription of the first part of J. S. Bach's Sonata in E-flat Major for Pedal-Clavier composed for Friedemann Bach.

Thomson Leads Philharmonic in Own Work

FEBRUARY 23 (1945), *NEW YORK HERALD TRIBUNE*

The program at the Philharmonic-Symphony Orchestra's Carnegie Hall concert last night was not a usual one for that organization. Dr. Rodzinski had got together a list of works that looked far more like a program one might have heard fifteen years ago at the Salle Pleyel in Paris, and it was a splendid idea. Nineteenth-century Germanic music can get to sound most unvaried.

Not content with inviting Virgil Thomson to conduct the first performance of his Symphony on a Hymn Tune, Dr. Rodzinski brought in Wanda Landowska to perform not only on the harpsichord but also on the piano, both of which instruments she handled, as always, with utter comprehension as to their maximum sonorous possibilities.

Only Miss Landowska can get those full, clear sounds from the piano that one heard last night when she played the Mozart F Major Concerto (K. 413). Visually she appeared to be scarcely touching the keys, quietly moving her fingers with a gentle firmness, yet each figure as it came out in sound proved the presence of infinite control, being exercised in a constant and equal manner at every moment.

Concerto Is Applauded

It was, however, the Haydn Concerto for Harpsichord and Orchestra (D Major, op. 21) which brought a storm of prolonged applause such as is seldom heard at concerts here. The combination of the artist's technical perfection and manifest reverence for the work, along with an unusually fine reading by the orchestra resulted in what the audience obviously felt was a truly great performance. As soon as the music stopped, they broke into cheers. It is a magnificent work, rich in harmonic subtleties and varieties of sound, and it would be hard to conceive another performance quite so fine as last night's. Everything was audible down to the tiniest trills of Miss Landowska's cadenzas; as a matter of fact, the instrument sounded rather better with the ensemble than the piano used for the occasion, because the latter's pitch was not quite up to that of the other instruments.

Virgil Thomson's Symphony on a Hymn Tune, the greater part of which was composed nearly two decades ago but had not previously been played, is a difficult number to get into if approached in the usual unintellectual sitting-back fashion; it offers nothing which is generally considered attractive to the ears.

The lack of a continuous melodic line or even of orchestral texture makes active listening essential. Still, it is one of the composer's most personal works; it sounds like the music of no one else. One might even say that it is conceived as no other music is conceived. Much of what it means has to do with extramusical things. Its references are literary, but its method of unfolding its form and argument recalls the technique of Cubist painting. The decorative juxtapositions and overlappings of contrasting harmonic and sonorous surfaces and the manner in which these component parts are held together suggest canvases of that period by Braque or Picasso. Such an analogy is viable only in attempting to work out a feasible manner in which to listen to a work that has so little in common with the rest of the symphonic repertory.

Homely Quality Noted

The piece is as American and ungainly as the wood stove and pump in the kitchen on the farm; it eschews the slick and insists on the homely. There is none of the streamlined mindlessness and spurious culture of present-day urban life. Its sounds are dry, with no suggestion of the lush or exotic. Sometimes one is reminded of the fact that the composer has written extensively for percussion; the music becomes wholehearted noisemaking. The hymn tune passages suggest the untrained voices of the backwoods. Often there is very little for the orchestra to do, but always there is something unexpected happening somewhere among the instruments. It is music which is awkward, droll and rough, but it is not static.

In conducting it Mr. Thomson could have made it clearer by waiting between the movements, to set them off a bit from each other in time; otherwise the performance was well managed.

Kenneth Gordon Makes Debut as Violinist at 15

FEBRUARY 26 (1945), *NEW YORK HERALD TRIBUNE*

Kenneth Gordon, fifteen-year-old violinist, made his New York debut last night at Town Hall before a responsive audience which apparently did not mind witnessing the unfair treatment he was undergoing at the hands of whoever planned his program.

Here was a young artist of undeniable talent and feeling faced with the obligation of performing one of the longest, dullest, and most difficult pieces in the repertory, the Paganini D Major Concerto, a work which, even if played well by a far more experienced instrumentalist, could scarcely elicit more than polite interest in the technique which made a good performance possible. There is no point in listening to complex passages in harmonies and multiple stops unless they are well-nigh perfect, since at any point this side of that state they sound most unpleasant. So that Mr. Gordon's efforts to present that virtuoso work last night operated distinctly to his disadvantage. And this was regrettable, because his readings of the other, shorter works on the program were highly commendable, showing a remarkable instinct for handling his instrument, as well as an intuitive musicianship.

In the Handel E Major Sonata, his pitch was firm, his tone equable although it will doubtless be fuller, his bowing sure. Only his rhythm was a bit headlong and eager. These qualities were again in evidence in his authoritative handling of the Kreisler *Praeludium and Allegro* and the Saint-Saëns *Rondo Capriccioso.*

Without the inclusion of the lengthy Paganini opus, the artist would have made a far more favorable impression. He may well turn out to be a brilliant violinist. Maurice Nadelle provided the accompaniments.

Zino Francescatti Gives Town Hall Violin Recital

FEBRUARY 28 (1945), *NEW YORK HERALD TRIBUNE*

A lively violin recital was given Monday night at Carnegie Hall by the French violinist Zino Francescatti, who, with the able assistance of Emmanuel Bay at the piano, drew warm and prolonged applause from the large audience for his rich-sounding performances of the Brahms Sonata in D Minor, op. 108, and the wistful, sensuous Violin Sonata of Debussy.

Even when Mr. Francescatti is being the virtuoso, which technically he is fully equipped to be, his musical product is wide awake and satisfying. However, his tone is less hard (though just as healthy) and his readings are somewhat subtler when he is not engaged in airing his facility.

The two sonatas, which formed the nucleus of his program, were also the most rewarding. In the Adagio movement of the Brahms work Mr. Francescatti showed his fine feeling for the pure, lyrical line, which in the playing became unequivocally eloquent and whose reading evoked particular applause. More of the same simple approach was evident in the Debussy work, only here the interpretation was highly dramatic and emotionally more persuasive. It was here, too, that the artist's beautifully exact rhythmical sense and impeccable pitch bore their finest fruit.

In the Chaconne of Vitali there was a great deal of sound and no small amount of fury. Of Mr. Francescatti's own arrangements of a Chopin Tarantella and Mazurka, the first was the better, the latter being rather unrelieved in its writing. The Dushkin arrangement of Gershwin's *Short Story* was pretty, but the piece is just Dvorák's *Humoresque* brought partially up to date.

Ormandy Leads Philadelphians in Final Concert

APRIL 4 (1945), *NEW YORK HERALD TRIBUNE*

Eugene Ormandy led the Philadelphia Orchestra in the season's final Carnegie Hall concert by that organization last night. The program offered the first New York concert performance of a cantata for chorus, contralto solo and orchestra made by Prokofieff from his film score for Eisenstein's *Alexander Nevsky,* produced in the Soviet Union in 1938. If the work in its new form inevitably suggests the visual images it was originally intended to accompany, it thereby becomes no less impressive as a piece of atmospheric music; indeed, there is little doubt that this cantata will be fresh, vigorous and inspiring long after the film has faded from the memory of all but the archivists.

The only recent choral work of like clarity and stature that comes to mind in considering *Alexander Nevsky* is Stravinsky's *Symphony of Psalms,* which, in certain places (notably the distant and archaic-sounding "Crusaders in Pskov") it strangely resembles. Prokofieff's vocal line is, however, more reminiscent of secular folk song than of ecclesiastical material. The instrumental melodies, too, are simple, and the complexities which arise exist more as atmospheric garnishments than as an integral part of the musical conception. But the brilliant instrumentation, which provides the vivid feeling of place and time in the work, is in no way extraneous to it, for the piece itself is the embodiment of atmospheric delineation. Prokofieff here points the way to the writing of this kind of monumental folk work: no melodic distortions, and the retention of the basic original harmonic feeling.

Mr. Ormandy outdid himself in getting from the orchestra a magnificent, viscera-rending performance. The Westminster Choir provided a stirring vocal sound of the "symphonic" variety, which is to say that the stress seemed always placed on massed sonorities rather than on diction. This was logical here, since the text, which offers little in the way of poetic interest, was sung in an English translation which did noting to ameliorate the commonplaceness of its expression. Two sections, "The Crusaders in Pskov," supposedly chanted by adherents of the medieval order of the Knights of Saint Mary the Virgin, and "The Battle on the Ice," have a Latin text. Rosalind Nadell, who sang the touching solo, "Field of the Dead," managed from her place far upstage to make herself heard above the orchestra.

The program began with a lucid and beautifully balanced performance of the Bach Brandenburg Concerto no. 2, for violin, flute, oboe, trumpet, and string orchestra. Soloists and ensemble played with utter perfection. Mendelssohn's Fifth ("Reformation") Symphony came between the Bach and the Prokofieff. Aside from the fact that it received a suave reading, it seemed little more than a filler, being, in the last movement especially (which might be called "The Tonic Triad Forever"), ponderous and incredibly redundant.

Little Symphony Plays Work by Virgil Thomson

APRIL 7 (1945), *NEW YORK HERALD TRIBUNE*

The New York Little Symphony, Joseph Barons director, offered a varied and diverting program last night at Carnegie Chamber Music Hall. Each of the four works played represented a different century.

A charming little group of dances called *Ouverturen-Suite,* by Philipp Heinrich Eriebach, started off the procession down the centuries, being of the seventeenth. Then came the B-flat major cello concerto of Boccherini, with Avron Twerdowsky, young New York cellist, playing the solo part with aplomb, including a strong, wide tone and a generally excellent control of pitch. The nineteenth century was left until last, being present in the form of Schubert's Fifth Symphony.

It was the contemporary work last night that caused a mild sensation, the first New York performance of Virgil Thomson's *Sonata da Chiesa,* written nineteen years ago for a quintet consisting of clarinet, horn, trumpet, trombone, and viola, and conducted by the composer. Musically the work stems unashamedly from Stravinsky, with both *L'Histoire du soldat* and the Octet (for the last movement) coming immediately to mind. The idiom is stark and dry, making concessions only to those who love their music naked and don't care how bony it is. The method is typically perverse in its dogged insistence upon following sequences beyond the point of necessity conditioned by habit, pushing the logic ahead to some point well outside the circumstances of expectation. Considered together with the circumspect dissonances embroidered upon a mock-Gregorian harmonic background and the wily and outlandish combinations of sonorities which have been worked out by the composer with an ear to extremes of sound and exaggerations of their ensemble incompatibility, this all makes an absurd and delightful little altarpiece (the middle section was called "Tango"), and one would like to see the church where it might be played.

Mr. Thomson is one of the few contemporaries who can write a truly funny piece. The *Sonata da Chiesa* was, to this reviewer, high comedy, ridiculous comedy. He was put in mind of Lewis Carroll, and of the dry biscuit given Alice for her thirst, and the solicitous but matter-of-fact query put to her after she has managed to choke it down: "Thirst quenched, I hope?"

Shostakovich Trio Receives U.S. Premiere

APRIL 28 (1945), *NEW YORK HERALD TRIBUNE*

A benefit concert was given last night at Carnegie Hall by Vivian Rivkin, pianist. The program was sponsored by Sweethearts of Service Men, and featured the first concert performance in the United States of the new Shostakovich Trio in E Minor for violin, cello, and piano. The work is elegiac in nature, having been written in memory of a personal friend of the composer.

While unmistakably a Shostakovich product, the Trio as heard last night is by no means one of his most compelling works. Some of its melodic material gives the impression of having been made up of unused odds and ends left over from more inspired pieces. However, in the first movement there is a certain atmosphere of mystery which is convincingly set forth. The cello starts the piece off in faint harmonics and presently the violin comes in two octaves lower.

As usual, the composer takes his time developing the ideas. The movement is painted in long, relaxed strokes, and has a certain effectiveness. This is more than can be said of the succeeding sections, save perhaps of the first part of the last movement, which is full of the typical Shostakovich ostinatos in polka-like rhythm. Miss Rivkin was ably assisted by Joseph Fuchs, violinist, and Nikolai Graudan, cellist.

The piano solos included three unfamiliar works: Twenty-two Variations on an Original Theme, by the English composer Richard Arnell; Cradle Song, by Alan Shulman, U. S. N., M 2/c., and Toccata, Song, and Dance, by Private First Class Sol Kaplan. The Kaplan Toccata was accorded a more muscular performance than the preceding two works; still it too gave the impression of being rushed through in a helter-skelter fashion. All Miss Rivkin's performances were curiously impersonal, as if the music were situated at a great distance from her consciousness.

Walden Quartet Gives Concert at Music Festival at Columbia

MAY 14 (1945), *NEW YORK HERALD TRIBUNE*

The third concert of the first annual Festival of Contemporary Music now in progress at Columbia University took place yesterday afternoon at the McMillin Academic Theater. It was a chamber-music concert played by the Walden String Quartet of Cleveland, with Alvin Etler, oboist, as assisting artist.

The music consisted of works by four contemporary American composers: Frederick Jacobi, Robert McBride, Alvin Etler, and Wallingford Riegger, who have in common the fact that they all are music instructors. The resultant pedagogical approach to music, exemplified in their placing of emphasis on writing rather than idea, does much, despite their obvious stylistic dissimilarities, toward making for a sort of unity of expression in their music.

One Quality in Common

Yesterday there was something else the different pieces had in common, and that was that invariably the slow passages meant more than the first ones. Various conclusions could be drawn from this, the most cynical being that the result of such concerts upon the listener is a state of mind to which the lulling, slow sections naturally form a more appropriate accompaniment. A more serious explanation might be that a fast movement demands more harmonic sureness and imaginativeness than a slow one; the temptation to fake is always more present when there is rhythmical patter to draw away the attention.

A feeling of amorphousness, intensified by lack of definitely established harmonic limits, generally is more or less present in contemporary music. It was most present yesterday in the Jacobi String Quartet no. 2 and the Riegger String Quartet. However, in the Jacobi work there were passages of Debussyan logic, notably in the second movement; and there was pleasure in hearing the opening Lento ma non troppo, with its oblique sentimentality, and the flowing, decorative writing of the first part of the last movement.

Fun for the Audience

In the Riegger quartet, the question of easily perceived form was less upsetting, because the absence of it seems more apposite to the twelve-tone idiom. This "international neurotic style," along with most international ideologies, however functionally designed, is likely to give pretty drab results. However, the piece contains many expressive moments, the second movement proving particularly interesting. It presents rhythmical and intonational difficulties to instrumentalists, and these were expertly solved by the Walden Quartet.

Robert McBride's Quintet for Oboe and Quartet provided fun for the audience. His pieces usually do, but apart from the taken-for-granted, not-necessarily-expressed underbeat of popular American music (which incidentally was not observed with enough incisiveness by the performers), there was little to signal as very original in the work.

Six From Ohio, by Alvin Etler, in which the composer also was oboe soloist, was a group of short, pleasant, pastoral-sounding pieces which combined an occasional folk-like phrase with proficient string writing of the horizontal sort. To sum up: The Etler work provided lyrical atmosphere for the concert; Riegger gave it recherché sonorities; Jacobi, melodic charm; and McBride listenability.

The Quiet Don Is Presented at Carnegie Hall

MAY 28 (1945), *NEW YORK HERALD TRIBUNE*

> *The Quiet Don,* opera by Ivan Dzerzhinsky based on Sholokhov's novel *Quiet Flows the Don*; first New York performance by Dmitri Chutro's Russian Opera Company in Carnegie Hall last night.

Since the presentation of *The Quiet Don* last night at Carnegie Hall cannot with justice be called a performance of that work, it seems only logical to preface any remarks that one is going to make about the opera with a reminder that the remarks necessarily refer to the piece only as it appeared last night.

If it had been given in oratorio form, it doubtless would have sounded far better, since the singers would have been facing the audience and there would not have been the painful problem of stage direction, and the entire pacing would have been much faster. The spectator would have been spared the attempts at delineation, the twitching, lantern-slide scenery, the wistful spotlights hurrying after singers, the inept dancing, and all the rest of the amateurishness.

There remains the music itself, its writing and its performance. Fortunately neither Mr. Dzerzhinsky's score nor the playing of it by the orchestra, under Mr. Fiveisky, had any amateurish quality. True, the music is not in the least inventive, nor could one tell which of half a dozen contemporary Soviet composers might have been its creator, but it is completely workmanlike both in its details and in its general construction. Its principal virtue, in fact, is its mobility. It is never episodic; it gathers momentum and pushes ahead to whatever emotional spot it wishes to reach. The work's proportions are mature, and there is the feel of real opera. The music is fresh, not in the sense that it contains a single discovery, but rather in that it is ingenuous, blissfully unconscious of its utter lack of style and originality and intent on carrying along its story as directly as possible.

The formal writing is conventional. There are set pieces, and spoken and sung recitativo with instrumental punctuations. Occasionally the composer lets the orchestra finish out a number all by itself after the vocal line is done. In the present production, this device exists at the expense of the action's continuity. Everything proceeds at a leisurely pace. Arias are highly melodic; most of them are in a minor mode and some have charm. The idiom uses Russian folk music in a haphazard, partially digested form, rather as Gershwin, for instance, uses American folk music in *Porgy and Bess,* although Dzerzhinsky succeeds less well in giving it a personal flavor. The orchestration is dark and brassy, and last night it covered much of the singing.

There probably is a story, but it would be best not to discuss it until a later production is seen. The three best voices belonged to the protagonists in a love triangle. Two women contend for the affections of one gentleman, one of them getting him, at least to the extent of being able to carry about a bundle which presumably was his child. However, neither contender was very happy at any point, and both had occasion to sing several touching arias. The two women were sung by Maria Maximovitch, whose voice at its best was full and rich, and Nadia Ray. The gentleman was sung by Arsen Tarpoff.

Popular Records

JUNE 24 (1945), *NEW YORK HERALD TRIBUNE*

In an album issued by Victor, Leonard Bernstein conducts the "On the Town" orchestra in several of the ballet numbers from his epoch-making score for that brilliant musical. The instrumentation is often phenomenal in its cleverness, and the recording does justice to the rich sonorous textures. This is not the case in the vocal pieces, sung by the Collegiate Chorale, which make up the rest of the volume. These are choral arrangements, not by Mr. Bernstein, of *Some Other Time, Lucky to Be Me,* and *Lonely Town,* and they all fall wide of the mark, both as recordings and as arrangements purporting to convey the spirit of the individual numbers or of the show as a whole.

In the realm of traditional blues singers, Bluebird offers such old standbys as Lil Green, singing *Boy Friend* in her typical shrill, indignant voice; Roosevelt Sykes, who used to bill himself as "The Honey Dripper," doing *Jivin' the Jive,* a boogie tune, on the piano, with spoken interpolations; and "Big Boy" Grudup, the most basic of these and also the most interesting, in *Rock Me, Mama.* Okeh has new disks by two celebrated blues singers, Memphis Minnie and Big Bill, these of the good old-fashioned shouting variety. Minnie sings *When You Love Me,* and Big Bill *When I Get to Thinkin'.*

Two other popular singers who contribute vocal performances above the average are Jo Stafford, a lady with suavity, clear, easy diction, precise pitch, and no small amount of persuasiveness in her voice; and Peggy Lee, a little more to the hot side. Both have recent recordings by Capitol. Miss Stafford is one of three vocalists who have chosen to record the season's best sentimental song: *There's No You*. For Capitol she does a straight version, very good. Frank Sinatra does it to perfection for Columbia, and Martha Stewart for Victor. In the same category, if not of the same degree of quality, come *I Should Care, Out of This World,* and *If I Loved You*. There is a version of each on practically every company's label.

Nothing having appeared during the spring in the way of inspired ensemble playing that makes any sense when compared with the magnificent Victor album of Jelly-Roll Morton reissues, we are forced to content ourselves with admiring whatever is good in what exists at present. There is plenty of technique in instrumental execution, and there is a certain amount of good arranging. Indeed, it is a characteristic of the times that the carefully arranged pieces surpass in interest those which may lay claim to some degree of spontaneity. A thing like *Grabtown Grapple* by Artie Shaw's Gramercy Five (Victor) leaves even less room for improvisation than the old Goodman Sextet numbers after which it is modeled; still, the small ensemble's possibilities seem generally to be more nearly realized than those of the large band with the "sections," where very little in the way of experimentation ever takes place.

On Columbia, Gene Krupa has a virtuoso *Dark Eyes,* where his drums back up nice piano and tenor sax work. And along this line, if not better, is the King Cole Trio's *If You Can't Smile and Say Yes,* on Capitol. John Kirby has done an album of little pieces for Asch Records, all neatly arranged and neatly played. No revelations at any point, but at least the material is new, the titles ranging from such likelihoods as *J. K. Special* and *K. C. Caboose* to the less expected *Maxine Dengoza*.

The nearest thing this trip to good ensemble improvisation is Commodore's recording of *How Come You Do Like You Do* by George Wettling and his Rhythm Kings. The kings are the same men we have been hearing around town for the last few years, including Billy Butterfield, trumpet; Edmond Hall, clarinet; and Bob Haggart, bass.

A smooth tune smoothly set and played by Benny Carter and his orchestra on Capitol is *Malibu,* in praise of the wretched little beach in California. Mr. Carter wrote it and plays it—who did the simple and effective arrangement that puts it across, this the label does not tell. Actually, in such cases it should, since the arranger is often responsible for whatever quality a number may have, be it pleasant or otherwise. Witness Victor's *June Comes Around Once a Year,* played by Tommy Dorsey and his orchestra. It is not a bad tune in itself, but by dint of a few skillful harmonic additions by the brass it becomes a really eloquent number. Commodore does give Eddie Heywood credit for arranging *I Cover the Waterfront* for Billie Holiday and her orchestra. This is a variant of the setting he did last year of the same piece, and it makes a very slick harmonic backdrop for Miss Holiday's deceptively simple vocalisms.

For Victor, Tommy Dorsey lends his talents to Duke Ellington and his orchestra in *Tonight I Shall Sleep,* a suave Ellington melody, coupled with a noisy one, *The Minor Goes Muggin',* in which the Duke returns the compliment by using the Dorsey band as a backdrop for his pianistics. It is all fairly commercial, as is *Mood to Be Wooed,* another recent Ellington waxing for Victor. In *Mood,* Johnny Hodges does some of his inimitable soft sax work, but this is not quite enough to make the piece a good one.

For those who deplore the Duke's commercial leanings, perhaps the most encouraging Ellington recording since the lifting of the ban is the one of *Carnegie Blues* by Victor. It offers one more proof, if a small one, that careful and "personalized" arrangements need not produce stereotyped jazz if these present an intelligent attitude toward tradition, and a really homogeneous and tractable ensemble. This piece was conceived in the Victor studios during a recording of parts of *Black, Brown and Beige,* and put down on the spot, so that in one sense it is extemporaneous music.

Record Review

JULY 15 (1945), *NEW YORK HERALD TRIBUNE*

For those who deplore the Duke's commercial leanings, perhaps the most encouraging Ellington recording since the lifting of the ban is the one of *Carnegie Blues* by Victor. It offers one more proof, if a small one, that careful and "personalized" arrangements need not produce stereotyped jazz if these present an intelligent attitude toward tradition, and a really homogeneous and tractable ensemble. This piece was conceived in the Victor studios during a recording of parts of *Black, Brown and Beige,* and put down on the spot, so that in one sense it is extemporaneous music.

Having what I naturally consider a quite healthy loathing for anything that sounds like the orchestra of André Kostelanetz, I need only remark along the way that there is a very pretty-looking album put out by Columbia called *Music of Gershwin,* and played by the aforementioned organization. A step above this in the achievement of slickness (although not necessarily in the hierarchy of taste) is Morton Gould's album, *After Dark,* also a Columbia product, and also very attractively packaged. The item contains eight satiny transcriptions by this super-arranger; the material consists of such pieces as *Besame Mucho, Temptation, That Old Black Magic,* and *Speak Low.* To the profane listener, these all have a way of sounding the same, and surprisingly like the title and credits music used in contemporary grade-A feature films, which no doubt lends the album all the great glamour that adheres to that mysterious art medium.

Columbia gives us a Benny Goodman disk: *At the Darktown Strutters' Ball,* coupled with *After You're Gone,* both fine old tunes, and both sonorously tops in the field of synthetic inspiration. The same label had *Flatbush Flanagan,* written and played by Harry James. Erskine Hawkins's *Bear Mash Blues* on Bluebird is more fun. Victor has two recent albums of reissues. One, a companion volume to their *Up Swing,* is *Smoke Rings,* a collection of dreamy "away" numbers, among which are Ellington's excellent *I Got It Bad,* Goodman's eight-year-old *These Foolish Things,* Artie Shaw's version of his father-in-law's great song, *All the Things You Are,* and Larry Clinton's metamorphosed Debussy opus, *My Reverie.*

Bruch Violin Concerto Played at Stadium Concert

AUGUST 2 (1945), *NEW YORK HERALD TRIBUNE*

A small audience listened last night at the Lewisohn Stadium to Eugene Goossens conduct the Philharmonic-Symphony Orchestra. The program combined two numbers which had originally been listed for Tuesday evening's concert, with two others scheduled for last night. The assisting artist was Joseph Fuchs, violinist, who played the Bruch G Minor Concerto with a precision and gusto which drew shouts of applause after the final cadence. His performance in the last movement was particularly pleasurable in its clean, decisive attack. The uppermost register suffered a bit in the preceding movements; it seemed as though the artist, to be on the safe side, kept everything on the sharp side, and this was too consistently noticeable.

Mr. Fuchs' encore, a Bach unaccompanied number, provided the most agreeable sounds of the evening, being played to perfection, without imposing upon the listener the strain of following the hazardous vicissitudes met with throughout the evening by the insufficiently rehearsed orchestra.

The concert began with the Borodin *Polovtsian Dances,* and ended with the Moussorgsky *Pictures at an Exhibition* as orchestrated by Ravel. After the Bruch Concerto, Mr. Goossens offered Prokofieff's *Lieutenant Kije* Suite, a charming piece but not the sort to force into auditory competition with passenger planes from La Guardia Field.

Grace Moore Is Heard In *Bohème* at Stadium

AUGUST 3 (1945), *NEW YORK HERALD TRIBUNE*

One of the season's largest audiences crowded the Lewisohn Stadium last night to hear Grace Moore sing the part of Mimi in Puccini's *Bohème.* The occasion marked the artist's first appearance here since her return last week from a two-month U. S. O. Camp Show tour of Europe, the rigors of which would seem to have had no adverse effect on her vitality and voice. Miss Moore was in excellent form last night, and at more than one point, after an eloquently delivered aria, she was obliged to wait while the audience demonstrated its approbation. Her voice was consistently rich in tone, and the elements of her delineation were of a piece within the style she had set for herself. It is not a subtle characterization, but it is a believable and a sympathetic one.

Miss Moore was supported by Jan Peerce, who sang Rodolfo and received his share of bravos in the first act. His voice was not too well matched with hers; it is a smaller one, but the public address system helped minimize the disparity. Martial Singher was a likable Marcello. Mimi Benzel made an amusing Musetta; the voice, however, was a little shrill and wavering. Colline and Schaunard were sung respectively by Lorenzo Alvary and George Cahanovsky, and Lodovice Oliviero appeared as Benoit and Alcindoro.

The piece, which is always a pleasure to see and hear, even under the trying conditions imposed by an outdoor performance, was directed by the firm hand of Alexander Smallens.

Notes on an Unpleasant Subject

AUGUST 19 (1945), *NEW YORK HERALD TRIBUNE*

The sudden taking on of our popular culture by peoples who have not recently been in connection with the Occident involves in some measure a repudiation by them of their own. This would not be inevitably so if ours had anything at all in common with theirs, but the incompatibility is complete. Theirs are carefully elaborated human necessities; ours is the streamlined broadcast that advocates our national product, industrialism. And they rather like the idea of the product and are completely sold on its smart programs. Thus it is not surprising that in the case of music, at once the most emotionally direct and intellectually abstract of the conventions of human expression, systematic disparagement is directed by various peoples of the world toward their own folk musics, while these same spirits are placidly or even eagerly receptive to our commercial antimusic.

It is of course only to be expected that those countries which have been carefully creating themselves in our image should carry out their imitation of us to the point of being one up on us in the production of kitsch, musical, literary, and graphic trash. But folk culture in Europe, with the possible exception of a few backward countries such as Spain, Greece, or Albania, is pretty much lost anyway. The period of a quick cultural death exists particularly for those parts of the globe peopled by races other than the Caucasian, but where Western civilization enjoys more prestige than the indigenous. In Latin America, Africa, the Far East, progress is taken seriously, and this fact ineluctably entails the destruction of the present system of thought and artistic expression.

Perhaps one of the greatest bulwarks against human disintegration is the intransigent politico-religious attitude of the Hindus and the Moslems; but even in the case of the Moslems, the pattern is repeated, with a variation it is true, the tendency being to deprecate the regional art product to the advantage of the Egyptian. Cairo is both New York and Hollywood.

......

Local culture is in ill repute. Go to Andalucia and look among the middle classes for some one who likes *cante jondo*. Your questions will be answered by: "I'd rather hear a catfight!" "Such music is for people who live in caves and die in the gutter." Go to Fez, where in spite of their fierce nationalistic chauvinism the inhabitants play only Egyptian records, preferably song hits from Abd el Wahab's latest film, on the café juke boxes. (This, incidentally, would be fine if they did not really prefer their own music with words in Maghrebi, which they shamefacedly play and sing themselves in the privacy of their own dwellings.) And Japan, who up until this war bought a great percentage of the recorded Occidental art music, has her bastardized Verdi and forgets her own modes and subtleties of vocalization. Doubtless Italian opera and cheap movies from Cairo are only an intermediate step en route to Sammy Kaye and the Ink Spots.

In 1934, I went to Colombia to hear the music of the Indians of the Goajira Peninsula. What happened is difficult to appreciate unless one is accustomed to the violent hatred most Latin-American officials manifest toward their own native cultures. I was in Santa Marta, waiting for the weekly boat that used to sail to Riohacha. The company was openly incredulous when I explained why I wanted passage and proceeded to notify the police, who quickly arrested me and went through my luggage. All the while they kept repeating, as if trying to convince me by hypnotic suggestion: "There is no music in the Goajira," and even "There are no Indians in Colombia." I was forbidden to purchase a ticket, and finally had to go back to Barranquilla without having heard anything more indigenous than some *bambucos* and *cumbiambas*.

......

I went to buy Panamanian records in Panama and found several *mejoranas* I like, but the clerk almost tearfully insisted that those outlandish things were from Ecuador. And so it goes. All through Central America, and particularly Mexico, the musical styles which were easy to find ten or fifteen years ago are nearly extinct, thanks to the ubiquitous and urbanizing radio, whose talent scouts in the last-named country corral rural musicians, carry them to the capital, and ruin their delicate collaborative technique, which is to say their tradition, in literally a few days.

A case in point is Cuba, a land where one might reasonably expect to hear, at least in the cheaper dance halls, a certain amount of that Afro-Latin music, which, along with her cigars, the world has come to consider Cuba's most typical export. By Cuban music most of us mean *rumbas, congas, pregones, guarachas,* and *sones*. We have also got used to expecting a varied and active percussion section in the performing group. What do we find in July

1945? In the first place, looking for a *rumba* in Cuba is almost tantamount to instigating a search in this country for a turkey trot: the answer to one's inquiries is likely to be an amused and condescending explanation that the *rumba* is an outmoded dance form that everyone knows perfectly well is passé. If you do by chance find an orchestra playing one, it is likely to be in a place frequented by Americans, and the conjunto is certain to lack the percussion, save for one person who occupies himself indifferently with either *maracas* or *guiro*. One can scarcely object to a dance or song form's going out of style; it happens to the best of them—of all the aforementioned, the only one still functioning is the *guaracha,* a Cuban counterpart to the Mexican *corrido*—but what comes up in its place? American commercial music, for one thing. *Triste Lluvia,* recognizable to our ears as *Stormy Weather,* seems to be the island-wide hit this year. And secondly, something worse: Latin swing, a new hybrid commercial idiom being propagated in the radio studios of the torrid zone. Its words, prosody, and harmonic sequences are likely to be roughly on the Argentine side, its melodic devices are often Mexican-inspired, while underneath is an insistent but dull simplification of Cuban rhythm. The idiom, which is consciously being pushed in order to destroy the international barriers normally preventing foreign consumption of any given country's product, is as meaningless as our own commercial music, and if possible even less engrossing. Now, wherever you may be in Latin America, you can hear the same pseudo-music, the same poisonous clichés of melody and harmony, the same empty purple lyrics. It has all been made digestible for the radio and film audiences of the Latin American republics, and presumably everyone is happy.

. . . . . .

The Cubans are almost as loath as the Americans to admit that their folk music, at least that part of it which can be called distinctive, is primarily of Negro origin. They constantly point out Iberian turns of melody, much as people here insist on the modes from the British Isles. In the music which receives public encouragement (radio, theater, dance hall), there is as little as possible of the African element. Even those numbers now distinguished by the adjective "Afro-Cubano" circumspectly Europeanize the Negro elements.

Along the waterfront in Santiago or Havana, a group of Negroes will begin a vigorous bit of true Cuban music, complete with *marimbula, bongó,* and antiphonal *estribillo*. They seldom get very far. The police saunter past and suggest silence. Reason: Such music provokes "scandals." Or you, a foreigner, may happen by and catch them singing and playing something quite relaxed. Shamefacedly they will hurry to finish it and begin something from the radio. Reason: The other is "old-fashioned," or even "backward": you might deduce that Cuba is not that thing they have been taught is the ultimate good: a modern country. The same pattern prevails all over the world: the uprooting of natural culture for the implantation of an ersatz culture which can be controlled from headquarters. There is obviously no remedy.

Carmela Ippolito Heard in Concert at Town Hall

OCTOBER 23 (1945), *NEW YORK HERALD TRIBUNE*

An unusual and somewhat daring program was presented last night at Town Hall by Carmela Ippolito, American violinist. With the exception of the Vitali-Auer *Ciaconna,* the entire list of works offered was by contemporary composers, and included the first performance of a suite for violin alone, entitled *American Scenes,* by Eda Rapoport; the "Gregorian" Concerto by Respighi; the First Violin Sonata by Honegger; short works by Frank Bridge and Szymanowski; and three pieces by Miss Ippolito.

There is nothing which raises the listeners' hopes so much as the inclusion of unfamiliar works on a program. Recent works all too often are accorded mediocre performances. Miss Ippolito, however, is a fine technician, and no contemporary composer could ask for a more painstaking and enlightening interpretation than the one she gave the Rapoport suite. *American Scenes* consisted of four sections, called, rather arbitrarily: "The Melting Pot," "Brooklyn Bridge at Dusk," "Playground," and "Airport." This last part was played *sul ponte* with rapid tremolos. Would that all airports made so small and undisturbing a sound.

Miss Ippolito is an accomplished violinist. It is rare to find such complete lack of querulousness in intonation and such consistently generous and suave tone. With this accomplished technicianship, it was strange to find her choosing to play a piano arrangement of the Respighi Concerto. A more monumentally dull piece would be hard to dig out of the repertory, and the lack of rhythmic feeling in last night's performance did not enhance its interest. One would like to hear Miss Ippolito in a program of new works more deserving of her talents.

Reah Sadowsky

NOVEMBER 5 (1945), *NEW YORK HERALD TRIBUNE*

Reah Sadowsky, Canadian pianist, made her New York debut last night at Town Hall before an unusually enthusiastic audience.

Several things became immediately visible: Miss Sadowsky's intelligence, as exemplified by her choice of program; her dignified, almost distant, keyboard manner; and, most important of these, her uncommon ability to hold the listener's attention without indulging in dramatics of any sort.

This last, expressed by insistence upon absolute clarity in phrasing and by the use of great subtlety of nuance within the phrase (both of which devices indicated a high degree of musicality in the artist), was achieved above all because she had a lucid conception of each work as it progressed from beginning to end, and was capable of communicating this in a very exact manner to the audience.

Thus each piece emerged as a logical emotional entity, and not as a parade of semirelated episodes, some invested with interest and some meaningless in their relation to their context, as is likely to happen in the case of more subjective executants.

Miss Sadowsky is expert in playing "pure" music. This was evident in her readings of the Bach C Minor Partita and of Brahms's Variations and Fugue on a Theme of Handel, both of which were well orchestrated, clean in sound, and played with a marvelous ease.

Two first performances were forthcoming during the program. One of these, a Sonatina by the Brazilian Guarnieri, was a light, restless, elegant little work all of whose three movements were written high on the piano. The second movement was based on a Fado-like theme, romantic and sleepy, but not at all sensuous. The third was a canon, nervous and reiterative like the first, but without the sparsely used allusions to local folk material.

The other new work was a Capriccio in two sections by Arthur Berger, music critic at the *New York Sun*. This astutely made piece stems stylistically direct from the late Stravinsky (and occasionally in rhythmical implications even from the Stravinsky of the 'teens). One finds the much-admired truncation of line, the strictly noncommittal emotional attitude. Both the Berger and the Guarnieri works were admirably performed by Miss Sadowsky.

City Symphony Offers 3d Program of Season

NOVEMBER 6 (1945), *NEW YORK HERALD TRIBUNE*

Leonard Bernstein led the New York City Symphony Orchestra last night at the City Center in the municipally sponsored organization's third program of the season. This comprised the E-flat Major Symphony (K. 543) of Mozart, Schumann's Cello Concerto in A Minor (op. 129), and Randall Thompson's Second Symphony. The playing ensemble has been molded with startling rapidity by Mr. Bernstein into an excellent orchestra. The strings sound fuller and the brass far surer than a month ago at the opening concert. And the extraordinary rhythmic drive and exactitude of the orchestra is something to hear. To American ears, rhythm should be unequivocal, and the young conductor of the New York City Symphony has a particular genius for insuring clear-cut rhythm.

The high point of sonority in last night's concert came with the Mozart Symphony. Here the orchestra showed that it was no longer "good, considering," but good, period. The audience responded with rounds of applause. They also enjoyed Joseph Schuster's capable reading of the rather unconvincing Schumann concerto, for which the orchestra was dexterously kept in the auditory offing.

Five years ago at the Berkshire Festival, Mr. Bernstein made his first professional appearance, conducting the Thompson Second Symphony. Like most American music, the work is more inclined to action than to meditation, is noisy rather than restrained, and more intent upon direct, forceful expression than upon the subtleties made possible by partial withholding. Its musical ideas alternate between naive sincerity and the professor's classroom joke. Mr. Bernstein gave the work a bright, vigorous performance.

Kirkpatrick Recital

NOVEMBER 13 (1945), *NEW YORK HERALD TRIBUNE*

John Kirkpatrick, American pianist, played last night in a recital at Times Hall. One can always be certain of two things before going to hear Mr. Kirkpatrick: the program will be unusual and chosen with great care, and the music will be presented with maximum clarity of sound. These two things require musicianship and technique.

Mr. Kirkpatrick has in addition a personality which is easily projected in performance. The quiet, sincere intensity with which he approaches whatever he plays communicates itself to the spectator and makes listening that much pleasanter.

Last night the program contained a good many unfamiliar works. The Smaller Preludes of the Catechism Chorales of Bach are not regular recital fare, but they provided, as played by Mr. Kirkpatrick's sensitive fingers, many more delightful moments than the big transcribed organ works generally do. Nor is the average concertgoer particularly familiar with the nine *Slåtter* of Grieg which were offered at the end of the program, yet certain of these are completely charming in their attempts to approximate rural Norwegian dances, as played on the Hardangerfelen. Grieg's devices include the insistent use of the sharped fourth, repeated hitting of what would be open strings, use of baroque ornaments, and irregular rhythms. One hopes to have the opportunity of hearing the more robust of these dances again soon in the concert hall. They were perfectly suited to Mr. Kirkpatrick's light and admirably lucid technique.

Another work, unfamiliar because it had never been played until last night, was Sergeant John Lessard's Second Sonata, which was given a tight, forceful, well-integrated reading by the artist.

The piece harks back stylistically to Stravinsky of the *Sérénade en la* in its diatonism; sometimes also it comes from Stravinsky in a less direct manner, via Copland. This happens overtly in the final movement. The work is in general extremely contrapuntal, yet it is not very engaging to hear. It is restless and frustrated, studded with sudden violences that do little to change the mood.

Bernardo Segall Gives Recital in Carnegie Hall

NOVEMBER 17 (1945), *NEW YORK HERALD TRIBUNE*

Bernardo Segall, Brazilian pianist, played last night to a large audience at Carnegie Hall. Mr. Segall is an artist of great facility, and he has original ideas about how piano music should sound. His program listed familiar pieces from the repertory along with less usual material, such as *The Three Maries* of Villa-Lobos, and *Night Letter From Mars* of Stanley Freedman.

Naturally, his unexpected treatment of the accustomed works was a very noticeable feature of his recital; whether the Villa-Lobos pieces are generally played in some other way this reviewer cannot say. He can say, however, that it is impossible for him to imagine their being better played. These brief, birdlike, butterfly-like things are among the most delightful in the contemporary repertory of piano music. It may be, of course, that they would lose some of their enchantment under other fingers than Mr. Segall's. Certainly he outdid himself in the management of their sonorous complexities.

It was in the works where he could derive (and give to his audience) a sensuous pleasure in the sounds that he made that Mr. Segall seemed most happy. This delight in expert orchestration on the keyboard, and a fine sense of rhythm, gave his playing elements of great interest above and beyond his excellent technique. And these two qualities were apparent in his strange interpretation of the Beethoven Sonata "Appassionata," which was like suddenly seeing a familiar painting under ultraviolet light, so that, although there were those present who pretended they could not recognize the work, it was by no means a dull reading.

The novelties, along with a bright performance of the Mozart C Major Variations, a subdued, poetic, and completely satisfying reading of the A Minor Mazurka of Chopin, and a playing of the Prokofieff *Suggestion diabolique,* which was a tour de force of virtuosity, were the high points of Mr. Segall's concert. The Freedman *Night Letter from Mars,* a first performance, is clever, light, and almost Broadway in its combined treatment of boogie and rumba rhythms. Mr. Segall made the most of it, naturally, and the audience decided it was a success.

Lenchner Recital

NOVEMBER 28 (1945), *NEW YORK HERALD TRIBUNE*

It would be pleasant if all Town Hall debuts disclosed such sure talent as that evinced yesterday by Paula Lenchner, soprano, who sang there for the first time yesterday afternoon. Miss Lenchner, born in Vienna, is a winner this year of the Walter W. Naumburg Foundation Award, under whose auspices the concert was held.

She is fortunate, first of all in having an engaging personality and stage presence, and is already on the way to knowing how to canalize this personal charm for dramatic use in her interpretations. Her voice is powerful, varied in sonorous possibilities, and rich in quality, and she gave evidence, particularly in the five Schubert *lieder,* of considerable vocal control. This is not to say that the voice remained in a state of constant perfection throughout the songs. In general, her high pianissimo tones were less firm than those in the same register where more force was used. At the same time, such passages as the close of *Der Juengling an der Quelle* disclosed tones of such flawless limpidity that one could scarcely have wished for anything finer.

In languages other than German, Miss Lenchner's diction suffered a good deal from vowel distortion. Her version of *La Maja y el ruisenor,* by Granados, contained well-managed ornamentation, but her dramatic projection of the song was less convincing. Again in two songs in English by Nordoff it was impossible to understand a word of the text, and although some of the blame must undoubtedly be put on the composer, particularly in the second song, *Dirge for the Nameless,* where the line was unvocal, still, clearer enunciation would have helped. The songs are not ingratiating ones.

A still more unfortunate choice on the artist's part was that of Victor Babin's *Ritual,* for whose first performance the composer was on hand to supply the accompaniment. This started out like a piano concerto; when the voice finally began, one discovered an aggravation of the same malady from which the Nordoff *Dirge* had suffered: a quasi-instrumental and wholly unlyrical line for the voice. Thus the song's import, both musical and literary, was left to conjecture. Miss Lenchner also presented five songs by Brahms. Coenraad V. Bos accompanied at the piano.

With clearer diction outside her native German tongue, Miss Lenchner would undoubtedly be a "natural" for opera roles. She has the vocal power, awareness, and musicality, as well as the dramatic adaptability for delineation, and from the visual standpoint everything is in her favor.

Hilda Banks, Pianist, Appears at Town Hall

DECEMBER 12 (1945), *NEW YORK HERALD TRIBUNE*

Hilda Banks, seventeen-year-old Boston pianist who appeared here two years ago, was heard Monday night at Town Hall in an interesting and well-integrated program. Her interpretations were always original, if sometimes eccentric and arbitrary in their rhythmical distortions and excessive tempo observances. It would seem that the element in her playing which Miss Banks strives, and successfully, to emphasize is her own quizzical personality, and of this she has a plenty. In her readings of the Bach Italian Concerto and the Beethoven E-flat Major Sonata (op. 31, no. 3), she was vigorous, and occasionally unwontedly violent. Her tone at its best was forceful but mellow, and there was a tendency in these works to overorchestrate the sonorous effects.

The most imaginative and poetic music-making of the recital occurred in the two Brahms Intermezzi (op. 116, A Minor and E Major), where the artist's fancy led her into some very apposite lyrical commentary. These performances were followed by the Brahms Rhapsody in B Minor (op. 79), which abounded in instances of fine technicianship, and which could have been really impressive if that technique had been sufficient to permit absolute accuracy throughout.

Miss Banks's program included her own *Tom Sawyer Suite,* whose episodes were subtitled: "Tom Himself," "His Sweetheart Becky," and "Jim." Such a literary framing of a purely abstract Schoenbergian musical composition struck this listener as pretty much beside the point. The piece would have been better off as Three Twelve-Tone Preludes. Miss Banks played the work with assurance and expression.

Temianka Recital

DECEMBER 13 (1945), *NEW YORK HERALD TRIBUNE*

Henri Temianka, violinist, appeared last night in recital at Carnegie Hall. His program consisted of four works: the A Minor Sonata of Schumann (op. 105), Lalo's *Symphonie espagnole*, the A Major Sonata, no. 17, by Mozart, and Szymanowski's *Notturn de Tarantella.*

Mr. Temianka has a tone which is pleasingly free of querulousness, and a style equally devoid of excessive use of portamento and those partly visual, partly auditory flourishes so often used by violinists to denote passion.

His tone is silky, sweet, and suave, his intonation on the whole excellent. Last night in his playing he evinced care and proficiency in the tiniest details of a phrase, as well as in the bringing to light of the entire line of a movement.

What was missing in his readings was attack. His notes were practically never in the least percussive, even when it would have been desirable. This lack of accentuation, which ended by making the music sound edentate and soft, was evidently the result of the artist's insistence upon maintaining a permanently suave tone quality. However, it must be stated that this tone was a distinct boon in the case of such movements as the Allegretto of the Schumann Sonata and the Andante of the Lalo work, which he accorded an admirably smooth and compelling performance.

An example of fine technicianship occurred in the perfect articulation and intonation of the repeated descending scales in the first movement of the Mozart Sonata. The Presto movement suffered through a combination of unwonted speed and lack of accent.

In the same manner, the "Lebhaft" section of the Schumann Sonata gave the impression of being slightly glossed over in performance, because the requisite of absolute precision of concerted attack between violinist and pianist was wanting. This naturally robbed the reading of rhythm and gave it an unclear character. The accompanying pianist was Artur Balsam.

Angel Reyes

DECEMBER 19 (1945), *NEW YORK HERALD TRIBUNE*

Angel Reyes, Cuban violinist, appeared last night at Carnegie Hall in a carefully chosen program of works from the eighteenth- and twentieth-century repertories. The early works consisted of a reworked version of Jean Marie Leclair's Sonata in B Minor, by Mr. Reyes, and he performed it for the first time in public. It turned out to be a virtuoso piece of the quiet kind, full of double stops: its transcriber accorded it a firm and pleasurable reading, which was enhanced by the strangely rich and reed-like tone he evoked from his instrument. The Bach Chaconne, while well played, seemed just a little out of its element in a program of novel works.

One wishes there were more violinists like Mr. Reyes. He is an artist with an excellent technical equipment (and that includes an unusually fine quality of tone), who is interested enough in new music to include in his recital the first performances of three contemporary works. These were the

Third Sonata for Violin and Piano by the Czech composer Martinu, four Preludes by Anis Fuleihan, and Three Hebrew Melodies by Jacques de Menasce. They were all very different from each other.

The Martinu Sonata supplied the missing romantic element for the evening. It is a discursive piece, full of bright, confusing shimmer, vigorous dance rhythms, and very listenable bits of melodic writing. It is also eclectic in its influences, with Brahms winning out over other romantic and impressionistic contestants. Probably this stylistic mixture, more than any other element, makes the work seem episodic. Still, it is so well done that one's final impression is simply that he would like to hear it again.

Mr. Menasce's three short Hebrew Melodies should be popular. The first is spirited and direct, with an amusing little accompaniment; the quiet second one, too, has a noticeably clever piano part (somewhat in the manner of the young Milhaud); the third is vehement and somewhat less simple. They make a brief and pleasant trio, free of over-writing and development.

The four Preludes of Anis Fuleihan are scarcely more than statements of musical ideas, and as such seem slightly incomplete. In spite of their tempo differentiations, it was hard after one hearing to keep them separate from each other in one's mind: they all seemed to have the same character. This is a perfectly legitimate procedure, of course; but the result was inconclusive.

Artur Balsam deserved praise for his accompaniments, particularly in the Martinu work, in which he acquitted himself more than efficiently.

Dyer-Bennet Recital

DECEMBER 31 (1945), *NEW YORK HERALD TRIBUNE*

Richard Dyer-Bennet, folksinger, presented another of his successful recitals to an intent Town Hall audience Saturday night. This time the "twentieth-century minstrel" widened the scope of his material, which had heretofore been limited to songs of the British Isles and the United States, to include two ancient French ditties, *Douce dame jolie* and *Veillée de Noël;* a Minnelied from thirteenth-century Germany; and a Swedish shepherd's song, all of which were sung in the original. While these were done with a feeling for style and the usual charm which marks all Mr. Dyer-Bennet's performances, his most successful items are still those whose texts are in English, where his lucid diction can get the words and their meaning across to each person in the auditorium.

There were several numbers on the program which were familiar to those who have heard Mr. Dyer-Bennet on other occasions; these included *O, No John; The Charleston Merchant; The Two Sisters of Binnorie;* and *Go Tell Aunt Rhody*. There were also some unfamiliar items whose music and words delighted this listener. Two which seem particularly memorable were *The Old Maid* and *Old Joe Clark,* engaging American folk songs of humorous intent, the one sly and the other bawdy. Both rated high applause.

One of the reasons for the success of this sort of music, aside from Mr. Dyer-Bennet's very evident ability to sing it, is the fact that the idiom retains a high degree of potential personality projection in its performance. And the words of ballads such as these can still give the illusion that they are somehow directly identified with the individual who sings them, an element which has been largely lost in the development of the art song.

It is also pleasant to note that Mr. Dyer-Bennet is sparing with his use of the guitar in the accompaniments. Sparseness of sound is one of the healthiest qualities any music can have today, when the overwhelming tendency is toward music whose expressivity is almost in direct ratio to the volume of sound it uses. Like those of the harpsichord, these small, precise guitar-sounds have a therapeutic value in the concert hall; they enforce strict listening and concentrated attention, and they discourage that relaxed, "bathing-in-music" attitude bequeathed us by the Romantics, of which we have not yet been cured.

ARTICLES AND REVIEWS

......

1946

In the Tropics *Pages From a Journal*

WINTER (1946), *MODERN MUSIC*

Havana, June 1945—Until now I had never slept in Havana, only wandered about during the daytime stopovers for the boat en route to Vera Cruz. I am already wondering why Cuba has recently been built up in legend as one of the world's most intensely musical countries. In 1932, I used to go nearly every day to the Sporting d'Eté to listen to Don Azpiazu's Orchestra, imported, according to the posters, directly from Havana. While I never liked the *maracas* very much, the rest of the percussion section won me over completely and was my introduction to West Indian music. It was gratifying later to learn that the *maracas* were the one Indian component of a drum section which otherwise derived totally from Negro sources. It seemed natural to believe that if Azpiazu's Orchestra had retained this much of its original vigor in transplantation to a spot like Monte Carlo, those playing groups which had remained behind in Cuba must be something pretty spectacular. And in the hills of Puerto Rico the following year, I heard improvised orchestras of *marimbula, cuatros*, and *guiro* which convinced me I would turn out to be right. Doubtless I was, then. But I waited too long to come here to Cuba. Music, along with everything else, is subject to the vagaries of fashion; and now in 1945, percussive frenzy is démodé and Havana is full of "Stormy Weather," known as "Triste Lluvia." A *bongó* is sometimes rapped timidly in the dining-room of the Hotel Nacional, where American tourists, unaware of the arrival of the new chic, still want to hear an occasional rumba or conga.

Havana—Or do I exaggerate? This evening on the Muelle de Luz, waiting for the launch that carries late merrymakers across the harbor to Regla (where because of last night's murders there is a state of martial law), I came on a group of Negroes inventing an old-fashioned song with choral *estribillo,* the first I have heard since I arrived three weeks ago. Lacking drums, they used the wooden bench; in place of *claves* they used the palms of their hands. And being pleasantly drunk, they did not stop when they saw me.

Santiago de Cuba—The Provincia de Oriente, they say, produces the finest music of Cuba. Here I am; where is it? I remember a group called El Cuarteto de Caney. El Caney lies just inland, half an hour above Santiago. I take a bus. There is a corner cantina at the intersection of two dusty roads. People ride up on horseback. Inside, a monstrous jukebox is roaring. The pieces are all from Hollywood's 1943 crop of musical films, with a few Agustin Lara and Maria Grever ballads sandwiched in. I inquire about the famous quartet and discover the sad secret of Cuba's popular music. As soon as a *conjunto* is at all well known it is exported to one of the hundred corners of the earth. "Aren't you sorry about that?" "No, it gives us fame out in the world, and anyway we like your music better, the *suin.*"

Camagüey—Having missed the plane for Haiti in Santiago, I am waiting to go shipside here. This is the triumph of visual *cursilería*: every other store seems to be a gift shop dealing in glazed pottery figurines and poufs covered in rayon satin. Today is a holiday: the inauguration of the *fiesta guaracha.* The entire juvenile population, masked and attired in unimaginative approximations of Cuban rustic costume, storms screaming through the streets. And unexpectedly enough, out in a muddy suburb I found some music. A gang of white kids wandered from alley to alley, singing. In front of them, walking backwards in the manner of the Sudanese exhorters in the religious processions of North Africa, was a very young Negro. He extemporized the typical florid line of the verse while his flock provided the recurrent choral refrain: "Ah, eh, cómo va quedar?" The circumspect complexity of syncopation in the accompanying handclapping rhythms would have been the despair of a notating musicologist. This song continued a quarter of an hour as the impromptu procession moved from house to house, and then, the leader having apparently exhausted his ideas thereon, another was begun.

Havana—Today some of the Grupo de la Renovación came to lunch: Ardévol, and with him his young disciples, the bland Cuban Harold Gramatges, and the fanatical looking Spaniard Julian Orbon. Ardévol himself is from Spain; the idea of "reform" in his movement is pro-neoclassicism and is directed principally against the Cuban-Impressionist influences of Caturla and Roldan. That such a group should be functioning in Cuba is a healthy sign; it would be more convincing if Ardévol were a Cuban. A similar state of affairs would exist here if Schoenberg were to announce the twelve-tone system as the new, true, American idiom. We sadly discussed the decline of Afro-Cuban folk music, and they all agreed that it was no longer to be found, save on the gramophone recordings of a decade or two ago. I still am unable to believe this.

Havana—Each day my trip to witness a Lucumí rite, promised me by Lydia Cabrera, has had to be put off. Señorita Cabrera has collected and published a good many Afro-Cuban folktales and claims to have influence with various practicing *babalaos* of the cult. I finally went to Guanabacoa with her and spent the afternoon in a pink shack with the fetishes, but because we arrived there in a very large Rolls, and since a good many people seemed to be expecting us, I am inclined to discount the seriousness of the baffling proceedings which followed. Inasmuch as the drumming begins only after the sacrifices, and Señorita Cabrera preferred to leave just as the first victim, a white kid, was being dragged to the altar, I was obliged to miss that part of the rite which had promised to hold the greatest interest: the music. And so the young goat's outraged bleating mingled with the sound of the automobile horn and repeated farewells as we were hustled away; the drums were left to my imagination. The painter Wifredo Lam assured me that I had missed little of interest, since only the rival cult, the *ñàñigos,* have really good ritual music.

Havana—That part of Marianao where the dancehalls are is a long, sad boulevard lined with one-story shanties. The roofs continue to the street to form a shelter over the sidewalk; you have to weave your way around the tables and chairs as you walk down the street. Here are professional singers armed with guitars, demanding that you listen to them perform their *guarachas,* rural ballads which somehow have until now escaped the wretched musical metamorphosis that has set in. The songs are distinctly

Spanish in flavor; it is hard to find any trace of African elements there. Vocalizing is often reminiscent of *cante jondo.* Like the Mexican *corrido,* the subject matter is eclectic, sometimes deriving from the events and circumstances of the day. Behind the singers you can hear the insistent *claves* clicking inside the dancehalls and an occasional ecstatic trumpet phrase climbing above the confusion. Each dancehall has a jukebox and on Saturday nights an orchestra. These little bands make the nearest attempt I have heard so far to providing Afro-Cuban dance music. Many have retained the flute, all have trumpets and piano, a few (alas!) a saxophone, and most of them sport two drummers at least. They all play a great amount of international Latin American trash, but in between, if you wait long enough, you can hear some real Cuban music. Nothing, however, like the percussive orchestras that used to enliven certain nightclubs in Paris fifteen years ago. That day is apparently gone for good.

San Salvador—It is beautifully cool and clear here after Belize. There is great excitement over the fact that, in a recent marimba contest between Guatemala and Salvador, the Salvadoreans came out ahead. My informant modestly added that perhaps the victory was "conceded as a courtesy; who knows?" Here, as in other parts of Central America, the marimba is the national instrument, one might even say the national pastime. Boys of eight can be seen pounding away (generally at the bass end) on the same instrument, along with old hands who show their prowess at trilling the melody up at the treble end. I have been in villages where the practicing kept up all night in some butcher's or cobbler's shop, because a fiesta was approaching and the *marimberos* (by day tailors or barbers or students) wanted to perfect their new repertory. When a village develops a really good marimba, the players are very much in demand throughout the region and can bring in more cash by going "on the road" as musicians than by remaining at their original professions.

I once stayed on a ranch in Costa Rica where my room, in the manner of the houses of hot lands, was separated from the adjacent rooms only by eight-foot partitions. In the next cubicle lived a foreman named Raúl, who spent all his leisure time fashioning a marimba. Each bamboo key had to be razor-pared down to its proper size, and each resonating gourd had to be hung below its corresponding note, tested, and cut away or replaced to insure the attainment of a maximum vibration when the bar above it was struck. Raúl had an excellent ear, and before I left he had completed a perfectly-tuned, three-octave chromatic marimba, which he promptly sold to an admiring *vaquero* from a neighboring ranch up the river. "I used to make a great many," he said casually, "but now the fever is past, and I hope to learn soon how to make radios."

Guatemala—The marimbas here are objects of luxury, with cases enhanced by marquetry and box-shaped resonating chambers of varnished wood. Their visual aspect bespeaks a certain degree of mass production, and as a consequence they are less attractive to the eye. Performing ability, however, reaches its technical zenith here. Beside the capital, the larger towns like Quetzaltenango, Antigua, and Huehuetenango have impressive marimbas—the term is used to mean the band as well as the single-instrument—in which several dozen men play, and there is always a drummer as well. The music itself is of scant interest, consisting of hackneyed numbers from the international popular repertory, new Mexican song hits, and examples of the so-called native form, the *son chapín,* which is quite as undistinguished as the rest, and whose name implies simply that it has been written by a Guatemalan.

Chichicastenango—The dubious meaning our culture holds for the members of less evolved groups: this village, where during Holy Week in 1938 I heard some of the best autochthonous Indian music it had been my luck to encounter, has recently been presented with a loud but not very good radio, which is set up in the central *zocalo* opposite the temple with its famous steps containing the sacrificial ovens. Naturally the Indians from the neighboring countryside remain crowded around it for hours on end listening to a barbarous mélange of tropical static and soap operas in Spanish, a language which a few of them have learned. I stopped and pretended to listen awhile this afternoon; a record of American swing was being broadcast. From time to time a blurred riff peeked out from among the howls and crashing explosions of static. Feigning bewilderment, I asked the most sophisticated-looking group: "What is it?"

"A gift from the government," they said.

"Yes, but what's that noise?"

"A fight in the capital."

Fritz Kreisler

JANUARY 11 (1946), *NEW YORK HERALD TRIBUNE*

Fritz Kreisler, violinist, was soloist last night with the Philharmonic-Symphony Orchestra at the regular Thursday evening concert under the direction of Arthur Rodzinski. Carnegie Hall echoed with applause for a long time both before Mr. Kreisler had begun and after he had finished playing the solo part of the Mendelssohn Violin Concerto.

Aside from the fact that Mr. Kreisler has long been a great favorite of the public, there were many things to applaud in his performance last night: his unfaltering grasp of the long line of a movement, his large tone with its very personal quality, and his expressive phrasing. In general, the intonation was firmly handled, not becoming in the least ambiguous in the long passage using multiple stops in the middle section of the second movement. The third movement received an admirably vigorous, rhythmical, and sure-handed treatment, and it was here that the artist's qualities as a master violinist were most overwhelmingly evident.

The concert opened with the Symphony in A Major of Boccherini, whose Minuet and Andante movements, of slight but healthy sonority, are particularly delightful. The work as a whole would undoubtedly have derived benefit from further rehearsal, but this would probably have defeated the purpose for which it was selected—namely, that of saving rehearsal time to spend it on the other works. The reading, however, did have its share of rough edges. The last half of the program was devoted to the always stirring Tchaikovsky Fourth Symphony, of which Dr. Rodzinski achieved a truly exciting performance.

Music of Today

JANUARY 21 (1946), *NEW YORK HERALD TRIBUNE*

The National Association for American Composers and Conductors, Inc., last night presented the first in a series of four concerts to be devoted to contemporary American music, that poor relation in the family of musical repertory. It was interesting to note that every seat in Times Hall was occupied.

The program, which included works by Americans of varying tendencies, was a mouthpiece for no school or clique, and could be called an honestly representative list of selections. It was short and moved along with dispatch, the elimination of intermission helping considerably to expedite its progress. Most of the material, although new, had been presented before. The heretofore unheard works included the Second String Quartet of Samuel Gardner, ably played by Mr. Gardner, George Bornoff, Leon Barzin, and Herman Busch. The piece is sagaciously written and often effective, in the macabre second movement particularly. Stylistically there is a somewhat unsatisfying relationship between the dissonant and consonant elements, but this is by no means rare in today's music, the harmonic problem being the most difficult one of all to unsnarl at this point.

Of a group of songs sung by Janet Fairbank, all were new save *Bells in the Rain* by John Duke. The first performances included three short songs on texts of Blake by Jack Beeson: *I Laid Me Down, Never Seek to Tell Thy Love,* and *I Asked a Thief*. These are pleasant, and the prosody is notably better than it is in the general run of new art songs. Paul Bowles had two frankly popular, Broadway-inspired songs to words by Tennessee Williams: *Heavenly Grass* and *Lonesome Man*. As some songs go to folk material and "civilize" it for the concert hall, so these go to the juke-box and do the same. David Diamond's *On Death* (text by John Clare) has a profoundly mellifluous line: one was struck by its sustained graciousness. Also sung by Miss Fairbank was Lou Harrison's arresting, vigorous, quasi-oriental *Sanctus*. Carl Krits accompanied for the singer.

Among the other works previously heard were Six Little Duos for Oboe and Violoncello, by Margaret Starr McLain, and Douglas Moore's skillful *Down East Suite* for violin, expertly played by Henri Temianka, assisted at the piano by Arthur Hollander. Both works drew heavy applause from the audience.

The remaining three concerts in the series will be held at Times Hall on the Sunday evenings of February 17, March 31, and April 14.

Music

MARCH (1946), *MADEMOISELLE*

The expression "Latin American" in connection with music is likely to awaken in most minds the idea of a rumba or a samba, and a vague impression of palms and a wave-kissed beach. Certainly this kind of music exists in Latin America, but it by no means forms the more important part of Latin American music. At least half the music from south of the border (and the more "American" half, to be ethnographically correct) comes from the cold and often dreary regions of the cordillera stretching from Texas on down to Cape Horn, regions with neither palms nor languor, where most of the inhabitants would find a rumba or a samba a pretty strange-sounding piece of music.

In reality, "Latin American folk music" is too broad a term to mean much in any way except geographically. It is as if one were to speak of "European folk music." The music of Ireland, southern Spain, and Albania, for instance, have little in common. Nor can a *son jaliciense* from Mexico be easily confused with a Cuban *conga* or a Panamanian *mejorana.* Each region makes its own music, unmistakable and distinct from that of the neighboring region; ethnical frontiers coincide no more with political ones on this side of the Atlantic than they do on the other.

There are two general categories in which most true Latin American music can be placed: that group in which the non-European elements are principally of Negro origin, and that group where these elements are Indian. In each case there is interaction of influences: European melodies have been Indianized, and melodies which were originally Indian have become Westernized. The same is true of the Negro division. Since both Negro and Indian music are basically linear, the one element which is alike in both cases is the purely European innovation of harmony, of which the same fundamental sort, often based on progressions of guitar chords, is to be found nearly everywhere one goes below the Rio Grande, insofar as the music uses it at all. Rhythm, melody, and sonority are the variables, and they vary considerably.

A third category could be made of that transplanted European music which has undergone no true hybridizing metamorphosis. This is to be found in practically all parts of Latin America; however, in spite of the differences which may exist between it and its Old World counterparts, unless a mixing of culture has taken place, there would seem to be no reason to consider it anything but displaced European material that has been deformed by regional tradition. This may seem arbitrary, and tantamount to saying that all truly American folk music contains extra-European elements, and as a matter of fact, I am inclined to believe that such is the case.

It is the basic change from the European to the American (read Negro and Indian) conception of rhythm which makes the great and immediately perceived difference between the music of the Old World and that of the New. So that, even though a given form can often be traced directly back to a sixteenth- or seventeenth-century Spanish or Portuguese song or dance, the rhythmical viewpoint with which it is approached on this side of the water effects a transformation of character.

It was far more imperative for the early colonizers, when they arrived here, to obliterate all vestiges of previous cultures than it was for them to try to deprive the already subjugated African slaves of their songs and rituals. And (fortunately for the colonizers) the Indians in general were less highly evolved culturally than the Negroes, so that their music, along with the other elements of their culture, was less strong and durable. Thus it is not surprising that the comparatively few Negroes brought to America's shores should have had such a tremendous effect upon its music. Wherever a few Negroes landed, traits of their music left their mark, and at the same time the Indian musical characteristics became less prominent.

This by no means implies mutually exclusive influences. Many of the music types here contain elements of both the African and autochthonous musical cultures. Thus, in Mexico, while the basic rhythm of the *son veracruzano* is clearly Indian, the vocalization contains much that is Negro. Or consider the Indian gourd-rattle used in the Negro music of Cuba—the ever-present *maracas.* It is unknown in Africa. On the other hand, the marimba, a purely African invention, has become the national instrument of Guatemala and El Salvador, where it has been highly developed, and where practically every Indian village has its marimba orchestra. But this more complex hybridization is rather the exception than the rule.

Generally speaking, it is in the islands and along the coasts, particularly on the Atlantic and Caribbean side of the two continents, that the Negro strain is strongest, and in the western highlands that the Indian material has proved most tenacious. The music of the Antilles and Brazil, places of extensive Negro infiltration, are especially rich in African traits, while in Mexico, Ecuador, and Peru, where the destruction of the indigenous culture proved most difficult because of the mountains and the fact that the cultures themselves were the most evolved and therefore the most resistant of the pre-Columbian systems, the Indian tradition has continued; one might say it has to an extent absorbed the Latin elements, carrying them from the lowlands and valleys back up into the mountain fastnesses, there to digest and transform them.

Comparatively very little pure Indian music remains to be heard now by the casual voyager down there. Almost all of it, even when native texts are used (and the number of indigenous spoken languages between Texas and Tierra del Fuego is stupendous), uses some variation of simple European harmony. In Peru some native instruments have been retained for the playing of hybrid music. In Mexico and Guatemala they have not; the Indian music one can hear there is largely restricted to the inevitable *chirimía* (high flute) and drum, which every rustic festival seems to call forth. (There are also the Yaqui and Seri rituals in northwestern Mexico, if one can get to them. And the *chirimías* of Guatemala are more rewarding because there are often several of them playing at once, and not in unison.) Almost always, nowadays, the pure Indian music is used in connection with religious observances, whereas the hybridized music may serve any purpose.

With the Negroes too, that music which approaches the greatest purity of style (that is, the music in which harmony has little or no place, and where the rhythms have retained the maximum complexity) is to be heard at religious ceremonies; here drums are used for the same purposes of facilitating the working of practical magic as they are back in West Africa. In Cuba there are *ñañiguismo* and the *Lucumi* cult, in Haiti the *Vodoun* and *Petro* rites, in Brazil it is *Macumba* or *Babacuê,* or one of many other local animist sects. In Trinidad, the Negroes have conserved certain song forms, such as the *leggo* and *kalender* (cf. the *calinda* of New Orleans's heyday), which are certainly remnants of such ceremonies, and in which the emphasis is all on percussive rhythm of a clearly African cast. The Calypso songs of that island vary in the degree of their Europeanization, those sung in patois usually being more conscious of rhythm than those in English.

In Latin America, as elsewhere, the radio and cinema are systematically exterminating folk music before its creators and consumers are in a position to participate in the creation or enjoyment of art music. What fills the gap? Commercial music. But there are still thousands of small villages in that part of our hemisphere where radios and projectors have yet to arrive, and where the people still make their own music just as they have for centuries, not for entertainment, but because it is an absolute essential to their living.

Preface to an Interview with Paul Bowles

......

IRENE HERRMANN

Talking with Paul Bowles about music always opened an entryway into the rich world he inhabited, which actively included music composition, music criticism, and the interconnected spheres of the New York art scene of dance, theatre, music, painting. He cultivated professional ties with all of them, and in each one he seemed equally at home. So it is not surprising that Paul, ever the autodidact in all things musical, wrote over four hundred articles, which reveal his deeply educated and discerning ear. They reflect his attendance at seemingly endless recital evenings of unknown budding soloists, and orchestra concerts of the New York Philharmonic with conductors including Dimitri Mitropoulos, Artur Rodzinski, Leonard Bernstein, and Leopold Stokowski. He heard Frank Sinatra sing at Lewisohn Stadium, attended jazz concerts in Harlem and Carnegie Hall, enjoyed Wanda Landowska performing Scarlatti and Bach, and even reviewed the (in)famous Florence Foster Jenkins. His commentaries are succinct, highly descriptive, insightful, and exhibit a dry, understated sense of humor. They are writerly and intelligent, yet never draw the attention away from the performance and the music toward himself. Critics are notoriously at their best when they are truly critical of a composer or a performance and Paul was no exception. (See Bowles's comments on Strauss's *Till Eulenspiegel,* December 15, 1944.)

His appreciation for a performer's musicianship constantly guided his criticism, and one sees how exhibitionism, showmanship, and musical integrity were never lost on him. Paul seemed to know and be on a first name basis with just about everyone on the New York "scene." Maybe everyone was then—it was a smaller, more interconnected world, not yet overtaken by academia. Ideas were fresh, the personalities of Stravinsky, Bartók, Bernstein, Balanchine, Stokowski, Heifetz, Milstein (to name but a few) loomed large. Paul heard world or U. S. premieres of many pieces now well known—Shostakovich's E-Minor Piano Trio, Bernstein's "Jeremiah" Symphony (to name but two)—and heard countless young musicians, many of whom became the great artists and interpreters of the first half of the twentieth century.

Unique to this era of music in New York was that composers were the writers, essayists, and critics of their own scene. Their discussions about music excelled in clarity and knowledge of the genre and were consistently well written. This period quickly turned to a world where professional music or art or theatre critics, people who decidedly did not practice art, became the arbiters of taste and writers of their respective fields. But in Paul's day, *Modern Music* reveled in its undisputed world of composers-writing-about-music: Virgil Thomson about Gershwin, Copland about theatre music, Elliott Carter about the New York Opera season, and Paul, with the widest variety by far, about traditional music of Latin America and the Caribbean, film music, jazz, art music. The world of music criticism was never again so entertaining, insightful, or well expressed. Music criticism of this lively era offers the reader a vivid sense of the quality, variety, and abundance of musical life in New York during the 1930s and 1940s. Surrounded by a staff of other great writer-composers at both the *New York Herald Tribune* and *Modern Music,* Paul Bowles leaves a legacy of articles equal to any of his colleagues.

I visited Paul every summer from 1993 until his death in 1999. Our musical discussions were always lively and engaged, and his memory of his career as a music critic was clear and sharp. In the last few years, as his health became ever more fragile, the focus of our musical visits changed. As we listened together ever more frequently to his favorite composers—Stravinsky, Ravel, Tailleferre, Gershwin, Milhaud—I realized that he listened very differently than I did. As a composer, he possessed access to the music that was unavailable to my performer's sensibilities. That is to say, he heard the music with a composer's ears, connecting to the works in a way unavailable to me as a performer. While listening together, he would draw on his own experience of composing, sharing with me observations about form, texture, orchestration, even humor, in the music at hand; he seemed to have a direct link to the expressive impulse of the composer. The reader will instantly recognize this in Paul's writing about music.

When Tim Mangan and I approached Paul with the suggestion of coediting a book of his writings on music, he was at once highly skeptical and, I think, secretly pleased. Although he took his work seriously, he did not think it was of lasting quality or interest. I brought with me to Tangier several excerpts of his reviews and read them aloud to him every day during that visit. As was my custom, I came by at tea time. Over the many years of visiting him, I had become accustomed to the hot, rather unventilated apartment and always dressed for humid tropical conditions (inside his apartment) regardless of the outside weather. Reclining in bed and receiving visitors, Paul was consistently gracious and inviting, and seemed clearly to enjoy and look forward to our daily encounters. As I continued to read from a variety of his music articles, I was astonished at how precisely he remembered so many of the concerts, as he commented on one or another aspect of the performances that the reviews described. He answered the questions that Tim and I prepared for him almost eagerly, with precision and clear-mindedness, much as if he were still on the staff of the *Herald Tribune*! These conversations took place during my last visit to him, in June 1999, five months before his death. What a gift he has left us.

Interview

......

JUNE 6, 1999

IH How did you meet Minna Lederman?

PB Well. . . meet her? I used to correspond with her long before I met her because I did translations for her magazine, *Modern Music*. I translated from French and Italian—articles.

IH So she had Italian contributors?

PB Yes, she did. Not very often, usually they were French and German. But I don't know—I volunteered to do Italian, too.

IH So the magazine existed for a while before you started to write for it.

PB Oh, of course. Yes, yes. And I first corresponded with her, and then we had telephone conversations, and finally I went over and talked to her, face to face. But I don't know exactly when it was. Well, he [Tim Mangan] doesn't ask when it was—he asked "how."

IH I suppose a "when" could be part of the answer but if you don't remember . . . but his follow-up question is "Did she discover, form, and train you as a contributor to her magazine, as Virgil Thomson said she did?"

PB I don't think she did, but . . .

IH What was she like as an editor?

PB Oh she was rather—she was easy enough, but she got excited about . . . If I was correcting proof, she was very meticulous, which I liked. But I don't remember that she did anything like "train me." No.

IH Who decided on the subject matter that you wrote on?

PB Well, you don't mean the translations.

IH No, I mean your own.

PB I. She would never have suggested that I review jazz or film music.

Sometimes I simply did a series of pieces—oh, connected with each other by virtue of being scores accompanying plays being given in New York. Or, music accompanying films.

IH I remember when you did the one—do you remember you reviewed when Walt Disney's *Fantasia* came out? And I don't know if you remember but they're sort of bastardized, shortened versions of *Rite of Spring* and Beethoven's Sixth Symphony.

PB *[Laughs]* Yes.

IH I thought you were really at your best when you were criticizing it. Do you remember that one?

PB Well, I remember, yes. That was that mad film—oh, each part was based on a different piece of music.

IH Right.

PB It included the *Sorcerer's Apprentice*, yes, yes.

IH And Stokowski conducting.

PB Yes *[laughs]*.

IH Well, if you think about it, it was probably an introduction to that music for many people who'd never heard that kind of music before.

PB Well, they heard it that time, anyway.

IH *[Laughs.]* More or less.

PB Yeah. The wonderful one was full of—what was it? Gounod's *Ave Maria*?

IH Yes.

PB Ah, so awful.

IH That was the worst—the height of kitsch I would say.

PB Oh, wow. How high is kitsch?

IH I think it ends with that.

PB Yes, a whole series of little candles going up the hill.

IH You remember it well. Were there any writers that influenced you when you first started writing music criticism?

PB Well no, only Virgil. Virgil Thomson, of course.

IH Because you'd read his criticism? Or because he advised you or read yours and criticized?

PB I generally showed him what I was doing. He was then reviewing on the *Herald Tribune.*

IH But would he read your reviews, would he edit them and read through them before they were printed?

PB No, he didn't edit anything. If he read a piece, he would say, "I see you managed to express yourself." Because his idea always was never say you don't like something, because no one's interested in what you like. That was his story.

IH Well, this question kind of dovetails into that. In your reviews for the *Herald Tribune,* did you have a particular philosophy, perhaps dictated by Thomson, on verbs and adjectives?

PB "Philosophy" I wouldn't say, but he always said you must consider what you're doing is reporting on an event, like a fire in the Bronx or something. You go, he says, tell what you see, you don't say, "I didn't like the color of the fire. I don't like the smell of the burning rubber." Don't tell what you like or what you don't like because no one cares. That was always very important, not to push your person into the review by complaining. It's always considered that you were simply reporting on an event, which *is* what you were doing—a recital at Town Hall or Carnegie Hall was an event. What happened. And that was the important thing. He always stressed that: What happened?

IH Yes. As a composer do you think you were easier or harder on your composer-compatriots—when you perhaps reviewed a work by Thomson?

PB Oh, well, I didn't distinguish between them.

IH In some of the reviews that I was going through, I noticed that you did review some of his music.

PB Of Virgil's?

IH Yes, and some of Bernstein's, too.

PB I did. Yes, the First Symphony, the "Jeremiah." Yeah. And beforehand I got to know . . . what did she call herself, Tourel?

IH Yes, Jennie Tourel.

PB Well, her name is Davidson. She told me. And I said, "Why do you call yourself Tourel?" and she said, "Well I don't think Davidson is a very interesting name, but Tourel, yes."

IH What do you think are the advantages and disadvantages of the composer as critic?

PB Well, the advantages probably are that he sees music as it is—as music. And the disadvantages of course could be many. Because the personal element can enter into it, and it shouldn't. It really should be the same. I mean, if you're to review a fire in the Bronx and even if you happen to know the man who was burned alive in the empty lot, you don't say, "Oh, dear, oh dear, he was such a nice man." You simply say, "He was found dead."

IH Was that against some instinct of yours when you were writing? Or did it come pretty naturally, to write in that distanced way?

PB Oh, yeah. It seemed much better. I wouldn't have considered anything else. Yeah.

IH At the *Tribune,* what was your deadline after seeing a concert that you had to review?

PB Well, depending on which edition you wanted to make—because there was a city edition and then there was a late city edition—and of course you could do more in the late edition because you had more time. But the idea was to hit the early edition, my idea was anyway. And, I don't know, I don't remember the hour. There wasn't any strictly applied, not that I remember. Sometimes I didn't have time to call for a boy to come and collect it and take it down to the typographers. In that case, I went myself. But the time? I really don't know what time it was. It was fairly early. I remember the first reviews I did I was very nervous. Because I thought I'll never get this written and make sense and get the copy down to the typographers in time. So I got very nervous. But after a week or so, no.

IH Who made the assignments? Who decided which concerts would be reviewed by whom?

PB Virgil Thomson. After all, he was the chief. He made a point of varying mine a little. But in general, he did the pieces where he really wanted to attack and where he wanted to, you know, smooth the feathers. And that was good. I mean, I didn't want to review Jascha Heifetz, but he could. And he knew just what he wanted to say—where he wanted to put Heifetz and what he wanted to do to him.

IH It sounds like he already went there with an attitude.

PB Who, Virgil? He did. Ah. Yeah, well he reviewed Heifetz, the heading was "Silk Underwear Music" *[laughs].* Wonderful. Heifetz and his friends never forgave him, of course. He made an awful lot of enemies.

IH So he didn't practice what he preached. Well, Virgil didn't practice what he preached if he told you that no one's interested in your opinions and yet his were full [of them]. And so, were your pieces edited? Who was your editor when your handed in a review at the *Tribune?*

PB What do you mean, editor?

IH Did someone read it and delete or discuss it with you before it came out?

PB No. If anybody, Virgil. But he didn't bother me.

IH How much were you paid?

PB I don't know. Practically nothing. Very little.

IH Were the Sunday pieces better paid?

PB No, they were contributed free.

IH Really?

PB Yeah, I got a weekly salary, so whatever I wrote was paid for by that salary, which was $35 a week. And then eventually I was obliged to join the Guild—they called it the Newspaper Guild, I'm not sure. The minimum there was $50, so they had to raise my salary by $15.

IH But you didn't have to do any more work for the $15?

PB No, no. It had nothing to do with the amount I contributed. No. So it was in my interest to do the Sunday pieces because I got a big block, with the name big. The same size as Virgil Thomson.

IH And those were always your choice as well?

PB Yeah.

IH Did only one critic get that spot each week or were all the pieces on Sunday longer?

PB Yes.

IH Did you prepare in any particular way to review a concert?

PB Oh, it depended on the concert. Yeah, there were concerts where I wrote a big piece. And when I did that, I generally read a lot first about the music, or the composer, or the circumstances of its first performance and so on. You know.

IH Do you remember hearing a lot of pieces from even the nineteenth century for the first time when you were reviewing? Was that an introduction to a lot of the music that you were hearing?

PB Nineteenth-century music?

IH Well, I was noticing you would review orchestral concerts and there would be Brahms on it or early Mahler, whatever, music that I just didn't know if you were familiar with that much before your reviewed it.

PB No, a lot of it I wasn't. Not all of it. Some I was, some I wasn't. I had to do a lot of work for Wanda Landowska. It involved studying the music and going up to her studio and having her play the pieces for me. Yeah. She was very collaborative.

IH Does any particular piece come to mind when you say that?

PB Yes, I think of some of the—what do they call them, sonatas?—by Scarlatti. They were so beautiful on the harpsichord. And she did them so well.

IH Yes. She had sort of the "Rolls Royce" of harpsichords, I guess you'd say. Do you remember anything particular about her instrument?

PB Instruments? Only that there were girls all over the place, all over the studio, underneath the harpsichords.

IH Servicing them?

PB Yes. They all had to be serviced every day. Ah.

IH So what kind of shape was the harpsichord in by the end of a real concert?

PB I suppose it was ready to be retired.

IH So you would go over to her house or her studio and listen to her play the music in advance of the recital?

PB I was eager to do it and she was delighted, you know, to get the attention. After all, I don't know why she would be delighted since she was famous, but I guess she never really got enough fame.

IH The photos of her always showed a formidable profile. Was she that type of person?

PB Well, she was fairly formal. Yeah. But I think she laid it on when she gave a concert. Yes, she wore a strange sort of gown that came down to the floor and she walked very slowly over to the harpsichord, across the stage. She always had to come on the other side and proceed toward the instrument very slowly with her hands in prayer. I never believed it. Well, I guess it was natural enough, but . . .

IH Did it seem really artificial and affected?

PB It seemed theatrical. And then she'd sit down and take a long time arranging the height of the bench, then she would sit down and then she would just hold her hands up as if in silent prayer for quite a while.

IH Creating the right atmosphere.

PB Yeah. And people were sort of waiting—why the hell doesn't she begin? Oh, no, no, no. And when she finally decided that the right moment had come, she released her hands and then went boom! and began you know. And it was always wonderful. She played so well. She had a wonderful sense of rhythm. Especially for the Scarlatti.

IH Did you ever also hear her play the piano?

PB Oh yes. She played a long Mozart sonata. And she could play the piano just as well as she could play the harpsichord, of course. She had her own theories about all the music she played. And the main thing was that there should be no rubato ever anywhere; it must always be strict. I mean, she might have been playing jazz, the rhythm had to be so strictly observed. I liked that of course.

IH The one quote I remember reading of her was, "You can play Bach any way you like, but I play him his way."

PB "*His way.*" She inherited that, obviously, from her great-great-great-great-grandfather.

IH Did she speak with a thick Polish accent? What was her heritage?

PB It seems to me she spoke fairly normal English. In the studio. Of course, she didn't have to speak on stage. What was her name really? Landowska. That's not . . . Landauer, or something, I think. She just changed it into something a little more—well, it's the same name, I mean, but another version of the same name. I think it was Landauer. I must say, Landowska sounds better. It was like Stokowski. What was his name really? Stokes, Leo Stokes. Yeah.

IH Well, then and the other way around. Vernon Duke had a very very Russian name.

PB Well, yeah, Vladimir Dukelsky. He was hoping to go Broadway. He did, but . . . he wrote some pieces that were successful.

IH Actually, there's a renaissance of interest in his songs now. There are quite a few opera singers and recital singers who want to sing American music. There are quite a few recordings now of opera singers who sing American, Broadway melody. For better or worse. He's one of the composers—Cole Porter, Vernon Duke, Harold Arlen.

PB Oh yeah, there were some very good songwriters. Richard Rodgers did some very good ones. And not to mention our favorite, which is Gershwin.

IH Yes. Well, and Bernstein's Broadway pieces are wonderful.

PB Are they? I never heard them.

IH *On the Town*?

PB Oh that, yes.

IH And then *Wonderful Town*. Well, those are two of the early ones, anyway.

PB *On the Town*. What was that? Was that a play?

IH It was a musical on Broadway. It also had music excerpted from it and you could play some of the music as a suite.

PB Before that there was a ballet he did, it was called *Fancy Free*.

IH Did you see that?

PB Yes. Of course. I was a friend of Jerry Robbins and he was very busy doing it.

IH Did that have a premiere on Broadway or in a concert hall?

PB What? *Fancy Free*? Well, it was ballet, yeah. It was in a concert hall. I'm not sure where they gave it, Town Hall or Carnegie Hall. I don't think they did ballets in Carnegie Hall.

IH So you must have seen the first performance of it?

PB Yes, I did. It was good. It was very good. I remember *On the Town*. I had to review three concerts that night, I mean the night of the premiere of *On the Town*. And [*laughs*] my chair where I was typing was next to the typewriter of the man who reviewed plays, theatre. Now I can't remember his name. Crazy, my memory of the *Herald Tribune* is not very accurate. But I went down with my material to the typographer's room and I saw his review. I only saw the heading. It said, "Half a Show," and I knew that would not do at all. Because I wanted our friends all to be successful, Jerry and Lenny and the whole lot—and what was her name?—Walker, Nancy Walker. She was marvelous. She occasionally invented what was not in her script. Someone was supposed to be talking too much and she was supposed to say "Yackety, yackety." Instead of that she called out "Yach-et-uh, yach-et-uh!" [*Laughs.*] I thought it was very funny.

IH Did she startle all the rest of the actors because they weren't expecting that?

PB Yeah, of course. Ah, his name was Howard Barnes, I think, the drama critic on the *Herald Tribune*. And he married the fashion editor. What was her name? Katherine Vincent. So they were always dressed up, you know, leaving a first night. And of course she had to be fancily dressed, being a fashion editor of the *Herald Tribune*.

IH Didn't you have a good story about a coat and a concert, or a gift? Was it Florence Foster Jenkins?

PB Oh she was very funny. Well, yes, let's see. [An earlier music] critic on the *Herald Tribune* was named Lawrence Gilman. And she, in order to be nice to Lawrence Gilman, she bought a brand new mink coat for Mrs. Gilman. Which was certainly nice of her.

IH He wouldn't have been the reviewer of her concert?

PB He probably was. . . . So I saw what Howard Barnes had written. We were all at a party, I don't know where, maybe at Lenny's. We were waiting to know what the news would be—what else do you do on opening night? You wait to see what each one said about it. And of course the *Herald Tribune* was so much more important that the *World-Telegraph* or the *News,* which wasn't important at all. But the *Times* was very important. And I think they had Brooks Atkinson then. And he really decided on the fate of a lot of shows. I don't know what he had written because I didn't see it, but I saw the Barnes and I thought, that's too much. So when I went up to the party where we were sitting waiting, I told them what I had seen and that was terrible news. They just said, "Half a Show!" And [*laughs*] Nancy Walker said, "That schmuck!" [*Laughs.*] She was so funny. She was really a comedienne.

So I went back to the *Herald Tribune,* I was talking to Howard Barnes and I asked him, "How do you like it?" And he said, "Oh, I didn't wait to see the end, I just saw the beginning." Imagine! And I said, "Well, I was talking to . . ." and then I mentioned all the other drama critics that I had been talking to. And I quoted each one to Howard Barnes. He began looking a bit worried. Obviously he hadn't seen the show. How could he? So, he hurried down and he redid his piece, yeah, after reading the other reviews. So it turned out to be a full show, not a half a show.

IH I hope he didn't do that again—learned a lesson.

PB Well, I don't think people like that take lessons.

IH Did the music criticism ever influence the way you composed?

PB No, completely different. No, no.

IH In other words, did your life as professional listener influence your music in any way?

PB I don't think I was ever a professional listener.

IH I guess he means you got paid to listen and write about it.

PB I didn't get paid enough, so I wasn't very professional. [*Laughs.*]

IH Those were separate worlds for you?

PB Yeah, yeah. I don't think I was a very good critic. I know when Virgil resigned, he came to me and said, "Would you like to take over?" And I said no. I'd have made a lot more money, of course. But that wasn't important to me—I felt I didn't know enough to be a really important critic. And I told him that.

IH Did reviewing take so much time that it took away from composing? Writing reviews, just going to concerts at night, and meeting deadlines, did you find that you were sacrificing things you would have rather done?

PB No, I enjoyed it. I enjoyed what I did. But I wasn't eager to amplify it and become an important critic because I couldn't. I don't think I knew enough. Virgil knew all sorts of things. He'd studied music at Harvard and so on. I never studied at all, that's the point. I think I'd have been a catastrophe.

IH Is there anything important that you learned while writing music criticism that you have carried over into your fiction writing? Or vice versa?

PB No, I don't think so.

IH Separate worlds?

PB Well, yes, of course. No, I don't see it.

Index

DESIGNER: Nola Burger COMPOSITOR: Westchester Book Composition
TEXT: 11/13.75 Adobe Garamond DISPLAY: Franklin Gothic; Bodoni Book
PRINTER AND BINDER: Maple-Vail Book Manufacturing Group